George Ward Nichols

The Story of the Great March

From the Diary of a Staff Officer

George Ward Nichols

The Story of the Great March
From the Diary of a Staff Officer

ISBN/EAN: 9783337017019

Printed in Europe, USA, Canada, Australia, Japan

Cover: Foto ©ninafisch / pixelio.de

More available books at **www.hansebooks.com**

THE STORY

OF

THE GREAT MARCH.

FROM THE

DIARY OF A STAFF OFFICER.

BY

BREVET MAJOR GEORGE WARD NICHOLS,
AID-DE-CAMP TO GENERAL SHERMAN.

With a Map and Illustrations.

NEW YORK:
HARPER & BROTHERS, PUBLISHERS,
FRANKLIN SQUARE.
1865.

Entered, according to Act of Congress, in the year one thousand eight hundred and sixty-five, by

HARPER & BROTHERS,

In the Clerk's Office of the District Court of the Southern District of New York.

PREFACE.

My service as aid-de-camp on the staff of Major General Sherman began with the fall of Atlanta. The remarkable features and events of the campaigns of Georgia and the Carolinas, visible to me during the whole of the Grand March, were noted daily in my journal. From that diary this Story of the March is compiled.

Sherman's army rests upon the laurels it has bravely won. Its heroes are now in other fields of duty, and a grateful Nation thanks them for their gallant deeds. I have told their story simply, and, I hope, honestly.

G. W. N.

CONTENTS.

PART I.
THE MARCH TO THE SEA.

CHAPTER I.
The Opening Campaign... Page 15

CHAPTER II.
Pursuit of Hood.—The Defense of Allatoona.............................. 27

CHAPTER III.
Preparations for the Seaward March.—The Burning of Atlanta........ 34

CHAPTER IV.
Organization of the Army for the March................................ 42

CHAPTER V.
Breaking Camp.—A Day's March.—The Bivouac........................ 48

CHAPTER VI.
Capture of Milledgeville.—Howell Cobb's Plantation................. 56

CHAPTER VII.
Wayside Incidents in Georgia.—An Original Character.—Cock-fighting.. 68

CHAPTER VIII.
From Millen to the Sea-coast.. 78

CHAPTER IX.
The Storming of Fort McAllister....................................... 89

CHAPTER X.
Evacuation of Savannah by the Rebels.—Its Occupation by Sherman.—Interview between Secretary Stanton and the Colored Clergymen.—Talks with the People.. 95

CHAPTER XI.
Review of the Georgia Campaign..................................Page 109

CHAPTER XII.
General Sherman.. 116

PART II.
THE CAMPAIGN OF THE CAROLINAS.

CHAPTER XIII.
Movement of Troops.—Crossing the South Carolina Border.—The Army under Fly-tents 125

CHAPTER XIV.
Advance to the Salkahatchie.—In the Swamps.—Desolation 131

CHAPTER XV.
Occupation of the Charleston and Augusta Railroad. — Branchville Flanked. — Passage of the Upper and Lower Edisto. — Capture of Orangeburg 144

CHAPTER XVI.
Marching upon Columbia.—Saluda Factory.—A View of Southern Factory Operatives.. 152

CHAPTER XVII.
Occupation of the Capital of South Carolina.—A terrible Conflagration 160

CHAPTER XVIII.
The March resumed.—Crossing the Catawba River.—News of the Fall of Charleston.—Capture of Camden............................. 174

CHAPTER XIX.
Marching upon Cheraw.—Bridges taken.—General Sherman and the Negroes 187

CHAPTER XX.
Capture of Cheraw.—Destruction of Rebel Artillery and Supplies.—The Enemy still befogged.. 198

CHAPTER XXI.
Refugee Loyalists.—The Emigrant Train.—Charleston Rebels...Page 208

CHAPTER XXII.
Crossing the Pedee River.—The Army in North Carolina 215

CHAPTER XXIII.
Marching upon Fayetteville.—A Deluge.—An Adventure in the Woods. —A perilous Road. 224

CHAPTER XXIV.
Capture of Fayetteville. — The United States Arsenal retaken. — Talks with the Slaves.—Wade Hampton.—"Bummers" and their Peculiarities 235

CHAPTER XXV.
A Fight between Kilpatrick and Hampton.—The Army in Communication with Wilmington.—Destruction of the Fayetteville Arsenal.—The Army across Cape Fear River.—Refugees sent to Wilmington..... 247

CHAPTER XXVI.
The Battle of Averysboro' 254

CHAPTER XXVII.
The Battle of Bentonville.—Retreat of Johnston 260

CHAPTER XXVIII.
Entering Goldsboro'... 274

PART III.
THE SURRENDER AND THE END.

CHAPTER XXIX.
Smithfield.—The Beginning of the End................................... 291

CHAPTER XXX.
The Capital of North Carolina.—Its Surrender........................ 295

CHAPTER XXXI.
A Talk with a Rebel Colonel... 301

CHAPTER XXXII.
The Construction Corps of the Army .... Page 305

CHAPTER XXXIII.
Pursuit of Johnston.—Conference between Sherman and Johnston.—A Truce 308

CHAPTER XXXIV.
The End 317

Going Home 322

APPENDIX.

I. General Sherman's Report of the Georgia Campaign 323
II. Report of the Campaign of the Carolinas 336
III. General Sherman's Testimony before the Committee on the War 350
IV. General Sherman's Report of Operations in North Carolina, and Surrender of Johnston's Army 354
V. Testimony before the Committee on the War—Continued 367
VI. Major General Barry's Report of the Campaign of the Carolinas 382
VII. Report of Engineer's Department 385
VIII. Extracts from Colonel Poe's Report of Operations in the Campaign of the Carolinas 386
IX. Quartermaster Reports 388
X. Commissary Stores furnished the Army 392
XI. Staff of General Sherman 394

LIST OF ILLUSTRATIONS.

The Story of the March, with the Badge of General Sherman's Headquarters, which is a combination of the Six Corps serving in the Atlanta and subsequent Campaigns. The Arrow is the Badge of the 17th Corps; the Triangle, of the 4th; the Shield, of the 23d; the Star, of the 20th; the Cartridge-box, of the 15th; the Acorn, of the 14th Corps... *Title-page.*
Sherman and his Generals.. *Frontispiece.*
Allatoona Pass .... Page   31
Atlanta in Ruins...   39
Sports of the Army (Vignette)..   77
Rice-mill on the Ogeechee..   88
Fort McAllister..   93
Treasure Seekers... 113
Destruction of Columbia 168
Corduroying at Lynch's Creek... 190
Army Mule 205
Refugee Train 211
Headquarters Camp of General Sherman................................... 219
The Heroes that are not Gazetted....................................... 231
A "Bummer"... 245
Battle of Bentonville.. 270
The Conference between General Sherman and General Johnston.... 313
The Graves of our dead Comrades.. 321
The End.. 322

THE

STORY OF THE GREAT MARCH.

PART I.

THE MARCH TO THE SEA.

CHAPTER I.

THE OPENING CAMPAIGN.

It was a proud day for the soldiers of Sherman's army when they encamped in and around the city of Atlanta. Their previous campaign had extended through the hot summer months, and after their protracted manœuvring, marching, and fighting, they were glad enough to rest on the glorious triumphs they had so long anticipated and so nobly won.

In future years the thoughtful traveler in our Southern States may seek to trace the pathway of what is known as the "Atlanta Campaign;" and in surveying the field of operations, which extends from Chattanooga to Atlanta, must feel and acknowledge the military skill and tenacity which, step by step, contested the advance of a conquering foe, fought many a bloody battle, but ever retired in good order, never in demoralized flight. And if he be a friend of the restored Republic, his heart will thrill with admiration and pride for the gallant heroes who pushed forward day by day, bearing grandly at the head of their resistless columns the Stars and Stripes, until over hill and plain, and emerging firm amid the smoke of victorious battles, the national standard waved in triumph over the Gate City itself—over the long-vaunted "impregnable" Atlanta.

Emerging from the mountain district of Tennessee, where Chattanooga lies cosily sheltered in a valley by the riverside, the explorer who visits this region in peaceful times will descend among the lesser hills of Upper Georgia. On each side of his way, and still more frequently directly across it, he will see and meet long lines of fortifications. The soil which formerly was devoted to the peaceful labors of the agriculturist has leaped up, as it were, into frowning parapets, supported and surmounted by logs, and guarded in front by tangled abattis, palisades, and *chevaux de frise*. By some river's bank he will find evidences of defense still more carefully constructed. Forts and redoubts will be reflected in quiet, rippling streams; *têtes du pont* still remain to guard the approaches to the water; and, as he passes on, the upturnings of the earth will become more and more frequent, till it would seem as if some giant plowshare had passed through the land, marring with gigantic and unsightly furrows the rolling plains, laying waste the fields and gardens, and, passing on to the abodes of men, upturning their very hearths, and razing even towns and cities. The hills of Allatoona frown upon him, with their forts and curtains peering above the rocky elevations. Before him rises the solemn Kenesaw, with its grandeur of "everlasting hill" intensified by the mute records of human warfare—with its impregnable front furrowed and crowned with the marks of war.

To General Sherman and the Army of the Union, the Atlanta Campaign, speaking in military technology, was "offensive." To Johnston and the Rebels it was "defensive-offensive." With both, it was a magnificent exhibition of the grand tactics of the art of war.

In the great strategic combinations which had already taken shape in the far-seeing mind of General Sherman, this campaign was but an incident in the scheme. To Johnston, driven to the defensive, the series of operations embraced in his retreat from Chattanooga to Atlanta were tactical, and not strategical. It may be said, then, that in itself the Atlanta Campaign belongs to the art of Grand Tactics. It is essential to make this definition clear at the outset, because the subsequent operations of Sherman, including the pursuit of Hood's army and the campaigns of Georgia and the Carolinas, belong to the higher art in the conduct of war—that of Grand Strategy.

The months of August and September, 1864, passed in quiet, while the army rested at Atlanta, varied only by drills, dress parades, reviews, and the usual phases of camp life and duties. With the exception of temporary interruptions, the line of communication with Chattanooga was sustained, and the military world was astonished by some of the most remarkable quartermaster and commissariat feats ever known in the history of war. Here was a vast and hungry army of more than seventy thousand men, supplied not only for their daily wants, but with a surplus sufficient to provide rich and valuable stores of provisions at secondary bases. These supplies were forwarded over a line of railroad passing for four hundred miles through an enemy's country. This prodigious effort, which military men will appreciate better than others, will be a proud record for those to whom its inception and success are due—General Meigs, General Easton, Colonel Beckwith, and the various officers engaged under their command. The importance of the prudent foresight of General Sherman in establishing these secondary bases will be better understood at a later period of this narrative.

While affairs were thus satisfactory, and even enjoyable, in the Union lines, and the Federal soldiers, far away from their starting-point, and in the centre of a hostile country, were provided with every necessity of life and many luxuries, discouragement and discontent prevailed in the Rebel camp and councils. With singular fatuity, the Rebel leader who had usurped the title of President displaced General Johnston, who had the confidence of the Southern army and the people, appointing to his command a headstrong and impetuous officer, who was at once obnoxious and imprudent. With equally inexplicable willfulness, Jefferson Davis continued his support of Hood even when fully informed of the distrust with which he was viewed. Moreover, Davis made a personal visit to Georgia, and at Savannah, Macon, and Augusta made foolish speeches, in which he prayed a little, threatened much, and promised more.

Taking up the order of events in the grand campaigns, I shall draw liberally upon the notes entered in my diary. These memoranda were written during the midday rest of the army, on fences and stumps by the wayside, by the light of the camp-fires in the night bivouac, in cities or towns at which we halted, wherever or whenever a moment's release from pressing official duties afforded leisure to jot down the fleeting impressions of our long and wonderful march.

Atlanta, September 16*th*. To-day our master of transportation sent the following dispatch to Colonel Warner, of General Sherman's staff, in reply to an inquiry:

"We have made the arrangements to send a train to Rough and Ready to-morrow at 11 o'clock, which will transport several hundred of the citizens going south, but we will send you down on a locomotive at once if it is your order."

A flag of truce was pending between the opposing armies, and Colonel Warner was in charge of it on our side. An important question relative to the exchange of prisoners needed to be settled at once; so the order was given, and a few moments saw us mounted upon the engine, and rattling away over the shaky road which runs from Atlanta on the way to Macon. Our engineer was a young man, who pleasantly informed me that it was not the best policy to jump from the engine in the event of an upset. "Always stick to the machine," he said: "I have been overturned three times in the course of my experience, and never was injured beyond a light scratch on the nose. Always stick to the machine." With all respect to your opinion, I thought to myself, I shall jump at the first indications of danger; and I proceeded to impress upon the mind of Colonel Warner the fact of the superior management of railroads in England and on the Continent, where the engine-drivers are held to a strict accountability. Meanwhile our engineer, with a fixed, earnest gaze out of the side window, was holding firmly with one hand the handle of the throttle-valve, and with the other the "shut-off." I was busily engaged in digging the cinders out of my eyes, when we turned a sharp curve in the woods, and beheld a man by the embankment frantically waving a red flag, while a party of men not ten rods distant, who had just taken up a rail from the track, were waving their hats and shouting for us to stop. Our engine-driver—keen-eyed, alert, and clear-headed—at once saw the danger, reversed the machinery, put the tender-brake in operation, and the huge monster in an instant was quiet as a sleeping child. "A close rub, sir!" said my friend the engineer. "Six feet more, and we should have pitched into the ravine there; that flag should have been a quarter of a mile farther back." In justice to myself, I should say that I "stuck to the machine," and in justice to our engineer, it should be added that no farther remark was made upon that trip derogatory to American railroad management.

Twenty minutes of travel carried us over the ten miles which intervened between Atlanta and the neutral ground, where the banished citizens are handed over to the Rebel officers, and the exchange of prisoners takes place. Rough and Ready as completely answers to the first part of its name as one could imagine, and perhaps to the latter half; for it appears to have been getting ready to be a town since its foundation, and is likely to remain in that condition for an indefinite length of time. Two miserable shanties, the respective quarters of the Federal and Rebel guards, separated for a distance of about two hundred yards, constitute the burgh of Rough and Ready.

Dismounting from our engine, we approached the hut nearest the Confederate lines. It was a characteristic specimen of the habitations of the poor class of whites at the South. A few refuse boards fastened upon an irregular frame; a disjointed window in a shattered sill; a battered door swinging upon a single hinge, formed its striking features; while several swords and pistols, hanging upon the side of the house, indicated the presence of soldiers. The single room was half filled with smoke, puffing lazily from a fireplace around which were scattered sundry dilapidated pots and pans; but we had little time, and it was not our business to take an inventory of the goods and chattels in the establishment. A pale, sickly woman, seated in the rickety porch, answered our question as to the whereabouts of Major Clare, a staff officer of General Hood, who represents the Rebel party in the truce.

"He's h'yar somewhar; round the corner of the yard, I reckon. Say, Betsy! whar's Major Clare?"

We made the circuit of the corner and found the major; a handsome, polite gentleman, by the way, who was seated near some ladies, in the midst of a collection of baskets and household goods. We were presented to the ladies, when the two officers stepped aside for the discussion of the business which brought them together, leaving me to attempt the somewhat difficult task of entertaining persons who had evidently just been ejected from their homes in Atlanta.

Of course the conversation turned upon the war and the order of removal issued by General Sherman. The youngest, a lady of refinement, remarked:

"It is very hard to be obliged to leave our home. We have not felt the war before, except in the cost of the luxuries of life. We did not believe your army would ever penetrate so far south; but I suppose our removal is one of the necessities of the situation, and we would much rather give up our homes than live near the Yankees. We will get far enough away this time."

A sentiment of commiseration filled my heart, and I ventured the remark:

"May I ask where you intend to go?"

"To Augusta, where your army can't come," was the reply.

"I would not be sure of that," I replied. "It is a long way from Nashville to Atlanta, and we are here."

"Oh yes," she rejoined, with ineffable scorn; "you will '*flank*' us, I suppose?"

"Possibly, madam."

"Look here, sir; there are not two nations on the face of this earth whose language, customs, and histories are different, and who are geographically separated as widely as the poles, but what are nearer to each other than the North and South. There are no two peoples in the world who hate each other more."

"I hardly think there is the difference you describe," I answered. "It seems to me just as if you and I were Americans, with no vital points of difference between us which may not be settled some day. And then I protest against the idea that we 'hate you.' I understand public feeling at the North pretty well, and such a feeling does not exist there generally."

"Well, sir, *we hate you;* we will never live with you again. If you whip us, and any of these mean politicians in the South (and there are thousands of them who will be only too glad to do it) offer terms of reconstruction, we will throw ourselves into the arms of France, which only waits the chance to embrace us."

"Reconstruction will undoubtedly come about in time," I said; "but we shall not permit France or any other foreign power to interfere. France would embrace you without doubt, if she gets a chance; but it will be the hug of an anaconda that will swallow you whole, without mastication."

"Any thing rather than become subject to the North. We will not submit to *that* degradation."

"If you are defeated you will; and then you will have thoroughly learned what your people have never, before the war, in the slightest degree understood—how to *respect us.* I assure you friendship follows very close upon the heel of mutual respect."

"There is much truth in that, sir, and we are willing to confess that we never even believed the North would fight; and while there is a certain feeling of respect which has been forced upon us, we hate you all the more now, because we despised you before."

During this conversation, which I have written out because it is a fair picture of the opinions of the Georgians, frequently expressed to me, a long train of wagons and ambulances from Atlanta, provided by General Sherman, had driven into the space between the outposts, and deposited their freight of women and children, with their household furniture. These people seemed to be almost entirely of the lower class. The wealthier citizens removed from Atlanta when the firing began; those only remaining who were willing to take the risk of shot and shell, and the possibility of Federal occupation.

The dust from our wagons had hardly subsided when the sharp crack of the whip and the loud cries of train-master and mule-drivers announced the arrival of the Rebel convoy to remove the people whom General Sherman had refused to permit Hood to throw upon him as a burden. Bidding adieu to the ladies, and with a kindly grasp of the hand from Major Clare, we departed from Rough and Ready. For several miles from Atlanta our course lay through the encampment of troops comprising the armies of the Tennessee and Cumberland. To the right and left stretched long lines of splendidly-constructed rifle-pits; here and there, upon commanding points, heavily bastioned forts overlooked the country. The afternoon was slowly waning into evening. Groups of soldiers were scattered in the openings of the forests—some engaged in preparing supper, others watching the play of their fellows, and all enjoying a much-needed rest from the toils of a long and arduous campaign.

Atlanta, September 27*th.* The armed foot has pressed heavily upon this people, and they feel the unrelenting iron hand of Sherman grasping and holding their very life; and I am sure that, with a vivid consciousness of the terrors of the past, and a dread foreboding of the future, they are ready for peace on almost any terms. Neither the newspapers nor the leaders say this, but there are strong indications in that direction. One of their newspapers proceeds deliberately to discuss the propriety of Governor Brown's acceptance of Sherman's invitation to come to Atlanta. . A current report of such an invitation having been extended has thus much of truth—that while a prominent citizen of Georgia was dining with General Sherman one day, the former remarked, "I wish, general, that Governor Brown could see and talk with you." "Let him come," replied the general; "I have no objection to his coming within my lines. He shall pass safely in and out; there are valuable records here which he would no doubt like to get and preserve. Let him come; I would like to see him." I presume the invitation was duly delivered to the governor, but it is a question if he is prepared just at this moment to accept it. Perhaps we shall have the pleasure of finding him at Macon or Augusta.

The military situation is unchanged here, so far as our army is concerned. The soldiers are resting and enjoying themselves thoroughly; they glory in the past, and are as confident of the future as if it were their own. Their faith in Sherman is beyond all description. "He can't make a mistake," they say. "Wherever he puts us, we are going in, and we're just dead sure to whip the Rebs every time—*sure.*" In view of the campaign from Chattanooga to the Chattahoochee, and after an inspection of the strong defenses of Atlanta, it is not surprising that our men have such faith in their leader. Had Atlanta been captured by direct approaches and attack, it would have taken months or years to reduce these fortifications, prepared with so much labor and skill. On the southern side of the city, heavy bastioned forts, mounting ponderous sixty-four-pounders, were erected upon the hills, which are separated some two and three hundred yards from each other; they are connected, however, by carefully-constructed curtains, with occasional redoubts mounting field artillery. In order to get full sweep for these terrible missiles, the country for several hundred rods was cleared of heavy timber.

Approaching these defenses, if the brave assaulting columns, in struggling through the tangled brushwood and fallen trees, had not been torn in pieces by the fire of a hundred guns covering every point of advance, they would have met, some twenty yards from the fortifications, a carefully-constructed abattis, composed of the tops of small pine and cedar trees, placed one upon another, pointing outward; a few yards farther in there was a stockade of five or six rows of stakes driven firmly into the ground, their sharpened points viciously inclined outward; a few steps more, if able to break these or tear them from their places, our men would have found a *chevaux de frise*, over which a very meagre man or a small boy might crawl, but not one of our well-fed soldiers, with a musket in his hand.

But we will suppose all this surmounted; there is still a palisade of logs from eight to ten feet high, set firmly into the ground, pierced for musketry fire, with openings for the play of artillery. Now if, by some process—under the somewhat embarrassing circumstances a soldier at this point would probably find himself in—these palisades could be scaled or torn down, the assailants have yet to descend into a ditch, and surmount the scarp and parapet of the work in the face of the concealed and enfilading fire of a vigilant foe. The lines of works which I have here attempted to describe are the principal, but by no means the only fortifications. Exterior to them there are lines of rifle-pits,

B

with redoubts, surrounding the city, and interior lines of almost equal strength to the main line surrounding the whole.

Meanwhile, under Sherman's orders, the removal of the citizens of Atlanta outside of our lines was continued. The order was kindly but firmly executed, and the inhabitants, unfortunate, it is true, in being thus in the track of war, were allowed to choose which way they would go. If they wished to go North, they were freely provided with transportation; if they preferred to penetrate farther into rebeldom, they were conveyed in wagons, with their furniture and personal effects, to the lines of Hood's army at Rough and Ready Station. The Rebels howled forth threats and objurgations at what they termed a fiendish act of cruelty, but General Sherman little heeded their ravings. He had taken this step only after due premeditation. Atlanta was a captured city. He was at a great distance from his base of supplies, with a precarious line of communication, which was frequently interrupted by the Rebel guerrilla raids. It would have been an absurd incongruity daily to fill the mouths of the wives and children of men in arms against the government. The safety of his command was at stake; so he sent these people away, and the sober judgment of the Christian world has since justified him in the act.

CHAPTER II.

PURSUIT OF HOOD—THE DEFENSE OF ALLATOONA.

During the rest at Atlanta the army was not idle. All the time preparations were making for the coming campaign. The leading generals of the army had already discussed their future plans, and the soldiers — to whom a stationary camp, even were it pitched in a paradise, would soon become tediously monotonous—were inquiring of each other what was next to come, and anxiously looking forward to a farther march. But, though the plans had assumed shape, certain events were waited for before a fresh start could be made.

It is said that a mysterious power of divination is the gift of genius; that, if it can not lift the veil of futurity, it can at least see the shadows which coming events cast before them. What prophetic intuitions filled the mind of General Sherman as he paced the piazza of that house in Atlanta, utterly abstracted in thought, his head cast a little to one side, one hand buried in his side pocket, the other fitfully snapping the ashes from his cigar, are known only to himself; but certain it is that one bright morning we were awakened with orders to move. Hood had already crossed the Chattahoochee, and was forty-eight hours in advance. His objective point was then a mooted question, nor has the military problem yet been fully answered: perhaps he did not know it himself. There can be little doubt, however, that the leading purpose of Hood's march was to draw Sherman away from Atlanta by a bold movement in our rear, threatening not only our line of communications, but our base of supplies. He thought that he could retort upon Sherman his own tactics, and force him, for want of supplies, to give up the bravely-won victories of the summer's campaign, and force us back upon Chattanooga.

Hood is said to be a rash man, with more zeal than prudence, and his vivid imagination may have pictured to him the advantages of retaliating upon Nashville the fate of Atlanta. He saw in his mind's eye the Tennessee capital, with its parlors and saloons brilliant with fashionable society, its vast stores of clothing, its millions of rations, its store of provision, its ammunition, cannon, and other trophies of war—in fact, every thing which he and his army could desire. And in the background of this picture were the green pastures of Kentucky, rich in cattle; and, still farther in the dim and hazy distance, the steeples and domes which marked the populous and wealthy cities of Ohio, teeming with treasures, and defenseless before the wild incursion of the desperate Confederate invader. It was with these suddenly-inspired hopes, this scheme of invasion and retaliation not wholly impracticable, that Hood started off on the errand of his master, Jefferson Davis.

Meanwhile it should be stated that, from the initiatory steps of Hood's movements, Sherman was accurately informed of all his proceedings. In the first instance, General Thomas was sent back to Chattanooga and Nashville to reorganize various scattered detachments of troops, to be used as coming events might require. General Slocum, with the 20th Corps, was left in Atlanta, while the 4th, 23d, 14th, 15th, and 17th Corps moved leisurely across the Chattahoochee up the line of railroad. Hood was known to be in the direction of Dallas, looking out for our approach.

All this time Sherman was watching, ready to take advantage of the slightest false movement of his enemy; and knowing the danger of the latter, he "gave him rope," pushing his own column by the left well up to Kenesaw. It was on the morning of the 5th of October that he saw the head of column of his right centre pushing out toward Pine Knob, which stands intermediate between Kenesaw and Lost Mountain. Behind the latter Hood was supposed to be lying.

Upon this day was fought the battle of Allatoona. It was a contest of vast importance, though it has not been as prominently before the public as other battles of smaller consequence. The post which it secured was a vital link in our communications. Here were stored a million and a half of rations, and here was a pass of the Allatoona range of hills, through which ran our railroad and our line of communications. Here, at the head of only fifteen hundred men, General Corse fought, from early dawn till noon, a force of no less than six thousand Rebels. A hard, obstinate fight was this battle of Allatoona—where men contested their ground foot by foot—where our soldiers were driven by the desperate assaults of overwhelming numbers from intrenchments to the hill, and from the hill to the fort—where, with half their number killed and wounded, with their chief bleeding and at times insensible, they yet fought on, inspired by his indomitable courage, until the Rebels, repulsed with fearful loss, gave up the struggle and fled from the field, leaving their killed and wounded in the hands of the brave defenders.

Standing on the top of Kenesaw, General Sherman saw the white puffs of smoke which told of the contest raging at Allatoona. He felt confident of the result; for, anticipating the possibility of this rash attempt of the Rebels, he had ordered Corse down from Rome to hold Allatoona until his columns could come up. He knew Corse to be quick of comprehension, determined in execution, and brave as the bravest.

The Hero of Allatoona Pass need have no nobler epitaph than the words of Sherman upon that morning of doubt and misgiving: "I know Corse; so long as he lives, the Allatoona Pass is safe."

It may be truly said that Corse is the embodiment of the defense of Allatoona. His quick comprehension is only equaled by the celerity of execution which has distinguished him upon many a battle-field. He is brave almost to rashness, and with that quality combines indomitable energy and perseverance. Corse is one of a large number of officers in the Western Army of whom it is sometimes said, when the firing comes sharp and frequent from an indicated direction, "Oh, Corse is in there, is he? He'll take care of that front, sure; he will wake them up," etc.

General Corse is of medium height, rather good-looking, open-handed, open-hearted, and genial. He is one of that class of men who make friends easily and seldom lose them. At the time of which I write, he commanded the 4th Division of the 15th Corps, the soldiers of which will always remember with pride the gallant Hero of Allatoona.

The battle in question was the decisive point of the campaign in pursuit of Hood. The same night, Corse, though severely wounded and suffering, went to Rome with his remaining troops. After the failure of the rash assault, the Rebel general passed by Rome, and threatened, but did not attack Resaca, for Sherman was now close in his track. Hood effected a temporary lodgment at Dalton. Then, collecting his hungry, barefooted men, and gathering what little plunder he could find, he fled over the mountains and down the valley at the rate of twenty-five miles a day to Gayles-

ALLATOONA PASS.

ville, and thence to Gadsden, where he rejoined his trains, to make his fatal march toward Nashville.

General Sherman waited some time at Gaylesville, until fully assured of the direction taken by his late antagonist. He then detached the 4th Corps, and subsequently the 23d, with orders to join General Thomas, who received full instructions as to the course he was to adopt.

CHAPTER III.

PREPARATIONS FOR THE SEAWARD MARCH — THE BURNING OF ATLANTA.

GENERAL SHERMAN at once made preparations to abandon all the posts south of Dalton. From Gaylesville and Rome he issued his orders concerning the new movement. The sick and wounded, non-combatants, the machinery, extra baggage, tents, wagons, artillery, ammunition stores, every person and every thing not needed in the future campaigns, were sent back to Chattanooga. The army was stripped for fighting and marching.

The movement thus begun was purely strategical in its character.

It would be hardly proper to say that General Sherman had opened the door for Hood to enter Tennessee, for his previous calculations for the new campaign had included Hood in his front; yet there can be no question that, after the Rebel leader had wandered off in the direction of Florence, leaving the Union general free to complete his arrangements, the latter was well satisfied that there was nothing to interfere with his grand projected march to the sea. The consciousness of this freedom of action, the certainty that he had intrusted the Chattanooga and Nashville line to the wise and prudent Thomas, with an army sufficient to repel the proposed invasion and overthrow the desperate invader, added zest and absolute confidence to his future operations.

Let us for a moment look at General Sherman as he appeared at Gaylesville, seated upon a camp-stool in front of his tent, with a map of the United States spread upon his knees. General Easton and Colonel Beckwith, his chief quartermaster and commissary, are standing near. By his side are Generals Howard and Slocum, the future commanders of the right and left wings. General Sherman's finger runs swiftly down the map until it reaches Atlanta; then, with unerring accuracy, it follows the general direction to be taken by the right and left wings, until a halt is made at Milledgeville. "From here," the general says, "we have several alternatives; I am sure we can go to Savannah, or open communication with the sea somewhere in that direction." After studying the map a while, tracing upon the tangled maze of streams and towns a line from Savannah north and east, at Columbia, South Carolina, General Sherman looks up at General Howard with the remark, "Howard, I believe we can go there without any serious difficulty. If we can cross the Salkahatchie, we can capture Columbia. From Columbia"—passing his finger quickly over rivers, swamps, and cities to Goldsboro, North Carolina— "that point is a few days' march through a rich country. When we reach that important railroad junction—when I once plant this army at Goldsboro—Lee must leave Virginia, or he will be defeated beyond hope of recovery. We can make this march, for General Grant assures me that Lee can not get away from Richmond without his knowledge, nor without serious loss to his army."

To those who gazed upon the map, and measured the great distance to be traversed, from this quiet village away up in the mountains of Northern Alabama down to the sea, and thence hundreds of miles through a strange and impassable country away to the North again, and over wide rivers and treacherous bogs, the whole scheme, in the hands of any man but he who conceived it, seemed weird, fatal, impossible. But it was at that moment in process of operation. General Sherman at once communicated the first part of his plan to General Grant, subsequently receiving his hearty approval, with entire freedom to act as he should deem best. The army was at once set in motion; the numerous threads spreading over a wide field of operations were gathered up; out of confusion came exquisite order. Detachments guarding various dépôts were sent to their commands, outposts were withdrawn, the cavalry were concentrated in one division, under the lead of a gallant soldier. Compact, confident, and cheerful, this well-appointed host, guided by that master mind, moved grandly on to the fulfillment of its high mission. The field of operations now entered upon belonged, as has been said, to the genius of strategy. Those who have written of this campaign always date its commencement as from Atlanta. Inasmuch as we trod upon hitherto unconquered soil when we went out from Atlanta, this statement is true; but the march really began at Rome and Kingston, and it is from this point that we take up the diary of events which occurred within the experience and knowledge of the writer.

November 13*th*.—Yesterday the last train of cars whirled rapidly past the troops moving south, speeding over bridges and into the woods as if they feared they might be left helpless in the deserted land. At Cartersville the last communications with the North were severed with the telegraph wire. It bore the message to General Thomas, "All is well." And so we have cut adrift from our base of operations, from our line of communications, launching out into uncertainty at the best, on a journey whose projected end only the General in command knows. Its real fate and destination he does not know, since that rests with the goodness of God and the brave hearts and strong limbs of our soldiers. The history of war bears no similar example, except that of Cortés burning his ships. It is a bold, hazardous undertaking. There is no backward step possible here. Thirty days' rations and a new base: that time and those supplies will be exhausted in the most rapid march ere we can arrive at the nearest sea-coast; arrived there, what then? I never heard that manna grew on the sand-beaches or in the marshes, though we are sure that we can obtain forage on our way; and I have reason to know that General Sherman is in the highest degree sanguine and cheerful —sure even of success.

As for the soldiers, they do not stop to ask questions. Sherman says "Come," and that is the entire vocabulary to them. A most cheerful feature of the situation is the fact that the men are healthful and jolly as men can be; hoping for the best, willing to dare the worst.

Behind us we leave a track of smoke and flame. Half of Marietta was burned up—not by orders, however; for the command is that proper details shall be made to destroy all property which can ever be of use to the Rebel armies. Stragglers will get into these places, and dwelling-houses are leveled to the ground. In nearly all cases these are the deserted habitations formerly owned by Rebels who are now refugees.

Yesterday, as some of our men were marching toward the Chattahoochee River, they saw in the distance pillars of smoke rising along its banks—the bridges were in flames. Said one, hitching his musket on his shoulder in a free and easy way: "I say, Charley, I believe Sherman has set the river on fire." "Reckon not," replied the other, with the same indifference; "if he has, it's all right." And so they pass along; obeying orders, not knowing what is before them, but believing in their leader.

From Kingston to Atlanta the rails have been taken up on the road, fires built about them, and the iron twisted into all sorts of curves; thus they are left, never to be straightened again. The Rebel inhabitants are in agony of wonder at all this queer manœuvring. It appears as if we intended evacuating Atlanta; but our troops are taking the wrong direction for the hopes and purposes of these people.

Atlanta is entirely deserted by human beings, excepting a few soldiers here and there. The houses are vacant; there is no trade or traffic of any kind; the streets are empty. Beautiful roses bloom in the gardens of fine houses, but a terrible stillness and solitude cover all, depressing the hearts even of those who are glad to destroy it. In the peaceful homes at the North there can be no conception how these people have suffered for their crimes.

Atlanta, Night of the 15*th November.* A grand and awful spectacle is presented to the beholder in this beautiful city, now in flames. By order, the chief engineer has destroyed by powder and fire all the store-houses, dépôt buildings, and machine-shops. The heaven is one expanse of lurid fire; the air is filled with flying, burning cinders; buildings covering two hundred acres are in ruins or in flames; every instant there is the sharp detonation or the smothered booming sound of exploding shells and powder concealed in the buildings, and then the sparks and flame shoot away up into the black and red roof, scattering cinders far and wide.

These are the machine-shops where have been forged and

ATLANTA IN RUINS.

cast the Rebel cannon, shot and shell that have carried death to many a brave defender of our nation's honor. These warehouses have been the receptacle of munitions of war, stored to be used for our destruction. The city, which, next to Richmond, has furnished more material for prosecuting the war than any other in the South, exists no more as a means for injury to be used by the enemies of the Union.

A brigade of Massachusetts soldiers are the only troops now left in the town: they will be the last to leave it. To-night I heard the really fine band of the Thirty-third Massachusetts playing "John Brown's soul goes marching on," by the light of the burning buildings. I have never heard that noble anthem when it was so grand, so solemn, so inspiring.

CHAPTER IV.

THE ORGANIZATION OF THE ARMY.

Before fairly entering upon a recital of the incidents attending the great march seaward, it is important to glance at the organization of the army, and to gain at least a general idea of its main features.

The grand army under the supreme command of General Sherman is divided into two armies, called the Right and Left Wings, each of which has a separate army commander—General Howard, of the right wing, and General Slocum, of the left. Each of these armies is composed of two corps, which are subdivided into divisions and brigades, with their proper commanding officers.*

In the long marches, when the army has covered a vast extent of country, this organization proves to be of the highest practical use. Each column marches within supporting distance of the others. Yet exceptional instances have occurred where one wing may be forced to act in a measure independent of the others, as when the communication is cut off by a stream difficult to cross, or by a mountainous district which can be but slowly traversed. At such times there is a complete organization united in one command, ready to act as the emergency may require. But, as before said, these instances are exceptional. The conditions of our success are attended with such weighty

---

* In addition to these, there is a cavalry corps, under the command of General Kilpatrick, who takes his orders directly from General Sherman. This corps is the curtain behind whose gleaming folds our chief, marching with one or another column as circumstances dictate, gives his orders.

responsibilities and dangerous risks, that this great moving mass of men and material is never fairly out of hand.

The General commanding issues his orders, directed toward or including certain objective points, to reach which requires several days' marching. It is the office of the subordinate commanders to put in motion that apparently unwieldy, but really manageable, orderly mass of humanity, wherein every man has his place, and duties which must be performed; and by this beautiful and practical system an army of sixty or seventy thousand men is shifted from place to place with a safety and celerity almost magical.

The ease and rapidity with which an army of so great a magnitude as this moves through an enemy's country is a convincing evidence of the great perfection we have attained in the logistics of the art of war. It is impossible to appreciate this fact without understanding in some manner at least the system of military organization. From the distant stand-point of persons outside of the army, only the successive steps in the great military progress are noted. To-day the newspaper reader at home is informed that this town is occupied or that river crossed; the next week he hears of additional successes; now the army is at Milledgeville, six or seven days later it is on the Oconee, subsequently at Millen, and so on step by step; but to understand *how* each daily step is taken; how nicely all the parts of the machinery are set up and put in motion; to fully comprehend the "*savoir faire*," requires not only a knowledge of the art of war in logistics especially, but daily observations, and personal experiences.

General Sherman's intimate acquaintance with all this detail of the movement of an army, and the close attention he gives to it day by day, is one of the most notable traits of his character as a military man. Thus, while his genius for strategic combinations exhibits the highest order of mind, General Sherman possesses a marvelous faculty in this science of logistics; a fact the more remarkable, as these two qualities, in their very nature diverse, are but rarely developed to any large extent in the same person.

As we are starting upon this new campaign, let us see who are the leading characters engaged.

General Sherman has a personal staff of five officers, none above the rank of major. Attached to his headquarters, but not technically members of his staff, are the chiefs of the separate departments for the military divisions of the Mississippi. Brigadier General Barry, chief of artillery, is a veteran soldier of sagacity and experience, and a most companionable gentleman of the old school.

Brigadier General Easton, chief quartermaster, is a man somewhat reserved in manner, punctilious in the execution of his duties, thoroughly comprehending and conscientiously fulfilling them.

Lieutenant Colonel Ewing is Inspector General. No one better understands the organization of this army, down to its last battalion, than he. His position would permit an incumbent so disposed to be exacting, censorious, and hypercritical, but Colonel Ewing is of a far different character. Though firm, he is as courteous as he is efficient.

Captain Poe, the chief of engineers, is a man of genius, of wide scientific knowledge, and unfailing practical executive capacity. Few officers have made themselves of greater value to the cause and the country.

Captain Baylor, chief of ordnance, is a quiet, modest gentleman, full of character, and with most thorough knowledge of the technicalities of his branch of the service.

Dr. Moore is chief medical director. He is also an able army officer of wisdom and experience. It is astonishing how men of such large responsibilities accomplish so much work without making the machinery prominent. Perhaps, however, there is great power in being authorized to append to one's signature the words "by order of the General commanding." Dr. Moore, it may be added, is something more than a surgeon; he is an exquisite humorist, one of the dry, genial, Charles-Lamb-like wits, who delight the taste as well as excite the risibilities.

The most extraordinary working man in the army is perhaps Colonel Beckwith, chief of the commissary department. He has the exterior appearance of a subdued Methodist clergyman of the Church South. The interior of the man's brain it would be a curiosity to see. He does more work himself, and gets more work out of others, than any other man it has ever been my good fortune to meet. Beckwith is indeed a terror to evil-doers, and is the especial horror of lazy or indifferent workers. He has kept the army supplied with food under circumstances of peculiar difficulty, at which almost any other man would have been appalled. He requires few instructions, anticipates necessities, calculates closely, and executes with remarkable rapidity.

The Signal Corps is represented by Captain Bachtal, who is identified with the Army of the West during its entire history. It was he whose flag signaled over fifteen miles of hill and dale the order for Corse to fly to the defense of Allatoona. Captain Bachtal is a type of his corps, who are the ablest, coolest, and most daring men in the army. Standing in the most exposed positions, often in advance of the army, they waft from their little flags intelligence of the movements of friend or foe. Away from lines of travel, and in a mountainous country, these adventurous sentinels are indeed "like watchmen upon the hills," and their services are invaluable.

The right wing of the army is called the Army of Tennessee, and is commanded by General Howard. It is composed of two corps, the 15th and the 17th.

The 15th Corps is commanded by General John Logan. Its division commanders are General Woods, first division; General Hazen, second division; General Corse, fourth division. The third division exists only upon paper. It would take a volume larger than this to contain the magnificent record of this corps, which has been commanded successively by Generals Grant, Sherman, McPherson, Blair, and Logan. The fighting qualities of its men are unequaled, and they will march faster and farther, in a given time, than any equal number in the army.

The 17th Corps is commanded by General Blair. Its division commanders are General Force, first division; General Giles E. Smith, second division; General Legate, third division. General Legate, although laboring under severe chronic disease, always remained with his command until it became necessary to order him away to save his life. He is one of the most trustworthy officers in the army, doing his duty earnestly and faithfully.

The left wing of the army is called the Army of Georgia, and is commanded by General Slocum. It also contains two corps, the 14th and the 20th.

The 14th Corps is commanded by General Jeff. C. Davis. Its division commanders are General Carlin, first division; General J. D. Morgan, second division; General A. Baird, third division. General Baird is one of the most elegant officers of the army. Of medium stature, fine form, a prepossessing face, tawny side-whiskers and full mustache, a clear blue eye and a fair complexion, he personifies the ideal of a gentleman and a soldier. His manners are in perfect harmony with his appearance. Besides this, he is an accomplished soldier, distinguishing himself upon every occasion."

The 20th Corps is commanded by General Williams. Its division commanders are General Jackson, first division; General J. W. Geary, second division; General W. T. Ward, third division.

The cavalry corps is under the command of General Kilpatrick, who reports directly to General Sherman.

CHAPTER V.

BREAKING CAMP—A DAY'S MARCH—THE BIVOUAC.

AMONG the most characteristic features of the soldier's life is the important step of breaking camp, which is at once the close of a season of monotonous inactivity and the preliminary stage of a phase of exciting adventure. The same general details are on such occasions observed throughout the entire army, differing slightly in some of the corps, when the division which was in the centre or rear marches first, taking the place of the division which was in advance the day before.

The order of march is issued by the army commanders the preceding night, from them to the corps commanders, and then passed along until every soldier, teamster, and camp-follower knows that an early start is to be made. "The second division will be on the Milledgeville road promptly at five o'clock" reads an order, by way of instance.

At three o'clock the watch-fires are burning dimly, and, but for the occasional neighing of horses, all is so silent that it is difficult to imagine that twenty thousand men are within a radius of a few miles. The ripple of the brook can be distinctly heard as it breaks over the pebbles, or winds petulantly about the gnarled roots. The wind sweeping gently through the tall pines overhead only serves to lull to deeper repose the slumbering soldier, who in his tent is dreaming of his far-off Northern home.

But in an instant all is changed. From some commanding elevation the clear-toned bugle sounds out the *reveillé*, and another and another responds, until the startled echoes double and treble the clarion calls. Intermingled with this comes the beating of drums, often rattling and jarring on unwilling ears. In a few moments the peaceful quiet is replaced by noise and tumult, arising from hill and dale, from field and forest. Camp-fires, hitherto extinct or smouldering in dull gray ashes, awaken to new life and brilliancy, and send forth their sparks high into the morning air. Although no gleam of sunrise blushes in the east, the harmless flames on every side light up the scene, so that there is no disorder or confusion.

The æsthetic aspects of this sudden change do not, however, occupy much of the soldier's time. He is more practically engaged in getting his breakfast ready. The potatoes are frying nicely in the well-larded pan; the chicken is roasting delicately on the red-hot coals, and grateful fumes from steaming coffee-pots delight the nostrils. The animals are not less busy. An ample supply of corn and huge piles of fodder are greedily devoured by these faithful friends of the boys in blue, and any neglect is quickly made known by the pawing of neighing horses and the fearful braying of the mules. Amid all is the busy clatter of tongues and tools—a Babel of sound, forming a contrast to the quiet of the previous hour as marked as that between peace and war.

Then the animals are hitched into the traces, and the droves of cattle relieved from the night's confinement in the corral. Knapsacks are strapped, men seize their trusty weapons, and as again the bugles sound the note of command, the soldiers fall into line and file out upon the road, to make another stage of their journey—it may be to win fresh laurels in another victory, or perhaps to find a rest which shall only be broken by the *reveillé* of the last trump.

C

A day's march varies according to the country to be traversed or the opposition encountered. If the map indicates a stream crossing the path, probably the strong party of mounted infantry or of cavalry which has been sent forward the day before has found the bridges burned, and then the pontoons are pushed on to the front. If a battle is anticipated, the trains are shifted to the rear of the centre. Under any circumstances, the divisions having the lead move unencumbered by wagons, and in close fighting trim. The ambulances following in the rear of the division are in such close proximity as to be available if needed. In the rear of each regiment follow the pack-mules, laden with every kind of camp baggage, including blankets, pots, pans, kettles, and all the kitchen-ware needed for cooking. Here will be found the led horses, and with them the negro servants, who form an important feature of the *ménage*.

Having placed the column upon the road, let us now follow that long line of muskets gleaming in the rays of the morning sunlight, and ride, heedless of the crack of the rifles, to the head of the column. The flankers are driving a squad of Rebel cavalry before them so fast that the march is not in the least impeded. The flankers spread out, on a line parallel to the leading troops, for several hundred yards, more or less, as the occasion may require. They search through the swamps and forests, ready for any concealed foe, and anxiously looking out for any line of works which may have been thrown up by the enemy to check our progress. Here the General of the division, if a fighting man, is most likely to be found; his experienced eye noting that there is no serious opposition, he orders up a brigade or another regiment, who, in soldier's phraseology, send the Rebel rascals "kiting," and the column moves on. A large plantation appears by the road-side. If the "bummers" have been ahead, the chances are that it has been visited, in which event the interior is apt to show evidences of confusion; but the barns are full of corn and fodder, and parties are at once detailed to secure and convey the prize to the road-side. As the wagons pass along they are not allowed to halt, but the grain or fodder is stuffed into the front and rear of the vehicles as they pass, the unhandy operation affording much amusement to the soldiers, and not unfrequently giving them a poor excuse for swearing as well as laughing.

When the treasure-trove of grain, and poultry, and vegetables has been secured, one man is detailed to guard it until the proper wagon comes along. Numbers of these details will be met, who, with proper authority, have started off early in the morning, and have struck out miles away from the flank of the column. They sit upon some cross-road, surrounded with their spoils—chickens, turkeys, geese, ducks, pigs, hogs, sheep, calves, nicely-dressed hams, buckets full of honey, and pots of fresh white lard.

A Roman consul returning with victorious eagles could not wear a more triumphant air than this solitary guard. The soldiers see it, and gibe him as they pass:

"Say, you thar! where did you steal them pigs?"

"Steal!" is the indignant response; "steal!—perhaps you would like to have one of "*them*" pigs yourself."

An officer who is riding along gazes upon the appetizing show. He has recently joined, never has been on one of Sherman's raids, and does not know that a soldier will not sell his chickens for any price.

"Ah! a nice pair of ducks you have there, soldier; what will you take for them?"

Firmly, but respectfully, the forager makes answer, touching his cap the while, "They are not in the market. We *never* sell our stuff, sir—couldn't think of it."

The officer rides away through a battery of broad grins from the by-standers, and never again offers to buy the spoils of a forager.

There is a halt in the column. The officer in charge of the pioneer corps, which follows the advance guard, has discovered an ugly place in the road, which must be "corduroyed" at once, before the wagons can pass. The pioneers quickly tear down the fence near by and bridge over the treacherous place, perhaps at the rate of a quarter of a mile in fifteen minutes. If rails are not near, pine saplings and split logs supply their place. Meanwhile the bugles have sounded, and the column has halted. The soldiers, during the temporary halt, drop out of line on the road-side, lying upon their backs, supported by their still unstrapped knapsacks. If the halt is a long one, the different regiments march by file right, one behind the other, into the fields, stacking their muskets, and taking their rest at ease, released from their knapsack.

These short halts are of great benefit to the soldier. He gains a breathing-spell, has a chance to wipe the perspiration from his brow and the dust out of his eyes, or pulls off his shoes and stockings to cool his swollen, heated feet, though old campaigners do not feel the need of this. He munches his bit of hard bread, or pulls out a book from his pocket, or oftener a pipe, to indulge in that greatest of luxuries to the soldier, a soothing, refreshing smoke. Here may be seen one group at a brook-side, bathing their heads and drinking; and another, crowded round an old song-book, are making very fair music. One venturesome fellow has kindled a fire, and is brewing a cup of coffee. All are happy and jolly; but when the bugle sounds "fall in" and "forward," in an instant every temporary occupation is dropped, and they are on the road again.

This massing of brigades and wagons during a halt is a proper and most admirable arrangement. It keeps the column well closed up; and if a brigade or division has by some means been delayed, it has the opportunity to overtake the others. The 20th Corps manage this thing to perfection.

A great many of the mounted officers ride through the fields, on either side of the line of march, so as not to interfere with the troops. General Sherman always takes to the fields, dashing through thickets or plunging into the swamps, and, when forced to take the road, never breaks into a regiment or brigade, but waits until it passes, and then falls in. He says that they, and not he, have the right to the road.

Sometimes a little creek crosses the path, and at once a foot-bridge is made upon one side of the way for those who wish to keep dry-shod; many, however, with a shout of derision, will dash through the water at a run, and then they all shout the more when some unsteady comrade misses his footing and tumbles in at full length. The unlucky wight, however, takes the fun at his expense in the best of humor. Indeed, as a general rule, soldiers are good-humored and kind-hearted to the last degree. I have seen a soldier stand at a spring of water for ten minutes, giving thirsty comers cool draughts, although it would delay him so that he would have to run a quarter of a mile or more to overtake his company. The troops, by the way, kept their ranks admirably during this Georgia campaign. Occasionally, however, they would rush for a drink of water, or for a beehive which they would despoil of its sweets with a total disregard of the swarm of bees buzzing about their ears, but which, strange to say, rarely stung.

But the sun has long since passed the zenith, the droves

of cattle which have been driven through the swamps and fields are lowing and wandering in search of a corral, the soldiers are beginning to lag a little, the teamsters are obliged to apply the whip oftener, ten or fifteen miles have been traversed, and the designated halting-place for the night is near. The column must now be got into camp.

Officers ride on in advance to select the ground for each brigade, giving the preference to slopes in the vicinity of wood and water. Soon the troops file out into the woods and fields, the leading division pitching tents first, those in the rear marching on yet farther, ready to take their turn in the advance the next day.

As soon as the arms are stacked, the boys attack the fences and rail-piles, and with incredible swiftness their little shelter-tents spring up all over the ground. The fires are kindled with equal celerity, and the luxurious repast prepared, while "good digestion waits on appetite, and health on both." After this is heard the music of dancing or singing, the pleasant buzz of conversation, and the measured sound of reading. The wagons are meanwhile parked and the animals fed. If there has been a fight during the day, the incidents of success or failure are recounted; the poor fellow who lies wounded in "the anguish-laden ambulance" is not forgotten, and the brave comrade who fell in the strife is remembered with words of loving praise.

By-and-by the tattoo rings out on the night air. Its familiar sound is understood. "Go to rest, go to rest," it says, as plainly as organs of human speech.

Shortly after follows the peremptory command of "Taps." "Out lights, out lights, out lights!" The soldier gradually disappears from the camp-fire. Rolled snugly in his blanket, the soldier dreams again of home, or revisits in imagination the battle-fields he has trod. The animals, with dull instinct, lie down to rest, and with dim gropings of consciousness ruminate over "fresh fields and pastures new." The fires, neglected by the sleeping men, go out, gradually flickering and smouldering, as if unwilling to die.

All is quiet. The army is asleep. Perhaps there is a brief interruption to the silence as some trooper goes clattering down the road on an errand of speed, or some uneasy sleeper turns over to find an easier position. And around the slumbering host the picket-guards keep quiet watch, while constant, faithful hearts in Northern and Western homes pray that the angels of the Lord may encamp around the sleeping army.

CHAPTER VI.

CAPTURE OF MILLEDGEVILLE—HOWELL COBB'S PLANTATION.

Milledgeville, November 24th.—We are in full possession of the capital of the State of Georgia, and without firing a gun in its conquest. A few days ago, the Legislature, which had been in session, hearing of our approach, hastily decamped without any adjournment. The legislative panic spread among the citizens to such an extent as to depopulate the place, except a few old gentlemen and ladies and the negroes, the latter welcoming our approach with ecstatic exclamations of joy: "Bress de Lord! tanks be to Almighty God, the Yanks is come! de day ob jubilee hab arribed!"—accompanying their words with rather embarrassing hugs, which those nearest the sidewalks received quite liberally.

General Slocum, with the 20th Corps, first entered the city, arriving by way of Madison, having accomplished his work of destroying the railroads and valuable bridges at that place. The fright of the legislators, as described by witnesses, must have been comical in the extreme. They little imagined the movement of our left wing, hearing first of the advance of Kilpatrick on the extreme right toward Macon, and supposing that to be another raid. What their opinion was when Howard's army appeared at M'Donough it would be difficult to say; and their astonishment must have approached insanity when the other two columns were heard from—one directed toward Augusta, and the other swiftly marching straight upon their devoted city.

It seemed as if they were surrounded upon all sides except toward the east, and that their doom was sealed. With the certain punishment for their crimes looming up before them, they sought every possible means of escape. Private effects, household furniture, books, pictures, were conveyed to the dépôt, and loaded into the cars until they were filled and heaped, and the flying people could not find standing-room.

Any and every price was obtained for a vehicle. A thousand dollars was cheap for a common buggy, and men rushed about the streets in an agony of fear lest they should "fall victims to the ferocity of the Yankees."

Several days of perfect quiet passed after this exodus, when, on a bright, sunshiny morning, a regiment entered the city, with a band playing national airs, which music had long been hushed in the capital of Georgia.

But few of the troops were marched through the city. Two or three regiments were detailed, under the orders of the engineers, to destroy certain property designated by the General Commanding. The magazines, arsenals, dépôt buildings, factories of various kinds, with store-houses containing large amounts of government property; and about seventeen hundred bales of coton, were burned. Private houses were respected every where, even those of noted Rebels, and I heard of no instance of pillage or insult to the inhabitants. One or two of the latter, known as having been in the Rebel army, were made prisoners of war, but the surgeons at the hospitals, the principal of the Insane Asylum, and others, expressed their gratitude that such perfect order was maintained throughout the city.

General Sherman is at the executive mansion, its former occupant having, with extremely bad grace, fled from his distinguished visitor, taking with him the entire furniture of the building. As General Sherman travels with a *ménage* (a roll of blankets and a haversack full of "hardtack"), which is as complete for a life in the open air as in a palace, this discourtesy of Governor Brown was not a serious inconvenience.

Just before his entrance into Milledgeville, General Sherman camped on one of the plantations of Howell Cobb. It was a coincidence that a Macon paper, containing Cobb's address to the Georgians as General Commanding, was received the same day. This plantation was the property of Cobb's wife, who was a Demar. I do not know that Cobb ever claimed any great reputation as a man of piety or singular virtues, but I could not help contrasting the call upon his fellow-citizens to "rise and defend their liberties, homes, etc., from the step of the invader, to burn and destroy every thing in his front, and assail him on all sides," and all that, with his own conduct here, and the wretched condition of his negroes and their quarters.

We found his granaries well filled with corn and wheat, part of which was distributed and eaten by our animals and men. A large supply of sirup made from sorghum (which we have found at nearly every plantation on our march) was stored in an out-house. This was also disposed of to the soldiers and the poor decrepit negroes which this humane, liberty-loving major general left to die in this place a few days ago. Becoming alarmed, Cobb sent for and removed all the able-bodied mules, horses, cows, and slaves. He left here some fifty old men—cripples—and women and children, with nothing scarcely covering their nakedness, with little or no food, and without means of procuring it. We found them cowering over the fireplaces of their miserable huts, where the wind whirled through the crevices between the logs, frightened at the approach of the Yankees, who, they had been told, would kill them. A more forlorn, neglected set of human beings I never saw.

General Sherman distributed to the negroes with his own hands the provisions left here, and assured them that we were their friends, and they need not be afraid that we were foes. One old man answered him: "I spose dat you'se true; but, massa, you'se 'll go way to-morrow, and anudder white man 'll come." He had never known any thing but persecutions and injury from the white man, and had been kept in such ignorance of us that he did not dare to put faith in any white man.

This terrorism, which forms so striking a feature of slavery, has had marked illustrations ever since we left Atlanta. The negroes were told that, as soon as we got them into our clutches, they were put into the front of the battle, and were killed if they did not fight; that we threw the women and children into the Chattahoochee, and when the buildings were burned in Atlanta we filled them with negroes to be roasted and devoured by the flames. These stories, which appear so absurd to us, are not too extravagant for the simple, untutored minds of the negroes. They are easily scared, and full of superstition. In almost any other instance such bloody tales would have frightened them entirely out of our sight to the woods and other hiding-places; but they assert, with much earnestness and glee, that "massa can't come dat over we; we know'd a heap better. What for de Yankees want to hurt black men? Massa hates de Yankees, and he's no fren' ter we; so we am de Yankee bi's fren's." Very simple logic that, but it is sufficient for the negroes.

Near Covington there was a certain large plantation. Before we arrived it was well stocked; I can't answer for its condition afterward. A jollier set of negroes I never saw than these were when the blue coats came along. Horrible stories of our cruelty to the negroes were also told by their masters to frighten them, but the negroes never put faith in one word. I asked the head man: "Well, how do you like the Yankees?"

"Like him? Bully! bully! bully! I'se wanted to see 'em long time; heard a heap 'bout 'em. Say, Sally, dese here be gemmen dat's passing"—a compliment to our soldiers which they no doubt would have appreciated could they have heard it.

"Yass, sar, I'se hope de Lord will prosper dem, and Mr. Sherman."

"Why do you hope that the Lord will help the Yankee?"

"Because I tinks, and we'se all tinks, dat you'se down here in our interests."

"You're about right there; did you ever hear that President Lincoln freed all the slayes?"

"No, sar, I nebber heard sich a ting. De white folks nebber talk 'fore black men; dey mighty free from dat."

In other parts of the South the negroes I have seen seem to understand there is a man named Lincoln, who had the power to free them, and had exercised it. In this neighborhood there is a stratum of ignorance upon that subject. All knowledge of that nature has not only been kept from the blacks, but only a few of the whites are well informed. The lieutenant commanding the escort of General Sherman was born and has always lived in Milledgeville, is an officer of the first Alabama cavalry regiment, and tells me that he never saw a copy of the New York Tribune until he joined our army. His history, by the way, is a most interesting one, and will one day be worth the telling. His adherence to the Union grew out of his natural abhorrence of slavery, whose horrors he had witnessed from childhood. His name is Snelling—a young man of good education, of high integrity, simple-hearted, and brave, who has been most useful to the cause of his country.

We are continually meeting with comical incidents illustrative of the ignorance of the people, and more especially of the funny side of negro character.

One old woman stood at her gate watching, with wondering eyes, a drove of cattle as they passed. "Lor', massy," said she, "whar did all them beef come from? Never seed so many in all my life."

"Those cattle were driven all the way from Chicago, more than one thousand miles."

"Goodness, Lor'; what a population you Yanks is!"

General Sherman invites all able-bodied negroes (others could not make the march) to join the column, and he takes especial pleasure on some occasions, when they join the procession, in telling them they are free; that Massa Lincoln has given them their liberty, and that they can go where they please; that if they earn their freedom they should have it, but that Massa Lincoln had given it to them any how. They seem to understand that the proclamation of freedom had made them free; and I have met but few instances where they did not say they expected the Yankees were coming down some time or other, and very generally they are possessed with the idea that we are fighting for them, and that their freedom is the object of the war. They got this notion hearing the talk of their masters.

"Stick in dar," was the angry exclamation of one of a party of negroes to another, who was asking too many questions of the officer who had given them permission to join the column. "Stick in dar, it's all right; we'se gwine along; we'se free."

Another replied to a question, " Oh yass, massa, de people

hereabouts were heap frightened when dey heard you'se coming; dey dusted out yer, sudden."

Pointing to the Atlanta and Augusta Railroad, which had been destroyed, the question was asked, "It took a longer time to build this railroad than it does to destroy it?"

"I would think it did, massa; in dat ar woods over dar is buried ever so many black men who were killed, sar, yes, killed, a workin' on dat road—whipped to death. I seed 'em, sar."

"Does the man live here who beat them?"

"Oh no, sar; he's dun gone long time."

At a house a few miles from Milledgeville we halted for an hour. In an old hut I found a negro and his wife, both of them more than sixty years old. In the talk which ensued nothing was said which led me to suppose that they were anxious to leave their mistress, who, by the way, was a sullen, cruel-looking woman, when all at once the old negress straightened herself up, and her face, which a moment before was almost stupid in its expression, assumed a fierce, almost devilish aspect.

Pointing her skinny black finger at the old man crouched in the corner of the fireplace, she hissed out, "What for you sit dar? you s'pose I wait sixty years for nutten? Don't yer see de door open? I'se follow my child; I not stay. Yes, anudder day I goes 'long wid dese people; yes, sar, I walks till I drop in my tracks." A more terrible sight I never beheld. I can think of nothing to compare with it, except Charlotte Cushman's Meg Merrilies. Rembrandt only could have painted the scene, with its dramatic surroundings.

It was near this place that several factories were burned. It was odd to see the delight of the negroes at the destruction of places known only to them as task-houses, where they had groaned under the lash.

General Sherman's opening move in the present campaign has been successful in the highest degree. First marching his army in three columns, with a column of cavalry on his extreme right, upon eccentric lines, he diverted the attention of the enemy, so that the Rebels concentrated their forces at extreme points, Macon and Augusta, leaving unimpeded the progress of the central columns. In this campaign—the end of which does not yet appear—it is not the purpose of the General to spend his time before fortified cities, nor yet to encumber his wagons with wounded men. His instructions to Kilpatrick were to demonstrate against Macon, getting within five miles of the city. That able officer has fulfilled his orders to the complete satisfaction of General Sherman.

The roads each column was to follow were carefully designated, the number of miles each day to be traveled, and the points of rendezvous were given at a certain date. All of these conditions were fulfilled to the letter. Slocum, with the 20th Corps, arrived at Milledgeville on the 22d instant, preceding Davis, with the 14th Corps, one day. On the same day Kilpatrick struck the Macon and Western road, destroying the bridge at Walnut Creek. The day following, Howard, with the 15th and 17th Corps, arrived at Gordon, and began the destruction of the Georgia Central Railroad.

It was near here that the most serious fight of the campaign has occurred up to this date. General Walcott, in command of a detachment of cavalry and a brigade of infantry, was thrown forward to Griswoldville, toward Macon, for demonstrative purposes merely. The enemy, about five thousand strong, advanced upon our troops, who had thrown up temporary breastworks, with a section of battery in position. The cavalry fell slowly back on either flank of the brigade, protecting them from attack in flank and rear. The Rebels were chiefly composed of militia, although a portion of Hardee's old corps was present, having been brought up from Savannah.

With the ignorance of danger common to new troops, the Rebels rushed upon our veterans with the greatest fury. They were received with grape-shot and musketry at point-blank range, our soldiers firing coolly, while shouting derisively to the quivering columns to come on, as if they thought the whole thing a nice joke. The Rebels resumed the attack, but with the same fatal results, and were soon in full flight, leaving more than three hundred dead on the field. Our loss was some forty killed and wounded, while their killed, wounded, and prisoners are estimated to exceed two thousand five hundred. A pretty severe lesson they have received. It is said, "*Ce n'est que le premier pas qui coûte.*" This first step has been a most expensive one, and, judging from the fact that we have not heard from them since, they seem to have interpreted the proverb otherwise than in the recognized sense.

Near Tennille Station, on the Georgia Central Railroad, November 27th.—Since writing the above the army has moved forward all along the line. The Rebels seem to have understood, but too late, that it was not Sherman's intention to make a serious attack upon Macon. They have, however, succeeded in getting Wheeler across the Oconee at a point below the railroad bridge. We first became aware of their presence in our front by the destruction of several small bridges across Buffalo Creek, on the two roads leading to Sandersville, over which were advancing the 20th and 14th Corps..

We were delayed but a few hours. The passage was

also contested by the Rebel cavalry under Wheeler, and they fought our front all the way, and into the streets of Sandersville. The 20th Corps had the advance, deploying a regiment as skirmishers, and forming the remainder of a brigade in line of battle on either side of the road. The movement was executed in the handsomest manner, and was so effectual as not to impede the march of the column in the slightest degree, although the roll of musketry was unceasing. Our loss was not serious—about twenty killed and wounded.

As the 20th Corps entered the town they were met by the 14th, whose head of column arrived at the same moment. While these two corps had found the obstructions above mentioned, the army under General Howard was attempting to throw a pontoon across the Oconee at the Georgia Central Railroad bridge. Here they met a force under the command of General Wayne, which was composed of a portion of Wheeler's cavalry, militia, and a band of convicts who had been liberated from the penitentiary upon the condition that they would join the army.

The most of these desperadoes have been taken prisoners, dressed in their state prison clothing. General Sherman has turned them loose, believing that Governor Brown had not got the full benefits of his liberality. The Rebels did not make a remarkably stern defense of the bridge, for Howard was able to cross his army yesterday, and began breaking railroad again to-day. In fact, all the army, except one corps, is engaged in this same work. Wayne, with his army, was hardly able to reach this point, where he met General Hardee, who had managed to get around here from Macon. Our troops struck the railroad at this station a few hours after the frightened band escaped.

We had been told that the country was very poor east

of the Oconee, but our experience has been a delightful gastronomic contradiction of the statement. The cattle trains are getting so large that we find difficulty in driving them along. Thanksgiving-day was very generally observed in the army, the troops scorning chickens in the plenitude of turkeys with which they had supplied themselves.

Vegetables of all kinds, and in unlimited quantities, were at hand, and the soldiers gave thanks as soldiers may, and were merry as only soldiers can be. In truth, so far as the gratification of the stomach goes, the troops are pursuing a continuous thanksgiving.

In addition to fowls, vegetables, and meats, many obtain a delicious sirup made from sorghum, which is cultivated on all the plantations, and stored away in large troughs and hogsheads. The mills here and there furnish fresh supplies of flour and meal, and we hear little or nothing of "hard tack"—that terror to weak mastication. Over the sections of country lately traversed I find very little cultivation of cotton. The commands of Davis appear to have been obeyed; and our large droves of cattle are turned nightly into the immense fields of ungathered corn to eat their fill, while the granaries are crowded to overflowing with both oats and corn.

We have also reached the sand regions, so that the fall of rain has no terrors; the roads are excellent, and would become firmer from a liberal wetting. The rise of the rivers will not trouble us much, for each army corps has its pontoon, and the launching of its boats is a matter of an hour.

Frequent occasions occur for conversations with the people. In the upper part of the state, meeting with none but the poorer and more ignorant class, I was led to believe that the rich and refined class had fled farther south;

but, although I have made diligent search for the intelligent, intellectual aristocracy, I have met with failure and disappointment. There are rich men, whose plantations line the roads for miles: men and women who own, or did own, hundreds of slaves, and raised every year their thousand bales of cotton; but their ignorance is only equaled by that twin sister of ignorance, intolerance. I now understand as I never did before why it was that a few persons, who every year represented the South in Congress, were able to wield that influence as a unit. To be sure, the interest of slavery was all-controlling, yet it never would have brought this people to the pitch of civil war had the common people received the most common benefits of education. The solemn truth is, that the Southern people have never had any conception of the National Idea. They do not know what it is to be an American.

It must not be supposed that we do not meet many persons who claim to have been Unionists from the beginning of the war. The vote of Georgia was undoubtedly given by a large majority against secession, and almost every old man, when he sees his pigs and poultry killed in his very door-yard, and gazes with mournful eyes upon the wagons that are filled with his corn, protests that *he* always was a Union man. It seems hard, sometimes, to strip such men so clear of all eatables as our troops do, who have the art cultivated to the most eminent degree; but, as General Sherman often says to them, "If it is true that you are Unionists, you should not have permitted Jeff. Davis to dragoon you until you were as much his slaves as once the negroes were yours."

CHAPTER VII.

WAYSIDE INCIDENTS IN GEORGIA—AN ORIGINAL CHARACTER —COCK-FIGHTING.

November 28*th.*—Last night we camped near the house of a Mr. Jones, who has represented his district in the Legislature of Georgia. Mr. Jones may have been a good legislator, but he was certainly neither a valiant nor extremely affectionate man, for he ran away at the approach of our army, leaving behind him a sick wife and a child only a few days old. He also carried away with him all his able-bodied slaves, leaving some fifteen or twenty helpless blacks, kindly informing the latter that "they were welcome to their liberty." Several of these negroes—old, decrepit, and destitute—came to see General Sherman soon after our arrival, soliciting his advice. One of them had lost a leg; another was bent with rheumatism; another was suffering under chronic chills and fever; all were ill from diseases contracted during the long period of their hard work and no pay. These poor creatures said to our General, "We un'stan' dere is perfec' freedom to every body, and dat we'se free wid de rest. Massa told us we might go along wid you. He t'ought you might want him, so he runned away. But you see, Mister Sherman, we'se not well; we shall only be an encumberance on you'se. You has a mighty long road to go ober, and we should be in de way. We'se cum to you for advice and opinion."

The General answered them with the utmost kindness. He said:

"I approve of your resolution. It is excellent. As you said, you are already free; yet, in your condition, if you are well treated, you had better remain where you are until the means of transportation are more complete. We hope to remove all of you one of these days; meanwhile do your work cheerfully and honestly, and you will be much happier for so doing."

Tennille Station, November 28th.—The destruction of railroads in this campaign has been most thorough. The work of demolition on such long lines of road necessarily requires time, but the process is performed as expeditiously as possible, in order to prevent any serious delay of the movement of the army. The method of destruction is simple, but very effective. Two ingenious instruments have been made for this purpose. One of them is a clasp, which locks under the rail. It has a ring in the top, into which is inserted a long lever, and the rail is thus ripped from the sleepers. The sleepers are then piled in a heap and set on fire, the rails roasting in the flames until they bend by their own weight. When sufficiently heated, each rail is taken off by wrenches fitting closely over the ends, and by turning in opposite directions, it is so twisted that even a rolling-machine could not bring it back into shape. In this manner we have destroyed thirty miles of rails which lay in the city of Atlanta, and all on the Augusta and Atlanta Road from the last-named place to Madison, besides the entire track of the Central Georgia line, from a point a few miles east of Macon to the station where I am now writing.

Near Johnston, south side of the Georgia Railroad, November 29th.—We have not heard from that part of the army which is operating on the north side of the railroad since it left us at Sandersville, nor from Kilpatrick until to-day, and that only indirectly, through a negro who reports that his master's son rode all the way from Louisville in great haste, reporting that Wheeler was fighting the Yankees, who were advancing on Augusta. General Sherman's second step in this campaign will have been equally successful with the first, if he is able to cross the Ogeechee to-morrow without serious opposition. The movement of Davis and Kilpatrick has been a blind in order to facilitate the passage over the Ogeechee of the main body of the army, which for two days past has been marching on parallel roads south of the railroad. Thus far we have reason to believe that the Rebels are ignorant of our principal movement, and are trembling with the fear that Augusta is our objective.

Kilpatrick is doing the same kind of work which he accomplished with such high honor when covering our right flank in the early days of the campaign. His column now acts as a curtain upon the extreme left, through which the enemy can not penetrate. He has a yet grander aim in view. If he succeeds, his name will not only stand at the head of our great cavalry generals, but it will be uttered with the prayers and blessings of the wives and children of the prisoners whom he may liberate at Millen, which is the point he aims for, and where have been incarcerated many thousands of our brave comrades. Kilpatrick started on the same day that our army left Milledgeville, the 25th instant. I have not mentioned the fact before in this diary, for fear that it might, in the casualties of war, get into the hands of the Rebels, and interfere with the movement. Heaven prosper it, say I.

All day long the army has been moving through magnificent pine-woods — the savannas of the South, as they are termed. I have never seen, and I can not conceive a more picturesque sight than the army winding along through these grand old woods. The pines, destitute of branches, rise to a height of eighty or ninety feet, their tops being crowned with tufts of pure green. They are widely apart, so that frequently two trains of wagons and troops in double column are marching abreast. In the distance may be seen a troop of horsemen—some General and his staff—turning about here and there, their gay uniforms and red and white flags contrasting harmoniously with the bright yellow grass underneath and the deep evergreen. War has its romance and its pleasures, and nothing could be more delightful, nor can there be more beautiful subjects for the artist's pencil than a thousand sights which have met my eye for days past, and which can never be seen outside the army. There is, by the way, a most excellent artist accompanying the expedition, who is working for the Harpers. His sketches are artistically executed, and he has the genuine spirit of an artist in his choice of subject; but I would have wished that Johnson, Hennessey, or Kensett might have been here also, to give us, in enduring colors, scenes now passing away, which belong to the history of the great day in which we live.

The most pathetic scenes occur upon our line of march daily and hourly. Thousands of negro women join the column, some carrying household goods, and many of them carrying children in their arms, while older boys and girls plod by their side. All these women and children are ordered back, heartrending though it may be to refuse them liberty. One begs that she may go to see her husband and children at Savannah. Long years ago she was forced from them and sold. Another has heard that her boy was in Macon, and she is "done gone with grief goin' on four years."

But the majority accept the advent of the Yankees as the fulfillment of the millennial prophecies. The "day of jubilee," the hope and prayer of a lifetime, has come. They can not be made to understand that they must remain behind, and they are satisfied only when General Sherman tells them, as he does every day, that we shall come back for them some time, and that they must be patient until the proper hour of deliverance arrives.

The other day a woman with a child in her arms was working her way along among the teams and crowds of cattle and horsemen. An officer called to her kindly: "Where are you going, aunty?"

She looked up into his face with a hopeful, beseeching look, and replied:

"I'se gwine whar you'se gwine, massa."

November 30*th*.—With the exception of the 15th Corps, our army is across the Ogeechee without fighting a battle. This river is a line of great strength to the Rebels, who might have made its passage a costly effort for us, but they have been outwitted and outmanœuvred. I am more than ever convinced that, if General Sherman intends to take his army to the sea-board, it is his policy to avoid any contest which will delay him in the establishment of a new base of operations and supplies; if he is able to establish this new base, and at the same time destroy all the lines of communication from the Rebel armies with the great cities, so that they will be as much isolated as if those strong-holds were in our hands, he will have accomplished the greatest strategic victory in the war, and all the more welcome because bloodless. Macon, Augusta, Savannah, or Charleston are of no strategic value to us, except that they are filled with munitions of war, and that the two latter might be useful to us as a base of supplies, with the additional moral advantage which would result from their capture. All these places, however, are vitally important to the enemy, as the source of a large part of their supplies of ammunition and commissary stores.

We have heard to-day from Kilpatrick and from Millen. Kilpatrick has made a splendid march, fighting Wheeler all the way to Waynesboro, destroying the railroad bridge across Brier Creek, between Augusta and Millen. It is with real grief that we hear he was unable to accomplish the release of our prisoners in the prison-pen at Millen. It appears that for some time past the Rebels have been removing our soldiers from Millen; the officers have been sent to Columbia, South Carolina, and the privates farther south, somewhere on the Gulf Railroad.

We have had very little difficulty in crossing the Ogeechee. The 20th Corps moved down the railroad, destroying it as far as the bridge. The 17th Corps covered the river at that point, where a light bridge was only partially destroyed. It was easily repaired, so that the infantry and cavalry could pass over it, while the wagons and artillery used the pontoons. The Ogeechee is about sixty yards in width at this point. It is approached on the northern or western side through swamps, which would be impassable but for the sandy soil, which packs solidly when the water covers the roads, although in places there are treacherous quicksands which we are obliged to corduroy.

This evening I walked down to the river, where a striking and novel spectacle was visible. The fires of pitch pine were flaring up into the mist and darkness; figures of men and horses loomed out of the dense shadows in gigantic proportions; torch-lights were blinking and flashing away off in the forests; and the still air echoed and re-echoed with

D

the cries of teamsters and the wild shouts of the soldiers. A long line of the troops marched across the foot-bridge, each soldier bearing a torch, and, as the column marched, the vivid light was reflected in quivering lines in the swift-running stream.

Soon the fog, which here settles like a blanket over the swamps and forests of the river-bottoms, shut down upon the scene; and so dense and dark was it that torches were of but little use, and our men were directed here and there by the voice.

"Jim, are you there?" shouted one.

"Yes, I *am* here," was the impatient answer.

"Well, then, go straight ahead."

"Straight ahead! where in thunder *is* 'straight ahead?'"

And so the troops shuffled upon and over each other, and finally blundered into their quarters for the night.

To-day I encountered an original character; an old man whom I will not name, but call him W. In the days when the railway was in operation he occupied the position of dépôt-master at this station. A shrewd old fellow, with a comical build, he was evidently born to be fat and funny—as he was. I first saw him sitting by a huge fire our men had kindled out of a pile of pitch-pine timber, originally cut for railroad ties. His face was grave as a Quaker's, but his eyes and the lower portion of his torso laughed most infectiously. He seemed to comprehend the war question perfectly, and expressed his opinions with a quaint volubility which kept his auditors in a roar of merriment. His speech ran thus:

"They say you are retreating, but it is the strangest sort of retreat I ever saw. Why, dog bite them, the newspapers have been lying in this way all along. They allers are whipping the Federal armies, and they allers fall back after the battle is over. It was that ar' idee that first opened my eyes. Our army was always whipping the Feds, and we allers fell back. I allers told 'em it was a d—d humbug, and now by —— I know it, for here you are right on old W.'s place; hogs, potatoes, corn, and fences all gone. I don't find any fault. I expected it all.

"Jeff Davis and the rest," he continued, "talk about splitting the Union. Why, if South Carolina had gone out by herself, she would have been split in four pieces by this time. Splitting the Union! Why" (with a round oath) "the State of Georgia is being split right through from end to end. It is these rich fellows who are making this war, and keeping their precious bodies out of harm's way. There's John Franklin went through here the other day, running away from your army. I could have played dominoes on his coat-tails. There's my poor brother sick with small-pox at Macon, working for eleven dollars a month, and hasn't got a cent of the d—d stuff for a year. 'Leven dollars a month and eleven thousand bullets a minute. I don't believe in it, sir!

"My wife came from Canada, and I kind o' thought I would some time go there to live, but was allers afraid of the ice and cold; but I can tell you this country is getting too cussed hot for me. Look at my fence-rails a-burning there. I think I can stand the cold better.

"I heard as how they cut down the trees across your road up country and burn the bridges; why, dog bite their hides! one of your Yankees can take up a tree and carry it off, tops and all; and there's that bridge you put across the river in less than two hours—they might as well try to stop the Ogeechee as you Yankees.

"The blasted rascals who burnt this yere bridge thought they did a big thing; a natural born fool cut in two had more sense in either end than any of them."

Then, with a deep sigh and an expression of woful resignation, he added:

"It'll take the help of Divine Providence, a heap of rain, and a deal of elbow-grease, to fix things up again."

As we journey on from day to day, it is curious to observe the attentions bestowed by our soldiers upon camp pets. With a care which almost deserves the name of tenderness, the men gather helpless, dumb animals around them; sometimes an innocent kid whose mother has been served up as an extra ration, and again a raccoon, a little donkey, a dog, or a cat. One regiment has adopted a fine Newfoundland dog, which soon became so attached to its new home that it never strayed, but became a part of the body, recognizing the face of every man in it. These pets are watched, fed, protected, and carried along with a faithfulness and affection which constantly suggest the most interesting psychological queries.

The favorite pet of the camp, however, is the hero of the barn-yard. There is not a regiment nor a company, not a teamster nor a negro at head-quarters, nor an orderly, but has a "rooster" of one kind or another. When the column is moving, these haughty game-cocks are seen mounted upon the breech of a cannon, tied to the pack-saddle of a mule, among pots and pans, or carried lovingly in the arms of a mounted orderly; crowing with all his might from the interior of a wagon, or making the woods re-echo with his triumphant notes as he rides perched upon the knapsack of a soldier. These cocks represent every known breed, Polish and Spanish, Dorkings, Shanghais and Bantams—high-blooded specimens traveling with those of their species who may not boast of noble lineage. They must all fight, however, or be killed and eaten. Hardly has the army gone into camp before these feathery combats begin. The cocks use only the spurs with which Nature furnishes them; for the soldiers have not yet reached the refinement of applying artificial gaffs, and so but little harm is done. The game-cocks which have come out of repeated conflicts victorious are honored with such names as "Bill Sherman," "Johnny Logan," etc.; while the defeated and bepecked victim is saluted with derisive appellations, such as "Jeff. Davis," "Beauregard," or "Bob Lee."

Cock-fighting is not, perhaps, one of the most refined or elevating of pastimes, but it furnishes food for a certain kind of fun in camp; and as it is not carried to the point of cruelty, the soldiers can not be blamed for liking it.

CHAPTER VIII.

FROM MILLEN TO THE SEA-COAST.

Millen, December 3d.—Pivoted upon Millen, the army has swung slowly round from its eastern course, and is now moving in six columns upon parallel roads southward. Until yesterday it was impossible for the Rebels to decide whether or not it was General Sherman's intention to march upon Augusta. Kilpatrick had destroyed the bridge above Waynesboro', and, after falling back, had again advanced, supported by the 14th Army Corps, under General Davis. South of this column, moving eastward through Birdsville, was the 20th Corps, commanded by General Slocum. Yet farther south, the 17th Corps, General Blair in command, followed the railroad, destroying the track as it advanced. West and south of the Ogeechee, the 15th Corps, General Osterhaus in immediate command, but under the eye of General Howard, has moved in two columns.

Until now, Davis and Kilpatrick have been a cover and shield to the real movement of the army. At no time has it been possible for Hardee to interpose any serious obstacle to the advance of our main body, for our left wing has always been a strong arm thrust out in advance, ready to encounter any force which might attempt to bar the way.

The Rebel councils of war appear to have been completely deceived, for we hear it reported that Bragg and Longstreet are at Augusta, with ten thousand men made up of militia, two or three South Carolina regiments, and a portion of Hampton's Legion, sent there for one month. It is possible, now that the curtain has been withdrawn, and as it may appear that we are marching straight for Savannah, that these generals, with their ten thousand men, may attempt to harass our rear, but they can accomplish nothing more than the loss of a few lives. They can not check our progress.

The work so admirably performed by our left wing, so far as it obliged the Rebels in our front constantly to retreat, by threatening their rear, now becomes the office of the 15th Corps, which is divided, and will operate on the right and left banks of the river. These two columns are marching, one day in advance of the main body, down the peninsula formed by the Savannah and Ogeechee rivers, with a detachment thrown over to the south side of the latter stream.

These flank movements are of the greatest necessity and value. They have taken place in the following order: first, the right wing, with Kilpatrick's cavalry, moved upon Macon, in the early part of the campaign; next, after disappearing from that flank, to the great amazement of the Rebels, the same troops marched across our rear and suddenly appeared upon our left flank, supported by Davis, and demonstrating savagely upon Augusta; and now Howard is performing the same office on our right. This style of manœuvring has not been practiced on account of any apprehension that we can not run over and demolish any Rebel force in Georgia, for all the troops of the enemy in the state could not stand for a moment against this army on any battle-field; but because General Sherman neither wishes to sacrifice life needlessly nor be detained. A very small force of infantry or cavalry in position at a river-crossing could delay a marching column half a day, or longer: our flanking column prevents this. Besides, our soldiers have tired of chickens, sweet potatoes, sorghum, etc., and have been promised oysters at the sea-side—oysters roasted, oysters fried, oysters stewed, oysters on the half shell, oysters in abundance, without money and without price. In short, the soldiers themselves don't wish to be delayed!

The railroad, which has received our immediate attention within the last week, is altogether the best I have seen in the state, though the rail itself is not so heavy as the T rail on the Augusta and Atlanta road. The rail on the Georgia Central is partially laid with the U, and partly with light T rail, but it is all fastened to parallel string-pieces, which are again fixed to the ties. The station-houses are generally built of brick, in the most substantial manner, and are placed at distances of fifteen or twenty miles apart. They have been destroyed by our army all the way along from Macon. The extensive dépôt at Millen was a wooden structure of exceedingly graceful proportions. It was ignited in three places simultaneously, and its destruction was a brilliant spectacle; the building burning slowly, although there was sufficient wind to lift the vast volume of smoke and exhibit the exquisite architecture traced in lines of fire. This scene was so striking that even the rank and file observed and made comments upon it among themselves—a circumstance which may be counted as unusual, for the taste for conflagrations has been so cultivated of late in the army that any small affair of that kind attracts very little attention.

An anecdote will illustrate this tendency to destruction. An Irishman, while engaged, a day or two ago, in the useful occupation of twisting rails, remarked:

"When the war is over General Sherman will buy a coal-mine in Pennsylvania, and occupy his spare time with smoking cigars and destroying and rebuilding railroads."

Other spectacles greet our vision as we march.

We daily traverse immense corn-fields, each of which covers from one hundred to one thousand acres. These fields were once devoted to the cultivation of cotton, and it is surprising to see how the planters have carried out the wishes or orders of the Rebel Government; for cotton has given way to corn. A large amount of cotton has been destroyed by our army in this campaign, but it must have been a small portion even of the limited crop raised, as our destruction has chiefly been upon the line of the railroads. As nearly as I can learn, two thirds of this cotton has been sent over the Georgia Central Railroad to Augusta by way of Millen; thence a limited amount has been transported to Wilmington for trans-Atlantic shipment; the remainder is at Columbia, South Carolina, at Columbus, Georgia, and at Montgomery, Alabama. I think it will be found, however, when the facts are known, that no large amounts of cotton are stored in any one place. The policy of scattering the crop is probably the wisest the Rebels could have adopted.

It is well ascertained that the country west of the Savannah River is expected to furnish supplies for the Rebel armies in the West; for although corn and beef are sent from this district to Lee's army, he draws the bulk of his supplies from the states east of the Savannah, and there is no region so prolific as that about Columbia. I note this fact because I wish to correct the impression, so general at the North, that the Eastern armies are fed from the Southwest. One thing is certain, that neither the West nor the East will draw any supplies from the counties in this state traversed by our army for a long time to come. Our work has been the next thing to annihilation.

Ogeechee Church, December 6th.—For two days past the army has been concentrated at this point, which is the narrowest part of the peninsula. General Howard is still on the west side of the Ogeechee, but he is within supporting distance, and has ample means of crossing the river, should it be necessary, which is not at all probable.

Kilpatrick has again done noble work. On Sunday last, while marching toward Alexander for the purpose of more thoroughly completing the destruction of the railroad bridge crossing Brier Creek, he found Wheeler near Waynesboro' and fought him several times, punishing him severely in each instance, driving his infantry and cavalry before him through Waynesboro' and beyond the bridge, which was completely destroyed. Kilpatrick, having performed this feat, rejoined the main body of our army, then marching southward.

One important object of this eccentric movement of Kilpatrick is to impress the Rebel leaders with the conviction that we intend to march upon Augusta. To divide and scatter their force is our main purpose. Let them keep a large army in Augusta until we reach the sea, and then they can go where they please!

In the course of our march to-day, we came upon a fine stately mansion, situated in a pleasant region, and surrounded by beautiful grounds, which were carefully and tastefully arranged. On entering the house, we found the reverse of a beautiful picture. It was a scene of shocking confusion: articles of furniture, soiled and broken, were strewn about the floors; household utensils lay in ill-assorted heaps; crockery, shattered into pieces, was beyond the mender's art. This was the work, not of our soldiers, but of Wheeler's Rebel cavalry, who had been on picket duty at this place on the previous night. The negroes left upon the place, who explained the cause of all this ruin, also told us that their master and mistress were hidden in the swamp, with sundry animals and articles of value. A party of our soldiers went in search of the fugitives, and found them in a dreadful state of fright. The negroes did not seem to sympathize with their late owners, and three of them discussed in my hearing the propriety of absconding. One of the three was an old woman who claimed to have come from Africa—a strange, weird creature, who spoke in a patois which I could not have understood perfectly but for the replies of her companions, two black men, who were busily engaged in appropriating to their own use such articles of household furniture as happened to strike their fancy. One of these men seemed somewhat unwilling to make the venture for freedom; the woman clutched him by the arm and spoke vehemently:

"Shame yer, black man, stay yere!—be whipped like der dog!"

She hissed the last words between the fangs protruding from her thick lips, while her wrinkled face and glaring eyes worked with terrible passion.

The man seemed frightened, and with reason. He took up the load of bedding which he had laid down, and replied:

"How you know dese people, mammy? Didn't massa say dese Yanks kill us all? Didn't de Yankee ball cum jus' yere," pointing to his head, "dis mornin'? I'se feard."

"You're fool, Sam! Dese—" retorted the woman. The rest of the sentence was lost in the distance, as the decrepit creature energetically led the way to the line of our soldiers then passing along the road.

A significant feature of this campaign, which has not before been mentioned in this diary, received a marked illustration yesterday. Except in a few instances, private residences have not been destroyed by the soldiers, but there has been at least one exception, for an excellent reason.

Yesterday we passed the plantation of a Mr. Stubbs. The house, cotton-gin, press, corn-ricks, stables, every thing that could burn was in flames, and in the door-yard lay the dead bodies of several bloodhounds, which had been used to track and pull down negroes and our escaped prisoners. And wherever our army has passed, every thing in the shape of a dog has been killed. The soldiers and officers are determined that no more flying fugitives, white men or negroes, shall be followed by hounds that come within reach of their powder and ball.

During our brief stay in Millen, we saw another sight which fevered the blood of our brave boys. It was the hideous prison-pen used by the enemy for the confinement of Federal soldiers who had become prisoners of war. A space of ground about three hundred feet square, inclosed by a stockade, without any covering whatsoever, was the hole where thousands of our brave soldiers have been confined for months past, exposed to heavy dews, biting frosts, and pelting rains, without so much as a board or a tent to protect them after the Rebels had stolen their clothing. Some of them had adopted the wretched alternative of digging holes in the ground, into which they crept at times. What wonder that we found the evidence that seven hundred and fifty men had died there! From what misery did death release them! I could realize it all when I saw this den, as I never could before, even when listening to the stories of prisoners who had fled, escaping the villains who rushed after them in hot pursuit, and foiling the bloodhounds which had been put upon their track. God certainly will visit the authors of all this crime with a terrible judgment.

Jeff. Davis knew that the people of the North would see the condition of the prisoners who were maltreated at the

Belle Isle Prison, and it is fair to suppose that, for the sake of humanity, and even with a slight regard for his own reputation, he would have sent for exchange the men who appeared to the best advantage—although there is a current theory that, with an atrocity which beggars belief, the starvation and exposure of our soldier prisoners is a settled policy, for the purpose of killing off as many of them as possible.

December 8th.—The army has been advancing slowly and surely, but as cautiously as if a strong army were in our front. The relative position of the troops has not materially changed during the past few days, except that we are all farther south. From fifteen to twenty miles distant lies Savannah, a city which is probably in some perturbation at the certainty of our approach. If the Rebels intend fighting in defense of the city, the battle will be an assault of fortifications; for as yet we have only skirmished with parties of cavalry, and the enemy has not yet seen the head of our infantry column, and can only judge of our strength through injudicious publications in the newspapers at the North. It can not well be conceived by those not in the field of operations what serious injury is caused by the publication of the number and contemplated movements of our armies. In a way which it is unnecessary to mention, such injuries have occurred during this campaign.

General Howard has just returned from a bold and successful movement. Fearing that we should detach a force for the purpose of destroying the Gulf Railroad, which they are using to its utmost capacity just now, the Rebels pushed a force across the Ogeechee. While this body was covered by a strong river-side line, General Corse, of Allatoona memory, shoved his division between the Little and Great Ogeechee, thirteen miles in advance of our main column, to the canal which runs from the Ogeechee to the Savannah River. He bridged the canal, crossed it with his division, and now holds a position out of which Hood's whole army could not drive him. This bold step has forced the Rebels to evacuate the line of works stretching from river to river, and they have now fairly sought refuge within the fortifications of Savannah.

December 9th.—We are gradually closing in upon the city. General Howard holds the position gained on the other side of the canal yesterday, and has advanced the larger part of his command in its support. Portions of our army are now within eight miles of Savannah. General Blair's column lost several officers and men, some of them by hard fighting, as the Rebels withstood the advance with pertinacity.

One officer and several men were severely wounded by the explosion of shells and torpedoes which the Rebels had buried in the road. This was cowardly murder. In the entrance to forts, or in a breach made in a line of works, such implements may be used to repel the assault, but the laws of war do not justify an attempt of the kind which has been so disastrous to-day. The Rebel prisoners were marched over the road, and removed ten of these treacherous, death-dealing instruments.

General Davis is to-night at Cherokee Hill, having crossed the Charleston Railroad, partially destroying the bridge spanning the Savannah. General Slocum is advancing upon our left, covering our front to the Savannah River. He has also been opposed by the Rebels, but, as with the other columns, the opposition only accelerated the progress of the troops, who hurry forward on the double-quick at the sound of the guns, eager to get into the fight. To-morrow we may expect to concentrate our army so as to form a continuous line about the city of Savannah.

December 10*th*.—The army has advanced some six miles to-day, and has met every where a strong line of works, which appear to be held by a large force, with heavy guns in position. Their line, although extended, is more easily defended because of a succession of impassable swamps which stretch across the peninsula. All the openings between these morasses and the roads which lead through them are strongly fortified, and the approaches have been contested vigorously, but with little loss to us. General Sherman seems to avoid the sacrifice of life, and I doubt his making any serious attack until he has communicated with the fleet.

We have now connected our lines, so that the corps are within supporting distance of each other. The soldiers are meanwhile in most cheerful spirits, displaying the unconcern which is the most characteristic feature of our troops.

The necessity of an open communication with the fleet is becoming apparent, for the army is rapidly consuming its supplies, and replenishment is vitally important. Away in the distance, across the rice-fields, as far as the banks of the Ogeechee, our signal-officers are stationed, scanning the seaward horizon in search of indications of the presence of the fleet, but thus far unsuccessfully. On the other side of the river, within cannon range, stand the frowning parapets of Fort McAllister, its ponderous guns and rebel garrison guarding the only avenue open to our approach.

This evening a movement of the greatest importance has begun. Hazen's division of the 15th Corps is marching to the other side of the river. Fort McAllister must be taken. To-morrow's sun will see the veterans whom Sherman led upon the heights of Missionary Ridge within striking distance of its walls. Warm words have been uttered by the Generals of the 15th and the 17th Corps because the second division has been assigned the honor of this expedition. The possibility of repulse, the fear of wounds and death, do not seem to be considered in the rivalry. These brave men of ours have seen too many wounds, and death has passed too near them to suggest any terrors now. The glory of the flag and victory is the noble thought which animates and stimulates officers and men alike.

CHAPTER IX.

THE STORMING OF FORT McALLISTER.

Fort McAllister, December 13*th.*—Fort McAllister is ours. It has been gallantly and bravely won. I saw the heroic assault from the point of observation selected by General Sherman at the adjacent rice-mill.

During the greater part of to-day the General gazed anxiously toward the sea, watching for the appearance of the fleet. About the middle of the afternoon he descried a light column of smoke creeping lazily along over the flat marshes, and soon the spars of a steamer were visible, and then the flag of our Union floated out. What a thrilling, joyful sight! How the blood bounded, when, answering the signal waved above us, we saw that the brave tars had recognized us, and knew that our General was here with his army!

The sun was now fast going down behind a grove of water-oaks, and as his last rays gilded the earth, all eyes once more turned toward the Rebel fort. Suddenly white puffs of smoke shot out from the thick woods surrounding the line of works. Hazen was closing in, ready for the final rush of his column directly upon the fort. A warning answer came from the enemy in the roar of heavy artillery—and so the battle opened.

General Sherman walked nervously to and fro, turning quickly now and then from viewing the scene of conflict to observe the sun sinking slowly behind the tree-tops. No longer willing to bear the suspense, he said:

"Signal General Hazen that he must carry the fort by assault, to-night if possible."

The little flag waved and fluttered in the evening air, and the answer came:

"I am ready, and will assault at once!"

The words had hardly passed when from out the encircling woods there came a long line of blue coats and bright bayonets, and the dear old flag was there, waving proudly in the breeze. Then the fort seemed alive with flame; quick, thick jets of fire shooting out from all its sides, while the white smoke first covered the place and then rolled away over the glacis. The line of blue moved steadily on; too slowly, as it seemed to us, for we exclaimed, "Why don't they dash forward?" but their measured step was unfaltering. Now the flag goes down, but the line does not halt. A moment longer, and the banner gleams again in the front. We, the lookers-on, clutched one another's arms convulsively, and scarcely breathed in the eager intensity of our gaze. Sherman stood watching with anxious air, awaiting the decisive moment. Then the enemy's fire redoubled in rapidity and violence. The darting streams of fire alone told the position of the fort. The line of blue entered the enshrouding folds of smoke. The flag was at last dimly seen, and then it went out of sight altogether.

"They have been repulsed!" said one of the group of officers who watched the fight.

"No, by Heaven!" said another; "there is not a man in retreat—not a straggler in all the glorious line!"

The firing ceased. The wind lifted the smoke. Crowds of men were visible on the parapets, fiercely fighting—but our flag was planted there. There were a few scattering musket-shots, and then the sounds of battle ceased. Then the bomb-proofs and parapets were alive with crowding swarms of our gallant men, who fired their pieces in the air as a *feu de joie*. Victory! The fort was won.

Then all of us who had witnessed the strife and exulted in the triumph, grasped each the other's hand, embraced, and were glad, and some of us found the water in our eyes.

In half an hour we were congratulating General Hazen, and in an hour more Generals Sherman and Howard were pulling down the stream, regardless of torpedoes, in search of the signaled vessel of the navy.

General Sherman opened the communication in person, sending a message home and appointing an hour of meeting for the next morning with Admiral Dahlgren and General Foster.

This evening we have enjoyed unrestricted opportunities of examining Fort McAllister. It is a large inclosure, with wide parapets, a deep ditch, and thickly-planted palisades, which latter are broken in several places where our men passed through. The dead and wounded are lying where they fell. Groups of soldiers are gathered here and there, laughing and talking of the proud deed that had been done. One said:

"If they had had embrasures for these guns," pointing to them, "we should have got hurt."

"It's of no use; you can't defend a work of this sort with guns *en barbette*," said another.

This soldier was right. There were twenty-one guns, large and small, in the fort, all mounted *en barbette*, and the deadly aim of our sharpshooters had killed many of the garrison at their pieces. The artillery did very little execution, for we have lost only ninety men killed and wounded, and many of these were injured by the explosion of the torpedoes which the Rebels had planted in the glacis of the work.

Major Anderson, who commanded the fort, tells me that he did not anticipate an assault to-night, and was hardly prepared for it when it came. In the history of the war there will scarcely be found a more striking example of the wisdom of quick and determined action than this assault. Had we waited, built intrenchments and rifle-pits, and made the approaches which attend siege operations, we would have lost many men and much time; and time at this crisis of the campaign is invaluable.

The victory of Fort McAllister, and the way it was done, is a grand ending to this most adventurous campaign. It is in reality the end, for here terminates our march. We set out for a new base, and we have found it. The capture of Savannah is another matter, and with its siege will begin a new campaign. Our soldiers are electrified by the brilliant episode just enacted, and are eager to go wherever the General directs.

General Hazen, the hero of Fort McAllister, is a West Point graduate, and not yet thirty-five years of age. In person, he is rather squarely built, is above the medium height, and has a fine, open, manly face; resolute withal, but that kind of resolution which does not seem to need constant assertion. You are impressed with it at the first glance, and rest there, always after, with confidence. His manner is that of an accomplished and refined gentleman. On the field of battle he is alert, self-assured, concentrated, brave, and capable. He has performed noble service during this war, from the bloody field of Shiloh until this day. He will never fail when the honor of the nation demands his presence in the front of the battle; but he can add few brighter leaves to his chaplet of fame than those of the storming of Fort McAllister.

FORT McALLISTER

CHAPTER X.

EVACUATION OF SAVANNAH BY THE REBELS—ITS OCCUPATION BY SHERMAN—INTERVIEW BETWEEN SECRETARY STANTON AND THE COLORED CLERGYMEN—TALKS WITH THE PEOPLE.

Savannah, December 20th.—The fall of Fort McAllister has been quickly followed by the evacuation of this great commercial city, which we gain without a battle. I have already written of the nature of the obstacles which confronted us, and the life-blood which must of necessity have been shed had we been forced to capture it by assault. I most devoutly thank God that, through the splendid strategy of our General, the lives of our brave soldiers are spared to their wives and homes, and for future use to dear old fatherland.

Two events combined to insure this important result: first, the capture of Fort McAllister by direct assault, a feat which seems to have impressed the Rebels in a manner which can only be appreciated by talking with the deserters who constantly come into our lines in squads, and who assert that the soldiers in Savannah did not hesitate openly to declare that it was a useless sacrifice of life to defend the city. This terror was shared by the citizens in a magnified degree; and now we know for a certainty that the mayor and alderman, with a large body of citizens, waited upon General Hardee and insisted upon the surrender of the city.

The second reason was a flank movement, which was in

process of operation. In two days more we should have had a division operating with Foster upon Savannah by way of Broad River, which would have rendered escape impossible. Practically, all avenues to the city were closed up by our army, which stretched from the Savannah to the Ogeechee rivers, and by Foster's troops, which covered the Savannah and Charleston Railroad.

The path by which Hardee finally escaped led through swamps which were previously considered impracticable. The Rebel general obtained knowledge of our movement through his spies, who swarmed in our camp.

It was fortunate that our troops followed so quickly after the evacuation of the city by the enemy, for a mob had gathered in the streets, and were breaking into the stores and houses. They were with difficulty dispersed by the bayonets of our soldiers, and then, once more, order and confidence prevailed throughout the conquered city.

We have won a magnificent prize—the city of Savannah, more than two hundred guns, magazines filled with ammunition, thirty-five thousand bales of cotton, three steamboats, several locomotives, and one hundred and fifty cars, and stores of all kinds. We had not been in occupation forty-eight hours before the transport steamer Canonicus, with General Foster on board, lay alongside a pier, and our new line of supplies was formed.

Christmas.—An incident connected with our occupation of the city illustrates the watchfulness and daring of our officers and soldiers. Colonel Barnum, of New York, commanding a brigade in the 20th Corps, a brave soldier, who bears scars and unhealed wounds from many a battle-field, was in command in the immediate front upon our extreme left, and near midnight crept out beyond his picket lines, which were only three hundred yards from the Rebel works. Not hearing the voices of the enemy, and not seeing their forms passing before their camp-fires, he suspected that they had evacuated their lines, notwithstanding that he could hear the boom of their guns, which echoed through the dark forests away off to the right. He selected ten of his best men, and cautiously scaled the parapets of the outside Rebel line; passing rapidly and silently from these to the fortifications from whose bastions frowned the black muzzles of ponderous 64-pounders. Although their camp-fires still burned brightly, no Rebels were to be seen. Sending back for reinforcements, he marched from earth-work to earth-work, and finally entered the city just as the early morning light appeared in the eastern horizon; while the forms of the retreating enemy could be seen flying into the gray mist across the marshes on the other side of the river.

The hero of this dashing exploit is one of the best soldiers in the army—a bold fighter, a rigid disciplinarian, the most generous of hosts, and one of the best of fellows generally.

General Frank P. Blair's corps was the first to reach the actual defenses of Savannah. As usual, he was with the advance. One who had never seen General Blair except in the field as a corps commander would find it difficult to realize that he has occupied so prominent a position in the political arena; for, while it may not be said that he is a born soldier, yet he possesses in a marked degree many of the qualities which constitute a good commander. Under all circumstances he never loses that perfect coolness and self-command which render him master of the situation and inspire the confidence of the soldiers. This imperturbability never deserts him. One day, when the Rebels renewed an attack upon his lines with furious vigor, although they

E

had already been repulsed several times, sustaining terrible losses, Blair removed his cigar from his mouth, as he watched their onset, and quietly observed:

"See the fellows! There they come again, right through the woods. What in thunder do they want?"

They wanted to carry his line, but they failed; and Blair continued smoking, as if nothing had occurred.

General Blair is one of the most hospitable and popular men of the army. As the commander of the 17th Corps he is identified with the history of the Army of the Tennessee —a gallant, heroic band of men, it may be added, the record of whose deeds yet remains to be written. The General wears a full sandy beard and moustache, which conceal the lower part of his face. His eyes are of a light hazel color, full of humor and good nature—an expression, however, that is somewhat qualified by the overhanging brow, which has a *noli me tangere* air, as much as to say, "If I must fight, it shall be war to the hilt." In height the General is about five feet eleven inches. His frame is finely proportioned; and he makes a good appearance on horseback. He selects excellent horses, and knows how to ride them. In the army he has the reputation of a kind, generous, discreet, and brave soldier.

General Geary, commanding a division in the 20th Corps, is now the military governor of Savannah. He is a tall, stalwart, soldierly man, with a full black beard and an open and inviting face. He has a hearty, hospitable manner which pleases every body; is sensible, discreet, and firm; understands precisely the nature of his duties, and executes them noiselessly but effectively. The citizens are delighted with him, and they may well be so; for no city was ever kept in better order. Clean streets, careful and well-instructed guards, perfect protection of property, and a general sense of comfort and security, indicate the executive capacity and the good judgment of the General.

Already the public squares which checker the city are filled with the wooden houses built by the ingenious hands of our soldiers. Very few of the citizens have left their homes, and officers and soldiers are in close affiliation with the people. The army is acclimatized in Savannah.

The people here re-echo the sentiment which has greeted us ever since we left Atlanta, that our uninterrupted march, ending with the conquest of this chief commercial city of Georgia, has closed the war so far as they are concerned. They hope and pray that our army will march through South Carolina, which region they denounce with bitter reproaches as being the cause of the war; and I have no doubt but that they would almost as readily fight for Massachusetts as for a state with which they have never been on terms of good-will and harmony.

We hear that the Rebel troops lately in occupation here are scattering. Hardee has already lost that portion of his troops who answered to the call of Governor Brown. After crossing the Savannah they left the ranks almost simultaneously, and their general, whose reputation rests chiefly upon his compilations from French works on military tactics, has now only the mere shadow of an army—that portion which had been drawn from every garrison between this point and the army under Lee in Virginia, including Macon and other posts beyond the call of Hood. I do not criticize Hardee for the course he has pursued. If he had followed the instructions of Beauregard, who, by the way, took good care to leave the city some days before there was a probability of its capture by assault, there might have been a host of dead men lying out in the cold moonlight; but the result would have been the same. If we had began an assault, we should have entered the city at whatever cost, and the garrison might not have met with the mercy generously shown to the brave defenders of Fort McAllister. Hardee acted wisely and well; he withdrew his troops at a critical moment, and saved his command, at the expense, it is true, of valuable material; but there is a large balance in his favor to the credit of good sense and humanity.

But I do not propose to enter into a discussion which, by this time, must be actively carried on between Jeff. Davis and Hardee; they may fight out the paper battle to their own mutual content or disgust, as it may be. We are in Savannah, in the full enjoyment of superb quarters, fish, oysters, and other good things, and our army relishes the condition of affairs.

January 1st, 1865.—Before the evacuation of the city, General Sherman had been busily engaged in planning a new flank movement; visiting Hilton Head in person for this purpose, and traveling night and day during his journey to that place and back. For a part of the way he was conveyed by steam-boats, but when that mode of conveyance failed him, pushed through swamps and creeks in rowboats and "dug-outs." And here I may properly bear witness to that faithful indefatigability which is one of the elements of greatness in this man. He is never idle in camp, and while he has the highest confidence in his generals, he always examines the situation with his own eyes. I do not know a man more indifferent to danger than he, although he never foolishly exposes himself; and there could not be a captain who, never hesitating in an emergency where a bloody sacrifice is essential, yet guards so well the lives of his soldiers. I know that it is his constant aim to gain grand results without paying the costly penalties of war. Certainly this campaign has been a signal illustration of this quality in the General's character.

Along the whole line of our march General Sherman has never lost an opportunity of talking with and advising the negroes who came to our camp, and his great heart has overflowed in kindly counsels to these poor people. Since his arrival in this city he has kept open house for all who choose to call upon him, white or black. His rooms in the splendid mansion of Mr. Green, a British resident, are constantly thronged with visitors, and the negroes are greeted by him with the same courtesy that is extended to the whites. In truth, I honestly believe the General entertains a more profound respect and love for these loyal blacks than for the rebellious white men who formerly called themselves masters.

The negroes all tell the General that the falsehoods of the Rebel papers never deceived them, and that they believed that his "retreats" were victories; that they would serve the Union cause in any and all ways that they could, as soldiers, as drivers, or pioneers. Indeed, the faith, earnestness, and heroism of the black men is one of the grandest developments of this war. When I think of the universal testimony of our escaped soldiers, who enter our lines every day, that in the hundreds of miles which they traverse on their way they never ask the poor slave in vain for help; that the poorest negro hides and shelters them, and shares the last crumb with them—all this impresses me with a weight of obligation and a love for them that stir the very depths of my soul.

A memorable interview has taken place here between the Secretary of War and the colored clergymen of the city. These good men represented almost every religious denomination. I was present during a portion of the interview, which occurred at General Sherman's headquarters, and I shall never forget the impressive spectacle. Mr. Stanton sat at a table, asking questions and making notes of the replies; now and then putting down his pen and adjusting his spectacles in a surprised way, as if he could not comprehend how these men came to possess such a clear consciousness of the merits of the questions involved in the war. Their replies were so shrewd, so wise, so comprehensive, that, as Mr. Stanton afterward observed, "they understood and could state the principles of this question as well as any member of the Cabinet."

General Sherman stood near the fireplace, occasionally walking to and fro, or making some pregnant suggestion, which would call forth new thoughts or start another train of remark.

In one corner of the room, watching with curious and interested gaze this singular interview, stood General Townsend, a gentleman who has for many years fulfilled with rare justness and courtesy the onerous duties of Adjutant General of the United States Army.

The black clergymen, fifteen or twenty in number, were grouped about the room, sitting and standing. With all due respect for the clerical profession, I doubt if twenty white ministers of the Gospel could have been called together so suddenly out of one of our Northern cities (certainly not in the South) who could represent so much common sense and intelligence as these men. Nor would an average score of clergymen present an array of nobler heads. In an artistic sense, the negroes would certainly have the advantage of color.

This conference lasted until the small hours of the morning, when the visitors were sent home with words of kindness and counsel.

It is surprising to all of us to see how admirably the negroes of the city behave, in view of their knowledge that our coming sets them at liberty from the control of their masters. They take no advantage of their freedom in any way in their conduct to those who ill treated them in former days, except that they leave them for the sake of obtaining remunerative employment. They put on no "airs," as the Southern people term it, but are uniformly quiet and respectful. One of them said to me:

"We don't wish to do any thing wrong. We know that you came here to set us free; we expect you to tell us what to do, and we shall act in accordance with that. Some of these masters have treated us shamefully, whipped, and imprisoned, and sold us about; but we don't wish to be revenged on them. The Bible says that we must forgive our enemies. They have been our enemies, and we forgive them. Thank God! we are slaves no longer."

It is shameful that the negro, even in a state of freedom, can not escape the cupidity and persecution of the white man. Since we have been here, negro men have rushed frightened to General Sherman's headquarters begging for protection from the "land-sharks," who, it appears, have seized all the able-bodied negroes they could lay their hands upon, and locked them up until they could be mustered into the service. The wretches who perpetrate this outrage take the names of these men and the evidence of their enlistment to the North, and sell them as substitutes for the army. General Sherman was exceedingly angry, and at once gave orders to have the negroes released, threatened the recruiting agents with severe punishment if violence was again used, and assured the negroes that they were free to go where they liked for work, and that they could become soldiers if they chose, but that they should not be forced into the army.

While the army is recuperating for another campaign, a crowd of civilians have found their way here from the North. They are eager creatures, seeking fortune in a cotton-bale. How they are able to run the blockade at the War Office is a wonder; but here they are in spite of the wise prohibition of Mr. Stanton; many of them with papers in their pockets signed by Mr. Lincoln, permitting them to purchase ten, twenty, or a thousand bales of cotton. General Sherman detests these speculators with all his soul. Several of them called upon him, and the interview was amusing.

"How are you, General?" said a black-haired, pale, hungry-faced man.

"Ah!" the General replied, "*you* are down here. What are you after in Savannah?"

"Well, General, I did so well in banking operations at Memphis that I thought I would try my hand in cotton. I have an order from Mr. Lincoln," etc.

Several others repeated in substance the same story. At last the General turned round, and with a manner any thing but agreeable to the individuals he addressed, said:

"You know that the Secretary of War is here?"

With some trepidation, his auditors replied in the affirmative.

"Well," he added, "I have peremptory instructions to arrest every man who came here without proper authority, and I shall execute these orders if I have to put in the guard-house the most intimate friend I have. You have come to the wrong place, gentlemen."

"You won't get me unless you do it in an hour, for I shall take the first boat to New York," said the Israelitish ex-banker.

The news of the order for arrest got about town in a few

hours. The next morning not one of the greedy speculators was to be found in the city.

January 2d.—The early colonists, when navigating the waters of Tybee, Ossabaw, and Warsaw Sounds, must have rejoiced greatly when they came to the high bluff where the substantial city of Savannah now stands. No matter how great the floods which descended the mighty river, overflowing the widely-extended swamp lands—it could never encroach upon the site they had chosen for their new settlement. Standing upon the balconies of the lofty warehouses which line the river bank, the spectator gazes toward the east and north over leagues of rice lands. Here and there a solitary tree or a negro hut breaks the monotonous level; in the far distance, toward the sea, groups of water-oaks, which have taken root in the sandy soil, fringe the horizon; below, the river rushes past, turbid with the washings from the myriad streams and creeks in the mountains of Tennessee. As we see it now, the surface of the stream is covered with hundreds of vessels. Ships are unloading at the piers; steamboats are surging painfully against the tide; rafts and rowboats are filled with curious soldiers, who are enjoying the novel spectacle of a sea-port for the first time. Down the river, where a line of dark spots marks the sunken "cribs" which the stupid people placed there to prevent the approach of the "Yankees," an object in the form of a tower lies gently reposing: it is a huge turreted monitor, which is best left sleeping. On the other side of the stream, snugly at anchor, swings the cutter Bibb, the flag at her stern showing that her worthy commander, Captain Boutelle, is on board. When a child, I remember hearing of Boutelle's surveys in Charleston Harbor and the Savannah River.

Little did I expect to meet him one day on the Ogeechee, fishing for Rebel torpedoes.

The wide piers, or wharves, at our feet are thronged with thousands of laborers in army blue. They are loading supplies with the long tiers of wagons which stretch through the admirably-built causeways to the main street above. Hundreds of them, thousands come here daily on a similar errand. Certainly in the most prosperous times there could not have been more life and movement in Savannah than we see here to-day.

Savannah is not so beautiful a city as Portland, in Maine, or Rome, in Georgia, where Nature has showered her graces with prodigal hand; nor has the artist here supplied the place of Nature. The city is not celebrated for its works of art, nor for fine architectural displays. A pretty fountain adorns one of the numerous parks; an unobtrusive monument to the memory of Pulaski occupies the centre of another; and one or two churches of substantial material and graceful form attest the wealth and good taste of the builders; but for all this it would be an extravagance of words to say that Savannah is beautiful.

There is a strong element of good society in the city. In the old time the port had excellent commercial advantages. Cotton and rice, in large quantities, were exported; and there grew up, with an active trade, a wealthy class of merchants, refined and cultivated. Then there were plantation owners, who made this place their home. Rich in lands, slaves, and gold, they lived luxuriously; and, like other people in other ages, who owned the human beings whose labor was the source of their wealth, they came to despise any man who gained his daily bread by the sweat of his own brow. In the course of time these people have come to believe themselves the aristocracy, born to rule their fellow-beings. If you choose to trace out the surroundings of the most violent of traitors, you will find that they belong to this class.

A highly cultivated lady said to me:

"It is terrible, sir! All my slaves have left me; my plantation is broken up. I don't know but the land will be given to my slaves. I have no money, or but little. I shall have to starve or work."

"Well, madam," I replied, "I really wouldn't advise you to starve. Supposing you do work?"

"But I never did such a thing in all my life!" she answered.

Mrs. ——, who had always passed her summers at the North, and had lived a life of perfect ease, found her income of $20,000 a year swept away at a single blow. With the most charming innocence she protested to me,

"I really fear, sir, that I shall have to submit to the disgrace of giving lessons in music."

I was rude enough to reply:

"Madam, I hope so."

While we occupied Savannah nothing occurred to interrupt the quiet and order which belongs to a large city. In truth, the citizens averred that never, even in peaceful days, was there so much of order; that they never felt so secure in the possession of their property and in the safety of life and limb as now.

While I have no doubt that the most of these people actually sympathize with their relatives and friends in the Rebel army, I am equally sure that they rejoiced that the city was in the hands of our army and under the government of the old Union. Not that they love the "Yankees" more than of yore, but they have learned to respect and even honor men whom in the days before the war they hated and despised. "*Nous avons changé tout cela*," and they have learned that we may be generous as enemies and gentle as friends, while they no longer suffer the deprivation of seclusion from the civilized outer world.

A foreigner visiting the city would not suppose that it was so lately a prize of battle. Ladies walk the streets with perfect confidence and security, and the public squares are filled with children at play; the stores and theatres are open; soldiers are lounging on the doorsteps of the houses in cheerful conversation with fair damsels; carriages whirl by, wherein the blue coat and brass buttons are in close proximty—any thing but warlike—to jockey hats and flowing ringlets. In truth, there is a delightful *entente cordiale* between the officers and ladies, which would never be disturbed, perhaps, could many of them be consulted. Yet to those who observe the movements in the different departments of the army there appear signs that this great host is unsettling its wings for another migration.

CHAPTER XI.

REVIEW OF THE GEORGIA CAMPAIGN.

IN a military point of view there is no precedent to the campaign through Georgia, for the history of war records no similar conditions. The uninterrupted success of twenty-seven days of marching was not due to the lack of an enemy to oppose our progress, for there were garrisons at Augusta, Macon, Charleston, and Savannah, which, had they been concentrated under the lead of a man like Johnston, might have stayed our steps for a while. But the direction of columns, the disposition of troops, the selection of lines of operations, so confused and deceived Beauregard that no concentration or effective opposition was made until the last moment, when it was too late.

There can be no doubt that the gravest error yet committed by the Rebel leaders was the dispatch of Hood's army to a field of operations north of the Chattahoochee. The capture of Atlanta by our forces was in reality the death-blow to the Rebel cause, for the downfall of that place proved that the two great strong-holds of the Confederacy, Richmond and Atlanta, could not both be held at the same time. Had not the Rebel chiefs been afflicted with that supreme selfishness, that arrogant pride, which impelled and fostered this traitorous war, the fall of Atlanta would have been the signal for a concentration of all their forces upon the plains of Georgia or in South Carolina. Had Richmond and the sea-coast been abandoned, and a rapid concentration of their armies and garrisons effected, we might not have been to-day in possession of Savannah, and the war would have been indefinitely prolonged.

It should not be inferred, however, that General Sherman would have remained in Atlanta, even if there had been a concentration of the Rebel forces. That city lost its military value the moment its machine shops, its arsenals, its factories, its system of railroads were destroyed; and it is a great error, or, rather, an under-estimate of the fertile brain of General Sherman, to suppose that the presence of Hood at Jonesboro' or any other place would have prevented our invasion of the South. The theatre for military operations was extensive. Whenever he had chosen to free himself from the vexatious guard of a line of communications two hundred miles in length, thus leaving the army at liberty to move, he had the choice of several important objectives. If he had deemed it imprudent or impossible to march upon Savannah direct, he had alternatives of equal value. There were ways of reaching salt water without marching straight toward the sea-coast. Skillful manœuvres would have been essential, some sharp fighting would have occurred, our march would have been slower, our work would have been delayed—nothing more. Sherman's army could not have been permanently arrested in the deed it meant to accomplish.

But the Rebels were not sufficiently sagacious to prevent us from doing as we intended. They presented a bold front near Atlanta; Hood crept up into Tennessee to meet the fate of a brave but desperate man when Thomas crushed him; Lee could not stir; and Sherman marched down to the sea.

Four co-operative movements of the Union forces took place during this campaign, but only two had marked significance.

1. General Foster was instructed to demonstrate upon the Charleston and Savannah Railroad, and, if possible, to make a lodgment at Pocotaligo or Grahamville. His soldiers made a brave attempt to effect this lodgment, but they were foiled. The Rebels were able to concentrate at the threatened point and drive our men back with some loss, defeating the object of the expedition.

2. A cavalry force left the banks of the Mississippi River, with instructions to move toward Selma, Alabama. This expedition returned after a short march without accomplishing any material results.

3. General Stoneman's cavalry started upon a similar expedition up the valley of the Tennessee. Stoneman was completely successful. He fought and routed nearly every force of the enemy who came in his way, capturing prisoners and stores, and destroying large and invaluable works erected for the manufacture of salt and saltpetre. He returned in safety, having admirably fulfilled his instructions.

4. The fourth and most important co-operative movement rose subsequently to the dignity of a separate campaign. A universally received rule in the art of war forbids the division of forces in the face of an enemy. Jeff. Davis and Hood's raid northward was undertaken in the belief that Sherman would not dare to violate this maxim. There were two reasons sufficient to justify General Sherman in the course he adopted. He knew that by detaching the 4th and 23d Corps to aid General Thomas, the re-enforcement, with the troops already within his control, would enable that General to oppose to Hood a largely superior army—an army not only sufficient to defend the line of the Tennessee, but at any moment to assume the offensive. More than this: the theatre of operations was not confined to the valley of the Tennessee. The vital strength of the rebellion

lay in that mighty army within the fortifications of Richmond. To break up and destroy the communications of that army, and thus to compel the evacuation of the Rebel strong-hold, was Sherman's mission and design. The future will decide whether or not the capture of Savannah and the victory of Nashville were steps toward that glorious achievement.

In closing this brief review of The March to the Sea, I can not refrain from noting one or two incidents of the campaign which naturally belong to this division of the subject.

As rumors of the approach of our army reached the frightened inhabitants, frantic efforts were made to conceal not only their valuable personal effects, plate, jewelry, and other rich goods, but also articles of food, such as hams, sugar, flour, etc. A large part of these supplies were carried to the neighboring swamps; but the favorite method of concealment was the burial of the treasures in the pathways and gardens adjoining the dwelling-houses. Sometimes, also, the grave-yards were selected as the best place of security from the "vandal hands of the invaders." Unfortunately for these people, the negroes betrayed them, and in the early part of the march the soldiers learned the secret. It is possible that supplies thus hidden may have escaped the search of our men; but, if so, it was not for want of diligent exploration. With untiring zeal the soldiers hunted for concealed treasures. Wherever the army halted, almost every inch of ground in the vicinity of the dwellings was poked by ramrods, pierced with sabres, or upturned with spades. The universal digging was good for the garden land, but its results were distressing to the Rebel owners of exhumed property, who saw it rapidly and irretrievably "confiscated." It was comical to see a group of these red-bearded, barefooted, ragged veterans punching the unoffend-

TREASURE SEEKERS.

ing earth in an apparently idiotic, but certainly most energetic way. If they "struck a vein" a spade was instantly put in requisition, and the coveted wealth was speedily unearthed. Nothing escaped the observation of these sharp-witted soldiers. A woman standing upon the porch of a house, apparently watching their proceedings, instantly became an object of suspicion, and she was watched until some movement betrayed a place of concealment. The fresh earth recently thrown up, a bed of flowers just set out, the slightest indication of a change in appearance or position, all attracted the gaze of these military agriculturists. It was all fair spoil of war, and the search made one of the excitements of the march.

CHAPTER XII.

GENERAL SHERMAN.

The relation of a staff officer to his chief is necessarily of an intimate personal nature: I desire to speak of General Sherman from this point of view. His military deeds have passed into the pages of history: his social characteristics can only be recorded by those who have been admitted to the privilege of his friendship.

Late in the summer of 1864 I was relieved from detached service in the West, and ordered to report to the General commanding the Military Division of the Mississippi. I found General Sherman at Atlanta, seated in the parlor of his headquarters, surrounded by several of his generals, and shall never forget the kindness with which he received me. When he heard that I was a stranger in the Western army, he said, "Very well; I will retain you on my staff." The expression of gentleness, sympathy, and consideration which accompanied this brief announcement, made an impression upon me which will be fully understood by any officer who has had the fortune to be suddenly ordered to a strange and distant field of duty, where anxiety and embarrassment awaited him. The incident is introduced here because it gives the key-note to a striking feature in the character of General Sherman.

Not only is the General sensitively considerate of the feelings of his friends, but he will not permit abuse or ridicule of any one attached to his person. This characteristic is well known to the officers of his army. It has been sometimes said that his strong personal attachments exert an influence over his official relations; but this is not true. In all his actions he is governed by a high and conscientious sense of duty, embracing all the questions involved in the subject under consideration. His decisions are rapid, alike on light and important questions; but he first weighs with care and judgment the arguments advanced on both sides.

A striking evidence of his sense of justice and his unselfishness may be seen in his refusal to accept the commission of a Major General in the Regular Army which was offered him previous to the fall of Atlanta. In his letter declining the honor, he said:

"These positions of so much trust and honor should be held open until the close of the war. They should not be hastily given. Important campaigns are in operation. At the end, let those who prove their capacity and merit be the ones appointed to these high honors."

General Sherman's memory is marvelous. The simplest incidents of friendly intercourse, the details of his campaigns, citations of events, dates, names, faces, remain fresh in his mind. A soldier who may have addressed him long years ago in the swamps of Florida; some heroic deed of an officer or soldier at Shiloh; a barn or a hillside in Georgia; a chance expression of your own which you may have forgotten; the minutest particulars in the plan of a campaign; whatever he has seen, heard, or read, he remembers with astonishing accuracy. Napoleon had a similar trait.

He is also remarkably observant, especially of the conduct and character of the officers of the army. He sees what many persons suppose it impossible for his eye to reach. In an army of seventy thousand men, it might be reasonably imagined that the commanding general is too far removed from the great mass to know or be known by them; but when it is remembered that Sherman has marched during this campaign alternately with one and another corps, it ceases to be a matter of surprise that he is thoroughly acquainted with the character of the different organizations. In truth, nothing escapes that vigilant and piercing eye, from the greatest to the minutest detail of the command.

General Sherman is sociable in the best sense of the word. When the responsibilities of the hour are cast aside—and he throws them off with the utmost facility—he enters into the spirit of a merry-making with all the zest and appreciation of the jolliest of the party. He has a keen sense of wit and humor, and not unfrequently he is the centre and life of the occasion. Sometimes he is familiar with others, but it would be a remarkable spectacle to see others take liberties with him. He converses freely, yet he is reticent to the last degree, knowing how to keep his own counsel, and never betraying his purposes. He is cautious, and often suspicious; yet no man ever accused him of deceit or dishonesty, either in word or deed. His unmeasured scorn and contempt are visited upon pretense, spurious philanthropy, arrogance, self-conceit, or boasting; but he never fails to recognize and pay a hearty tribute to unpretentious merit, courage, capacity, Christian manliness, and simplicity. He is not prodigal of promises, but his word, once given, is sacred as Holy Writ.

If the personal descriptions of the General given by the Rebel newspapers during his campaign were accepted as truth, he would appear as a creature of demoniac passion and cruelty, whose unrelenting spirit found pleasure in wreaking vengeance upon old men, women, and children; but Rebel journalism is known to be violent, unscrupulous, and libelous, as readily assailing the President with coarse vituperation as his generals with wholesale falsehood. General Sherman is terribly in earnest in his method of conducting war, but he is neither vindictive nor implacable. He once said to a Methodist preacher in Georgia who had, by voice and example, helped to plunge the nation into war:

" You, sir, and such as you, had the power to resist this mad rebellion; but you chose to strike down the best government ever created, and for no good reason whatsoever. You are suffering the consequences, and have no right to complain."

While the General was speaking, his soldiers were rapidly emptying the preacher's barns of their stores of corn and forage. The anecdote illustrates Sherman's ideas of the way to make war.

Again: Alfred Rhett, while speaking of the refugees who had escaped from the tyranny of the slaveholders' despotism, said to Sherman, with an oath:

"These miserable miscreants should every one be killed!"

"That is a favorite hobby of mine," replied the General, with a peculiar expression which was possibly lost upon Mr. Rhett; and then he added:

"There is a class of persons at the South who must be exterminated before there can be peace in the land."

Yet there is a depth of tenderness, akin to the love of woman, behind that face which is furrowed with the lines of anxiety and care, and those eyes which dart keen and suspicious glances. Little children cling to the General's knees and nestle in his arms with intuitive faith and affection. During our sojourn in Savannah, his headquarters and private room became the play-ground of hosts of little ones, upon whom the door was never closed, no matter what business was pending.

General Sherman's integrity seems to pervade every element in his character. His intense dislike of the men who have been interested in the war only to make money out of it is well known. From the first instant of the rebellion pecuniary considerations were cast aside by the General, and he has given himself wholly to the service of his country. He knows the value of money, but he can say, with honorable pride, that the atmosphere of integrity and honesty about him withers and destroys the lust of gain. Not even the taint of suspicion in this regard has ever been cast upon him, nor upon the officers associated with him.

His keen sense of commercial integrity finds an apt illustration in an incident of his career as a banker in California. At that time it was the habit of Eastern men to send funds to California for favorable investment, and Hardee and others of Sherman's old army friends sent remittances to him for that purpose. During the financial panic in 1857 the securities which had previously given the investors a high rate of interest suddenly became worthless; but Sherman refunded the money, which was accepted with the knowledge that the banker suffered the entire loss. He was under no legal or moral obligation to perform this act, but his strong feeling of conscientiousness demanded the sacrifice.

In person, General Sherman is nearly six feet in height, with a wiry, muscular, and not ungraceful frame. His age is only forty-seven years, but his face is furrowed with deep lines, indicating care and profound thought. With surprising rapidity, however, these strong lines disappear when he talks with children and women. His eyes are of a dark-brown color, and sharp and quick in expression. His forehead is broad and fair, sloping gently at the top of the head, which is covered with thick and light-brown hair, closely trimmed. His beard and moustache, of a sandy hue, are also closely cut. His constitution is iron. Exposure to cold, rain, or burning heat seems to produce no effect upon his powers of endurance and strength. Under the most harassing conditions I have never seen him exhibit any symptoms of fatigue. In the field he retires early, but at midnight he may be found pacing in front of his tent, or sitting by the camp-fire smoking a cigar. His sleep must be light and unrestful, for the galloping of a courier's horse down the road instantly wakes him, as well as a voice or a movement in his tent. He falls asleep as easily and quickly as a little child—by the roadside, upon the wet ground, on the hard floor, or when a battle rages near him. No circumstance of time or place seems to affect him. His mien is never clumsy nor commonplace; and when mounted upon review he appears in every way the Great Captain that he is.

When sounds of musketry or cannonading reach his ears, the General is extremely restless until he has been satisfied as to the origin, location, and probable results of the fight in progress. At such moments he usually lights a fresh cigar, and smokes while walking to and fro; stopping now and then to listen to the increasing rattle of musketry; then, muttering "Forward," will mount old "Sam," a horribly fast-walking horse, which is as indifferent to shot and shell as his master, and starts off in the direction of the fire. Dismounting near the battle-line, he will stride away into the woods, or to the edge of a creek or swamp, until some officer, fearful of the consequences, respectfully warns him that he is in a dangerous position, when, perhaps, he retires.

One afternoon, during the Atlanta campaign, the General paid a visit to General Hooker, who had pitched his headquarters in a place almost as much exposed to the fire of the enemy as any that could have been found along the line. The two Generals seated themselves comfortably, with their

F

feet planted against the trees, watching the operations immediately in front, and in full view of the Rebels. Very soon a Rebel shell passed them, shrieking overhead, clearing the crockery from the dinner-table with amazing rapidity, and frightening the cook Sambo, who afterward excused himself on the ground that his mate had been killed the night before by one of " them things." Another shell quickly followed, demolishing a chair which had just been vacated by an officer. Meanwhile the rifle-bullets were singing and "fizzing" about in a reckless way, chipping the bark from the trees and cutting their leaves and branches. Still the two Generals sat, discussing military questions, with the utmost indifference, until the sun went down; while the staff-officers, not seeing any fun in the business, carried on their own conversation as companionably as could reasonably be expected in a spot where the protecting trees were five or ten feet apart.

General Sherman asserts that he never needlessly goes under fire, and that he calculates all the chances, avoiding useless exposure, which is undoubtedly true. *Mais*, as the French say.

The General's habits of life are simple. Primitive, almost, as first principles, his greatest sacrifice will be made when he resigns campaigning for a more civilized life. He has a keen sense of the beauty of nature, and never is happier than when his camp is pitched in some forest of lofty pines, where the wind sings through the tree-tops in melodious measure, and the feet are buried in the soft carpeting of spindles. He is the last one to complain when the table fare is reduced to beef and "hard tack," and, in truth, he rather enjoys poverty of food, as one of the conditions of a soldier's life. I remember that he apologized to our guest, the Secretary of War, one day at Savannah, because certain luxuries, such as canned fruits and jellies, had found their way to his table.

"This," he remarked, "is the consequence of coming into houses and cities. The only place to live, Mr. Secretary, is out of doors in the woods!"

This simplicity of taste, which is so perfectly natural to the General, has served well in the campaigns of this war. It is easily seen that in making long marches, the most fatal clog to successful operations is excessive transportation, and the tendency of the army is constantly to accretion; but Sherman reduces baggage-trains to the minimum, and himself shares the privations of the common soldier.

General Sherman's patriotism is a vital force. He has given himself and all that he has to the national cause. Personal considerations, I am sure, have never influenced him. Doubtless he is ambitious, but it is impossible to discern any selfish or unworthy motive, either in his words or deeds. I do not believe it possible for a man more absolutely to subordinate himself and his personal interests to the great cause than he. His patriotism is as pure as the faith of a child; and before it family and social influences are powerless. His relatives are the last persons to receive from his hand preferment or promotion. In answer to the request of one nearly allied to him that he would give his son a position on his staff, the General's reply was curt and unmistakable:

"Let him enter the ranks as a soldier, and carry a musket a few years."

In no instance is it possible for the General to favor the advancement of soldiers upon mere political grounds; bravery and capacity are the considerations which weigh with him. When a paper is handed to him for indorsement, accompanied by questions relative to promotion, he leaves the selection of the candidate to army or corps commanders, reserving his own opinion until the proper time.

The character of General Sherman's mind is growth. Perhaps the process is slow, but it is not the less sure. Several of the great progressive ideas of the day have had to battle with his reason against old-established prejudices; but, having once gained entrance, they become a part of his nature. He has had as great responsibilities to meet as any man of the age, but there has never been an instant when he was not equal to the occasion, even to the acceptance of a new truth. Few men have so harmoniously united common sense and genius as General Sherman. He can hardly be styled a representative man, but he is altogether original, and is, at the same time, a pure outgrowth of American civilization. He is a Democrat in the best sense of that word. There is nothing European about him. He is a striking type of our institutions, and he comprehends justly the National Idea.

PART II.

THE CAMPAIGN OF THE CAROLINAS.

CHAPTER XIII.

MOVEMENT OF TROOPS—CROSSING THE SOUTH CAROLINA BORDER—THE ARMY UNDER FLY-TENTS.

EVERY thing was quiet in Savannah in the middle of January, and the most perfect order was maintained from day to day. It seemed as if Sherman and his army had determined to become permanent residents of the city, so smoothly ran the wheels of routine. Yet while each man in the army, with that easy philosophy of the soldier which teaches him to catch pleasure wherever he can, was making the most of his time, not one imagined that the march to Savannah had been made with no other purpose than to remain there. It was thoroughly understood by all the intelligent veterans who composed the legions of Sherman, that so long as Lee and his forces stood defiant at the Rebel capital, Richmond was the real objective of our campaign. How and when we were to reach that point were the questions discussed throughout the camp; but our men said that "while 'Uncle Billy' had the matter in his hands, it was sure to go right."

The new expedition had already been determined in the mind of our chief before we saw Savannah. So far back as the Alabama campaign, when Hood was racing toward the North, and the march of this army through Georgia was in its inception, and perhaps long before that time, when pressing his columns steadily forward to the Gate City, our Great Captain had studied the problem he meant to solve, grasping the grand plan of his campaign, mastering its details, and working out its probable results. The capture of Savannah was but a pivot upon which he swung his army; this campaign was but a part of the *grand idea*. The 15th of January saw the troops actually in motion for the new campaign, and it was soon known that South Carolina was to be the next field of operations. To those whom the world called wise and prudent this new invasion seemed the height of danger. "While," said some, "the campaign through Georgia was harmless and safe, this is a march into the jaws of destruction." Others saw that every step into the interior was a step toward Lee, who could throw his columns, by easy railroad transit, across our track. Hardee was already in our front with 30,000 men; a retreat to Savannah could not be accomplished over roads which we had already cut to pieces; our flanks would continually be exposed to surprise by the enemy; the approaches to Charleston by the land were infinitely more difficult than those of Savannah. Altogether, these good people in Savannah thought the undertaking hazardous in the extreme—in fact, impossible.

Nevertheless, the troops were in motion.

The better to see how and when it was done, it is essential to recur to the diary of the campaign.

Savannah, January 21*st.*—The grand movement of the right and left wings of the army, which has been going on quietly yet vigorously for several days, has received a severe check in the heavy rains of the past three days. Last week the 17th Corps and two divisions of the 15th were moved by water from Thunderbolt round to Beaufort, and from there to the main land. Advancing toward the Charleston Railroad, they met the enemy, who fell back after a sharp skirmish. Our loss was light, and the troops went into camp under the fire of the Rebel batteries. The next day preparations were made for a detour which would have flanked the position. The Rebels did not wait for this, but evacuated their works, leaving three guns behind them; so we now occupy Pocotaligo, with a loss of ten men killed and wounded. The attempt of Foster to carry the same position a month ago cost him twelve hundred or fifteen hundred men. The 20th, 14th, and two divisions of the 15th Corps remained here; two divisions of the 20th crossed the rice lands opposite to the city and reached Hardeeville, opening communication with Howard at Pocotaligo. Then the rains fell in torrents, and a freshet came down the river, and there was from ten to fifteen feet of water where our wagon trains passed along safely a week ago. We have attempted to march up the river on this side, but the water covers all the roads, until they also are impassable. Mules and wagons actually sink out of sight. At Purisburg, where the crossing is made, our soldiers are doing picket duty in boats and scows. It seems as if we must wait until the water runs off.

Beaufort, January 25th.—A portion of the army, with its trains, is yet in process of transportation from Thunderbolt here. Our soldiers, upon landing in what they suppose to be the State of South Carolina, have the idea that they can commence foraging at once, and so the hen-coops of the worthy Union men, who are safely and snugly settled down here in their cheaply-purchased mansions, have suffered somewhat. The men restrained themselves as soon as they found how the matter stood, and no more damage will be inflicted.

The inhabitants were easily satisfied when they fully understood the ignorance of the soldiers as to their status. An unfortunate major general, however, did not escape so easily. Assigned to the house of a government official, his servants foraged on the premises without his knowledge, quickly clearing them of chickens, turkeys, etc. The owner of the house thought himself wronged, and refused to be comforted, although all sorts of apologies were offered.

Pocotaligo, January 27th.—From Beaufort to this place there is the same character of country as in the rear of Savannah—impenetrable swamps and wide-extended rice-fields, crossed by raised dykes or causeways. The heads of these were defended by finely-constructed forts, where it seems as if a few men could hold at bay an army. How it is that our soldiers are able to outflank and outmanœuvre the Rebels it is hard to tell, unless we take into account an advantage which is illustrated in an incident which took place on the skirmish-line a short distance from here when the two lines came within speaking distance.

Johnny Reb. commenced the conversation with the remark, "Who the —— are you? Strikes me you're pushing things!"

"You're right there, Johnny. We're Bill Sherman's raiders; you'd better git—we're coming for you straight!" The Rebels left the same morning.

From present appearances I judge we shall not move for several days. The balmy South, which I have heard of so long, is something we have yet to experience. We have either very heavy rains, or a harsh, biting wind, such as is now sweeping over the country to our great discomfort.

The 14th Corps is by this time on its way to Sister's Ferry, much higher up the Savannah River than Purisburg, and at a much better crossing, having the additional advantage of reaching a high pine ridge which traverses the State of South Carolina as far north as Augusta, and nearly parallel to the river. The object of this movement of the left wing I can not understand, unless Branchville is our first objective. Many of the officers of the army think, and all of the navy hope and pray, that we are making direct for Charleston. I doubt it. We can not stay long before that city for want of supplies, unless we establish a new base in that vicinity, which is probably not anticipated; whereas, if we march into the northern and middle part of the state, our army can obtain supplies on the way, and accomplish its capture without a fight before its fortifications.

In the outset of the campaign orders of a general character were issued. All sick, wounded, and incompetent soldiers were left behind. Transportation was reduced to the smallest possible space. The amount of hard bread, coffee, and salt, the number of wagons for the different headquarters and for each regiment and battery, and the size of the supply-train, were specified. The number of officers to occupy a tent, and the kind of tent to be used, were also designated. Except for the uses of the adjutants' offices, the wall-tent, which we look back upon with tenderest gratitude, is forbidden, and two officers are permitted to share the "fly" which formerly was stretched over the wall-tent. This will answer when the weather is pleasant, for with half a dozen blankets one can sleep comfortably in the open air; but let the wind blow and the rain fall, and comfort in your fly is an open question. But we manage to rig up boughs and water-proofs, which keep out some of the wind and a limited amount of water.

When I think of the many hours passed in happy security in a wall-tent, no remorse embitters the recollection; for no shadow of doubt then crossed my mind but that I was enjoying the luxury of camp life, if not of all living.

Wall-tents are not the only luxuries now forbidden. Chairs, camp-cots, trunks, and all unnecessary personal baggage, are thrown out without exception. No officer is permitted to take with him more horses than the regulations allow, and he is also restricted in the number of his servants. In truth, General Sherman has reduced the army to its simplest and most effective fighting and marching conditions, rejecting as superfluities all that is not essential to its health, or that may clog its movements.

In all these personal sacrifices General Sherman demands nothing of his soldiers which he does not himself share. His staff is smaller than that of any brigade commander in the army. He has fewer servants and horses than the military regulations allow; his baggage is reduced to the smallest possible limit; he sleeps in a fly-tent like the rest of us, rejecting the effeminacy of a house; and the soldier in the ranks indulges in luxuries (the fruits of some daring forage raid, to be sure) which his chief never sees.

When we left Atlanta we thought the army had been stripped to the lowest possible point, but our experiences thus far prove that we can go several steps lower, and that a man may have but little and still be contented, if not comfortable. Farther than this, we discover how unnecessary, if not enervating, are the conventionalities and luxuries of city life.

CHAPTER XIV.

ADVANCE TO THE SALKAHATCHIE—IN THE SWAMPS—DESOLATION.

January 30*th.*—The actual invasion of South Carolina has begun. The 17th Corps and that portion of the 15th which came around by way of Thunderbolt and Beaufort moved out this morning, on parallel roads, in the direction of McPhersonville. The 17th Corps took the road nearest the Salkahatchie River. We expect General Corse, with the 4th Division of the 15th Corps, to join us at a point higher up. The 14th and 20th Corps will take the road to Robertville, nearer the Savannah River. Since General Howard started with the 17th we have heard the sound of many guns in his direction. To-day is the first really fine weather we have had since starting, and the roads have improved. It was wise not to cut them up during the rains, for we can now move along comfortably. The well-known sight of columns of black smoke meets our gaze again; this time houses are burning, and South Carolina has commenced to pay an instalment, long overdue, on her debt to justice and humanity. With the help of God, we will have principal and interest before we leave her borders. There is a terrible gladness in the realization of so many hopes and wishes. This cowardly traitor state, secure from harm, as she thought, in her central position, with hellish haste dragged her Southern sisters into the caldron of secession. Little did she dream that the hated flag would again wave over her soil; but this bright morning a thousand Union banners are floating in the breeze, and the ground trembles beneath the tramp of thousands of brave Northmen, who know their mission, and will perform it to the end.

February 1st.—The 15th Corps has reached Hickory Hill to-night, making a fine march of twenty miles from Pocotaligo. The roads are much better, for we have found higher ground in each mile of our march until we reached this "hill," which can not have received any such cognomen because of its elevation, for it is simply a rising plateau, and would perhaps become submerged in the event of a freshet. General Howard is with the 17th Corps, eight miles east of us, on the Salkahatchie River Road. General Slocum, with the left wing, has not yet crossed the Savannah. The river is up again, and unknown distances of bridging must be accomplished before he can get fairly on his appointed way. This remark, however, does not apply to two divisions of the 20th Corps, which crossed the Savannah below Sister's Ferry, at Purisburg, and are to-night at Robertville. They will be able to join us sooner than the others, who are likely to be delayed several days.

During the march to this point we have had opportunities of observing a barren agricultural region, and a population of "poor whites" whose brain is as arid as the land they occupy. The wealthy landholders, who formerly held this region by a sort of feudal tenure, have all run away on the approach of our troops, leaving a contingent remainder of ignorant, half-civilized people, whose ideas are limited, and whose knowledge of the English tongue is, to say the least, extremely imperfect. A family of this class I found in full and undisputed possession of the mansion of an escaped magnate (I came near writing the word convict). The head of this family was a weak creature, with pale face, light eyes, and bleached beard. His wife, a woman of about thirty years, was bowed, crooked, and yellow. She carried in her arms a dirty boy about three years old. A frightened young girl of thirteen, the woman's stepdaughter, completed the number of the household. The man entered freely into conversation on the subject of the war. He seemed to understand but little of the great principles which were at stake in the conflict, and, in point of fact, it is an open question whether he knew what a principle meant; yet even his dull intellect took in two points, namely, that the success of the Rebels would certainly establish the bondage of his own class to the aristocrats of the South, and that our own victories would secure freedom to the slaves. The emancipation of the blacks, he thought, "would be a derned shame;" but he immediately added: "I don't pretend to understand these questions; I don't know much anyhow!" To this remark I mentally gave my hearty assent.

He continued: "The poor whites aren't allowed to live here in South Carolina; the rich folks allus charges us with sellin' things to the niggers; so they won't let us own land, but drives us about from place to place. I never owned a foot of land all my life, and I was born and raised in this state. It was only a little while ago they cau't a man a sellin' to the nigs, so they tarred and feathered him, and put him into Georgia across Sister's Ferry. They hate the sight of us poor whites."

"And yet," said I, "you are the class that are now furnishing the rank and file of their armies. How absurd that is!" The man answered with a vacant, listless stare, and the remark, "It mought be so."

February 3d. — The 15th Corps have moved forward again, and are in camp at Loper's Cross Roads, the junction where the Sister's Ferry Road crosses the direct road from Hickory Hill. Two divisions are encamped on the Sister's Ferry Road, as far as the place formerly called Barker's Mills. This point was occupied yesterday by a division of the 17th Corps coming up from Whippy Swamp. General Howard was heard from directly to-day; we have had intimations of his position since yesterday morning through the sound of cannon in his direction. He has been trying to make a crossing over the Salkahatchie at River's Bridge, up to last accounts unsuccessfully. Several officers and men have been killed and wounded since he left us at Pocotaligo.

We have again had news from our left wing. The two divisions which crossed at Purisburg have come up, and are in camp two miles from this point. The other part of this wing is still at Sister's Ferry, waiting for means to march.

A journey of thirty miles which I made to-day again afforded opportunities to talk with the people. As usual, the negroes were by far the most interesting. Alert, witty, and sensible, their intelligence is in every way superior to that of the lower class of white men who share these abandoned lands with them. I found the blacks generally aware that the Rebels intended to put them in the army, and much conversation on this point elicited curious illustrations of the state of feeling among the slaves.

I remarked to a jolly-looking black that I had heard the Rebels meant to make a soldier of him.

"But I wouldn't go!" was his reply.

"Suppose they offer you your freedom."

"Oh, dey lies a heap! I'se not belieb 'em; I wouldn't fight."

"Then they will force you to go. What will you do

when they get you into their army, and put a musket in your hands, and tell you to shoot the Yankees?"

"I nebber will shoot de Yankees; de first chance I git I run away!"

Three very queer specimens of white women were at the corner of the road as our column wound around to cross Jackson's Creek at Barker's Mills. The day was cold and windy, and now and then the rain would fall in torrents, to be thirstily absorbed by the sandy soil, except here and there in the roadway, where it stood in huge puddles to warn the wary teamsters that a quicksand stood ready to engulf their mules and wagons. It was a wild day, and a dreary place for three lone women. Supposing that they had been burned out of house and home by the soldiers, I asked the old woman (the other two were not more than sixteen) if I could be of any service to them.

"Anan?" was the reply.

"Can I help you in any way?"

"Oh no; we jist cum out h'yar to see the soldiers go by; never seed so many men in all my life. We live back here off the road a spell."

"How do you get a living?"

"We spin, and make cloth, and do our own farming."

I noticed that they were standing in the cold mud with their bare limbs and feet exposed, and asked them where were their shoes.

"We ain't got none; the rich people won't let poor folks like us have shoes."

All this time the two girls were peering out at us from beneath the long hoods covering their faces, so that we could only see their eyes. There was a simplicity and bashfulness in this action which was not only odd, but really charming, although the surroundings strongly suggested the comical. I asked the old lady, who proved to be their mother, if they were frightened:

"Lor' bless you, sir, no; they are a little backward, that's all. They never seed so much company, sir, before to-day."

"I should think not," I replied. "If you don't look out, some of these blue-eyed Yankees will marry them and elope."

She nodded her head with satisfaction, and said, "May be."

I left them standing in the cold rain, gazing with curious, wondering eyes upon the long column of troops as it wound along the road and crossed the swollen river.

February 4th.—The army has had a remarkable experience in floundering through these South Carolina swamps; but Sherman's soldiers stop for nothing. Yesterday afternoon the swamps were conquered, the Salkahatchie was crossed, and a force of the enemy who offered a determined opposition to our passage of the stream were driven back. Under a heavy fire from Rebel infantry on the opposite bank of the river, Mower's division of the 17th Corps dashed through and obtained a footing on the east side. The river was too deep to ford, but our brave fellows spanned it by hand-bridges, or floats, upon which they launched themselves, regardless of the pelting storm of lead which was hurled upon them. The Rebels held strong intrenchments on the other side of the river, but, instead of remaining to defend them against our direct attack, ran away as soon as Mower had made a landing. Perhaps their flight was hastened by the fact that a lodgment was at the same time made some miles farther down the river. A division under General Giles E. Smith waded and swam the stream, and was fortunately able to effect a lodgment on the main

Charleston Road, just before the arrival of eight regiments which had been sent up to make good the position the Rebel commander had so successfully held. The gain of River's Bridge opened up the east side of the river as far as our army extends, so that this morning General Wood, commanding first division 15th Corps, found no enemy at Beaufort Bridge.

The bridge was partially destroyed, but not so much injured but that we can repair it before night. The woods resound with the music of the axes, and the cries of the pioneers, as they move timbers and other material to the river. On the other side of the bridge the Rebels had built a strong *tête du pont*, with embrasures and curtains, forming a work sufficiently capacious to contain a division of troops. The successful break made in one part of the Rebel line of defense is an illustration of the great principle in war, that when any part of an enemy's line is carried, and the foothold obtained is made permanent, the remainder of the line must be given up.

Major General Giles E. Smith, who commanded the division of the 17th Corps which swam the Salkahatchie below Mower's position, is a Western man, whose fame has been nobly won on almost every battle-field of this war west and south of the Blue Ridge. He is a manly and handsome soldier, nearly six feet in height, with a frame well-knit, genial blue eyes, light complexion, sandy hair and beard, and an open and cheerful countenance. With this prepossessing exterior, he is polite and hospitable, and of course is popular. As a soldier, he stands among the best. Always attentive to the wants of his command, his men are the last to be out of supplies or clothing. As a commander, he is brave and cool upon the field of battle, and manages his troops with admirable skill.

General Mower personally directed his part of the grand movement of yesterday. During the struggle to gain a footing for our troops on the opposite bank of the river, he stood or waded in the water, urging on the men, watching the course of events with keen glance, and frequently becoming the mark for the Rebel sharpshooters. He is a noble officer, and has won the admiration of his superior officers, and of none more than General Sherman.

No tidings from General Slocum or the left wing of the army have been received to-day. There is some speculation in the camp whether the delay of this column will endanger the main movement. Thus far, we have kept on our course without much regard to the left wing, but it is probable that we shall halt presently, in order to enable it to make a junction. As yet, the real objective of the campaign remains the secret of a few at head-quarters.

February 5th.—To-day I have examined the works at Beaufort Bridge, which were evacuated by the Rebels as soon as we made the crossing at River's Bridge. The place is remarkably strong, both in its natural advantages and in the line of works which defend the passage. A brigade, with a single section of artillery, could have held an army at bay. So it would seem, at least, when one wades and stumbles over the narrow road which leads for half a mile through the swamp. Emerging from the dense jungle before crossing the main branch of the stream, one may see upon its border a line of well-built works extending for a quarter of a mile on either side. Here are three embrasures, pierced for heavy guns, while the parapet is surmounted by the protecting head-log. If the enemy had not been flanked below, and could have defended this place, its capture would have cost us hundreds of lives.

As it is, we have gained the peninsula formed by the Salkahatchie and Edisto Rivers, and have now the choice of going to Augusta or Charleston. The latter place we can capture with less trouble than Savannah caused, even if a direct attack should be made upon the city, for the army could find an excellent base of operations at Bull's Bay. Still, I am certain that the General expects to take Charleston by operating a hundred miles away from its walls—a kind of strategy which has not always been practiced in this war.

General Williams is up with two of the divisions of the 20th Corps. Kilpatrick and his cavalry are at Allandale, and the remainder of the left wing have crossed the Savannah. The army here has made a short move to-day, and we are within a single day's march of the Charleston and Augusta Railroad. We hear that the Rebels intend defending it at several points, but they can not protect the whole line, and we will flank them somewhere.

The land improves as we advance into the interior. The region through which we are now traveling is rich in forage and supplies, and the army is once more reveling in the luxurious experiences of the Georgia campaign—turkeys, geese, ducks, chickens, nicely-cured hams, potatoes, honey, and abundance of other luxuries for the soldiers, and plenty of corn and fodder for the animals. The soil does not seem to be very prolific in Barnwell County, as it has a large proportion of sand, yet the planters, judging from their houses and the outbuildings, seem to have been wealthy. Nearly all these places are deserted, although here and there we find women and children, whom it is difficult to persuade they are not at once to be murdered. Wide-spreading columns of smoke continue to rise wherever our army goes. Building material is likely to be in great demand in this state for some time to come.

As we march on our way, incidents continually occur which for the moment call out the tenderest sympathies of our nature. It is grievous to see a beautiful woman, highly cultured and refined, standing in the gateway of her dismantled home, perhaps with an infant in her arms, while she calls upon some passing officers to protect her home from farther pillage; for the advance-guard, who have just been skirmishing with the enemy or some stragglers, have entered and helped themselves to what they needed or desired. No violence is done to the inmates, but household furniture is pushed about somewhat. The men of the house have all run away, as did Cain after killing his brother. Perhaps it is the best protection for their property to leave women at home, for the soldiers always respect a woman, even if they do sometimes enter a house. These people have one cry in common, now that they feel the bitterness of war. They pray God that it may cease upon any terms, any thing, any time, but give them peace. They say, with the most emphatic unanimity, that they never for a moment thought the war would come into South Carolina. Oh no, her sacred soil was forever to be free from the touch of the hated, despised Yankee!

But here we are; and where our footsteps pass, fire, ashes, and desolation follow in the path. When I hear their cries for help, their wails of pain, and gaze upon their faces pale with fear, I feel as I have never felt before how supremely selfish, how shameless and cowardly has been the action of this state from the first moment of rebellion up to this time. When urging and dragging her sister states into this hell of treason, she little dreamed that, encircled and protected by other states, by the mountains and the sea, her soil would be traversed by Union armies, or ever become the theatre of war. But we are on her soil, and she meets with the fate she deserves. An armed force marching through the land is a fearful scourge.

Our command is in splendid health. Marching and the open air have brought out all the invalids. Day before yesterday we sent back a train with all the wounded, so they will be well cared for, and will not encumber us in our onward march. This is more than well. To be effective for marching or fighting, an army must be stripped of superfluities and encumbrances, and thus the old soldier reduces himself to a few simple necessities. He travels light. You may distinguish him from his fellows in the column by his small, well-packed knapsack and blanket tightly rolled; his well-ordered musket and accoutrements; his fine springy step, his determined *nonchalance*. This man has learned the best philosophy of soldiering by practical experience. This daily experience of marching, scouting, foraging, skirmishing, drilling, manœuvring, and fighting, joined to other natural qualifications, makes the American the best soldier in the world. I affirm this with some knowledge, for I have seen the English, French, Austrian, and Italian soldiers. I do not believe there is an army in the world, outside the United States, that could make such a march as we are making now. Road and bridge building, which we have learned to perfection, would stop them the first day out.

This comparison of European and American soldiers suggests another. General Howard, who has command of our right wing during this campaign, has often been called the Havelock of the army; and the parallel is not unnatural, for both the hero of the Indian campaign and our own distinguished General will rank in history as perfect types of the Christian soldier. General Howard is a man whose religious convictions are intense, positive, entering into and coloring every event of his life. When exposed to fire, there is no braver man living than he. He does not go into action in the Cromwellian spirit, singing psalms and uttering prayers, but with a cool and quiet determination which is inspired by a lofty sense of a sacred duty to be performed. His courage is a realization of the strength of a spiritual religion rather than a physical qualification. The General is constantly censured for rashly exposing himself to the fire of the enemy; but it is difficult to say whether such censure is just or not, for every commander of a corps or an army should himself be the best judge of the necessities of the hour. Napoleon at the Bridge of Arcola was an example.

History shows that more battles have been lost or gained at heavy cost because the commanders did not know the nature of the ground they were fighting over than for any other reason. Such a criticism can never be applied to General Howard. He sees the whole field of operations, and has an admirable tactical knowledge of the best use to be made of its advantages. It is a high compliment to his worth as a man and a soldier that he should have been chosen by General Sherman to the command of the right wing of the army. General Sherman may not be a religious man in the sense that Howard is, but he valued and respected Howard all the more for his Christian faith and practice. In the direction of a march, in the accomplishment of an arduous or dangerous duty, when speed and certainty were required, he knew that Howard would never fail him. In the record of four campaigns, there stands no instance of his dereliction from duty; while many a march and battle-field bear witness to his energy, perseverance, soldierly skill, and manly courage.

Howard lost his right arm at Malvern Hill during the bloody Peninsular campaign. There is wondrous pathos in an empty sleeve; but regret for Howard's affliction ceases when one looks into that kindly face, with its loving eye and generous mouth—a face full of patience, gentleness, and manly resolve.

It is a beautiful tribute to General Howard and his professed Christian belief, that his influence upon those about him is positive. There is but little use of liquor, and a most gratifying absence of profanity, about his head-quarters. I shall never forget his gentle rebuke to a soldier who, in the very presence of death, was swearing in a decided manner: "Don't swear so, my man. You may be killed at any moment. Surely you do not wish to go into the next world with dreadful oaths upon your lips."

CHAPTER XV.

OCCUPATION OF THE CHARLESTON AND AUGUSTA RAILROAD —BRANCHVILLE FLANKED—PASSAGE OF THE UPPER AND LOWER EDISTO—CAPTURE OF ORANGEBURG.

February 6th.—We have occupied at least two positions on the Augusta and Charleston Railroad — at Louray's (Bamburg) and at Midway. The Rebels supposed we should march direct upon Branchville, which they fortified strongly, concentrating a heavy force to receive us; but as Branchville is of no especial importance to us, provided the railroad is cut elsewhere, we have wasted no time or strength before their fortifications.

Already our troops are at work on the railroad bending and twisting the rails. Although we severed the only connecting link between the East and West when we took Savannah, yet this road has been of very great importance to the Rebels, both as a means of communication and for forwarding supplies from Augusta and Northern Georgia to Richmond. Every tie burned and every rail twisted is an irretrievable damage to the Rebels.

Kilpatrick's cavalry is on the railroad at Blackville, about twelve miles from Bamburg; Logan is at Bamburg with the 15th Corps; and Blair, under the eye of General Howard, is at Midway. We are therefore in full possession of the railroad, with no fighting except slight skirmishing by the heads of columns, and no serious loss of life, having gained an important advantage without the opposition we expected. The real line of defense for the Rebels was the Big Salkahatchie, but, having lost that, they have now no strong defensible position this side of the Edisto. We learn that Wheeler, who is supposed to be in command of some eight thousand men, has retired across the Edisto. The refugees are moving generally in that direction, probably to make use of the Columbia Railroad. There is a rumor that one of Hood's corps is at Augusta.

Our left wing is yet in the rear. Yesterday it was at Duck Branch Postoffice, a point which it can have gained only by long marches. We should see their heads of column to-morrow, but for the heavy rain which commenced falling last night, and has continued throughout the day. How long they will be delayed by this intervention of Nature can not well be calculated. We have already cut up the roads, and the rain will make them much heavier.

General Corse, cutting loose from the left wing, has moved forward rapidly since he waded out of the river bottoms. He has found sandy roads which here and there give out, but the troops are so well used to corduroying, that a day's march would not seem complete without it.

February 10*th*.—Another important step is gained. We have crossed the south fork of the Edisto, and hold the main road beyond, while the left wing of the army, which has been delayed so long by the freshet that submerged the roads leading from Sister's Ferry, is at last coming into position with the remainder of the army. The fourth division of the 15th Corps, under General Corse, is coming rapidly forward by way of Hickory Hill and River's Bridge. Corse, however, has extraordinary disadvantages to contend against, marching, as he must, over roads already cut up by the preceding columns. Yesterday he made a severe march of

G

twenty miles; yet his troops joined their corps in fine condition, although somewhat fatigued.

The entire army, in a few days, will be once more united, or, at least, will be actually in co-operation. The heads of column of the different corps are all pointed northward, and it would seem as if the first grand movement of the Georgia campaign was to be repeated now. Then we threatened Macon and Augusta, and captured Milledgeville, the state capital. Now, wheeling this great force to the right, pivoted upon Savannah, we are marching north and east, demonstrating upon both Charleston and Augusta. Shall we continue the parallel, and advance upon Columbia, South Carolina's capital? A few days will tell the story.

Meanwhile the people of Charleston and Augusta are in great fear. Their newspapers are filled with frantic appeals to the citizens to resist the invader, and all sorts of preparations have been made for our reception. All the while we are perfectly sure that one or both cities are, beyond any possibility of doubt, within our power, even if we do not choose to go and take possession.

The crossing of the South Edisto was a feat worth mentioning somewhat in detail. It was Mower's fortune to have the lead. Upon the arrival of his division at the place known as Bennaker's Bridge, which he found burned, he was met with a sharp cannonading from the Rebels, who were in position on the other side. This was in the afternoon. He at once set to work to find means to cross the stream. A little lower down, by dint of wading and swimming, he managed to get into the water four pontoon boats. Upon these, about eight o'clock in the evening, just as the moon was rising, he crossed his division. This night attack was something the Rebels were not prepared for, accustomed as they are to the strange doings of the

"Yankees." The moon rose above the tree-tops in all her queenly splendor. Mower thought it was light enough to whip Rebels by. He was not well out of the swamp, and knew that the sooner he gained the high road the better. So, as we say in the army, he "went in," and the result was that the Rebels went out; that is, all who were not killed or captured.

Our first step in the campaign is an accomplished fact. A great result has been obtained with but little loss of life. Thank God for that! And it has all been done without cavalry and less than half our infantry. The detention of the left wing has not delayed the main operations. We wished to destroy the railroad, and, in any event, should have remained here the length of time it has taken the left wing to come up with us.

It is useless to conjecture what will be the next move. I think the army is altogether indifferent about the matter. It has such an abiding faith in General Sherman that it will go wherever he leads. "Leads" is the proper word, for he is always on the skirmish line, frequently pitching his camp there. He never rests contented with the reports of others; he must see the condition of affairs for himself, and so is generally to be found in the front.

Orangeburg, February 12th. — To-day another difficult task has been achieved. We have crossed the north fork of the Edisto, and occupy Orangeburg. At an early hour this morning the army was in motion, and soon afterward was actively engaged in skirmishing with the enemy all along the river, at different points, for fifteen miles. It is not easy to say who first crossed the river. Several lodgments were made at about the same hour, near noon. Generals Hazen and Woods, of the 15th Corps, got parties across, and, flanking the works at Shilling's Bridge, captured some eighty Rebels. At Orangeburg Generals Force and Giles E. Smith crossed their troops about the same moment, although Force was upon the flank of the Rebels, who had barely time to escape from their works and get away in the cars in the direction of Columbia, our skirmishers firing into the train as it sped away up the road. Ninety Rebels, not so fortunate as their fellows, were captured, having failed to discover the change suddenly made in the time-tables.

The passage of these rivers, even though there may not be a large force of the enemy to oppose, is a triumph of patience, skill, hard work, and true valor. Each new attempt and every success adds to my warm admiration of our noble army, and yet more to my unbounded enthusiasm for our great leader. His far-reaching dispositions bring about the desired result with the certainty of a mathematical problem.

The city of Orangeburg, with a population of three thousand, is prettily situated upon the north bank of the Edisto; and from its position upon the ridge of high lands upon which the railroad runs to Charleston, it was really of more importance than Branchville, which the Rebels had taken great pains to fortify, and which we have easily flanked. The small detachment of Rebels which was stationed at the Junction will probably run away as fast as possible. Had the enemy concentrated a large force at Branchville there would have been some reason in making it a point of defense, but, after they left wide open the door by which Sherman could move forward toward the state capital, Branchville was worse than useless. After the Salkahatchie, the Edisto was the next line of strength, and Orangeburg a salient point, with splendid tactical advantages. As already remarked, there is no especial object to be gained by occupying the Junction, when we can readily destroy both its diverging branches at other points.

Unfortunately a portion of the city of Orangeburg has been burned, but not by our soldiers. The fire was first started by a Jew, from a feeling of revenge upon the Rebels, who had destroyed fifty bales of cotton belonging to him. The high wind which prevailed spread the conflagration in spite of the efforts of our soldiers, who, under the orders of Generals Sherman and Howard, tried to extinguish the flames.

Although we obtain bountiful supplies for both our animals and men, yet the country we have passed through for two days past has been sterile and unfruitful. The land is higher and more rolling as we advance, and is covered with lofty pines and scrub oak. Near the rivers we find swamps where the roads are covered with water. More or less of corduroy has to be built, but the road was generally of sand, and our trains are not seriously delayed in their progress.

To-night we are encamped upon the place of one of South Carolina's most high-blooded chivalry—one of those persons who believed himself to have been brought into the world to rule over his fellow-creatures, a sort of Grand Pasha, and all that sort of thing. How the negro pioneers are making away with the evergreens and rose-bushes of his artistically arranged walks, flower-beds, and drives! These black men in blue are making brooms of his pet shrubs, with which they clear the ground in front of the tents.

We find very few wealthy planters; the inhabitants we meet, mostly women, are of the poorer class; they are frightened fearfully, and expect all sorts of outrages to be perpetrated, and appear to be correspondingly grateful that their lives and houses are spared. The stories they are told and believe are so absurd that I will not repeat them. It is enough that these foolish, ignorant people have believed them. The negroes in this city remind me more of Georgia experiences than any I have seen in South Carolina before. I suppose it is because they are house servants, and have always lived in a city, where there has been more or less of refinement and education. But the plantation negroes are the most ignorant and debased of any I have ever seen.

As nearly as I can ascertain, it has been the effort of the South Carolina master to degrade his slaves as low in the scale of human nature, and as near the mules and oxen which he owns in common with them, as possible. It makes one's blood boil to see the evidences of the heartlessness and cruelty of these white men. I firmly believe that we are God's instruments of justice, and that they are at last called to account for this shameless crime.

A curious incident connected with our occupation of the railroad at Midway illustrates the dashing spirit of the men of Sherman's army, and the close of this chapter is a good place in which to relate it. When the 17th Corps struck the railroad near Midway, it was known that the enemy had erected fortifications at that town, and a lively fight was expected. Our head of column had halted, to give the troops time to build a road through a swamp about five miles from Midway, and a foraging party, regularly detailed, had started on an expedition to obtain supplies, while General Howard and his staff seated themselves to wait patiently by the road-side. Suddenly a strange figure, mounted upon a white horse, with rope halter and rope stirrups, came tearing down the road from the direction where the enemy were supposed to be. Halting suddenly before the General, he shouted:

"General, we've got the railroad—we've captured the

railroad, and the foraging parties have formed line of battle, intrenched, and will hold it against any force until you come up!" Sure enough, foraging parties, in their wanderings, had come out upon the railroad, and knowing, with that intelligence which distinguishes our troops, the importance of the position, had dropped chickens, turkeys, and sweet potatoes, and at once went to work to make good their hold. The bearer of dispatches was a bold forager, who mounted his captured steed, and, with his hastily-improvised equipments, sped back to headquarters to deliver the news.

It is impossible to pass the columns of the army without observing the excellent condition of the animals. The abundant forage found upon the plantations, and the short marches which we make, have put the horses, mules, and beef cattle in the best possible condition. Aside from the fact that it is a pleasant sight, and a matter of the first importance for our successful progress, it is gratifying to know that we are saving millions of dollars to the government; a fact to which General Meigs has borne emphatic testimony in a general order published for the information of his department.

Each day, as the army moves forward, large additions are made to the droves of cattle. Our conscription is remorseless. Every species of four-footed beast that South Carolina planters cherished among their live-stock is swept in by our flanking foragers, and the music of the animal creation mingles with the sound of the footfall of the army.

CHAPTER XVI.

MARCHING UPON COLUMBIA—SALUDA FACTORY—A VIEW OF SOUTHERN FACTORY OPERATIVES.

Fifteen Miles on the Road to Columbia, February 14*th.*— Yesterday, after destroying the railroad from Orangeburg to Louisville, the right wing of the army swung swiftly round and marched upon roads parallel to the Congaree River, concentrating at this point, ready to be launched upon the capital of South Carolina. The Rebels have built heavy fortifications at Congaree Creek, a stream which empties into the river of that name, crossing the state road, upon which we are marching, in a line nearly east and west. We have made a short march to-day in order to give the left wing time to swing round by way of Stedman's and toward Lexington. If they succeed in this movement the Rebels will be obliged to give up the line of the Congaree, and fall back upon the capital itself. Even this step will not help their condition, for the left wing will most likely continue its flank movement until the city is completely encircled. It is possible that the fifteen thousand Rebel troops said to be gathered there will make resistance, but it seems that their best plan would be to follow the example of Hardee at Savannah and evacuate the place. Defense will be a needless sacrifice of life, for we are certain to capture the city, and their opposition may place the inhabitants in a most unpleasant position.

Columbia is vastly more valuable to us in this campaign than Milledgeville was during the march through Georgia.

It is a city quite as large as Savannah. It contains the largest printing establishment in the Rebel states. It is the centre of a number of railroads which stretch up into the most fertile and fruitful agricultural district in the South. It is the home of thousands of those wicked instigators to treason who have made this state so hated and despised, South as well as North. Manufacturers of powder, arms, cloths, and other materials, are there. Columbia, therefore, is a richer prize and more important capture than any city in the South; for Augusta, the place next in importance, has been cut off by our destruction of fifty miles of the Charleston and Augusta Railroad, and is, therefore, no longer valuable to us or the Rebels.

The magnificent spectacle of a fire in the woods was the striking episode of our march yesterday. The army moved through a tract of hilly country which was thickly clothed with pine forests. Many of the trees were dead, and all had been scarped in order to obtain the resinous substance which formed their fruit and life. Accidentally or otherwise, the dry leaves and pine cones had caught fire, which ignited these trees, and for miles the woods were on fire. It was grand and sometimes awful to see the flames flying over the ground like a frightened steed. As we approached one of these forests, filled with flames and pitch-black smoke, it appeared as if we were about to realize the imaginings of childhood, and see dragons and terrible beasts guarding the entrance to some forbidden ground. Wagons, horsemen, and foot-soldiers, one by one disappeared in the gloom, to reappear here and there bathed in lurid light. Within, the fire singed our hair and clothes, while our maddened animals dashed hither and thither in an agony of fear. There was a terrible sublimity in this scene which I shall never forget; but it subsequently partook largely of the ridiculous when the column went into camp, each man so sooty and begrimed that it was almost impossible to distinguish African from Caucasian.

On the State Road, eight miles from Columbia, February 15th.—We are gradually approaching Columbia, but not without a determined opposition. The Rebels successfully defended their strong line of works on the north side of Congaree Creek until about four o'clock this afternoon, when it was carried by our troops without much loss of life or limb. It was supposed that the enemy would make a determined stand at this point; but I think General Sherman trusted to the flank movement of General Slocum to force its evacuation, but that, for some reason not within our knowledge, Slocum has not come up in time. In fact, we have not heard from him or his column for three days past. The Rebels still hold a high hill three miles from the creek, which is crowned by an embrasured fort, with curtains leading off to the right and left into the woods. To-morrow we shall probably test the strength of this position.

Day before yesterday a brigade of the 17th Corps drove a force of the enemy up the Charleston and Columbia Railroad to the bridge crossing the Congaree, which was destroyed by the Rebels. As this was the chief object of the expedition, the party returned in good time.

We continue to find ample supplies of forage. In truth, there has not been a day of want since we started. Our experience in this campaign, like that of Georgia, proves the utter futility of attempting to force the inhabitants of a country to destroy supplies on what is supposed will be the line of march of an invading army. The people reason that the troops may not march over their roads; or if they pass that way and find forage destroyed, vengeance would be visited upon the offenders; and again, *all* might not be taken, but something be left for their sustenance. And this reasoning is true. Although pretty clean work is made by our army, yet the people are generally allowed to carry into their houses a sufficient supply of corn, potatoes, etc., to keep them from starving.

A great many negroes have joined our columns, but it has been from no lack of caution upon the part of the masters. Anticipating the approach of the Union army, the slave-holders have driven off their horses, and, when they were able, their negroes, to some safe place. The latter, however, when they could do so, have hidden in the swamps, coming out to join us as we passed along. As usual, they are our best friends, giving invaluable information of the roads and the movements of the enemy. They are always our safest guides, and their fidelity is never questioned.

In View of Columbia, February 16*th.*—The point where I am writing is in full view of the capital of South Carolina. Persons on foot and on horseback are visible, passing to and fro in one of the main streets of the city. The only hinderance to absolute occupation is the Congaree River, which flows between our army and the city. Yesterday afternoon, after serious fighting, our soldiers drove the Rebels from an admirably intrenched position, several divisions of the 15th Corps going into camp upon the ground held by the enemy during the afternoon. About midnight the Rebels commenced shelling the camp, guided by the fires which covered hillside and plain. This mean kind of warfare they kept up until the morning, killing and wounding several, and disturbing the rest of all. At early dawn our troops were again on the move, and before nine in the morning the whole southern bank of the river was in our possession. We have not taken advantage of our position, by which we could shell the city in every quarter, except to test the range of our guns, and to drive away persons who were removing stores from the dépôts. In these instances the result was comical to us, the lookers on, although it must have been any thing but agreeable to those aimed at, who scattered in every direction.

Our attempts to cross the river below the city have met with earnest opposition. These efforts, however, were feints to withdraw attention from the real point of attack, which was at Saluda Factory, three miles above. We here found the bridges crossing the Saluda burned. After sharp skirmishing, we managed to get a few men across the river in boats. I never saw more spirited, determined fighting than that of those few hundred brave fellows. Usually our foragers have the advance, but in this instance the skirmishers had all the fun to themselves. Gaining the shelter of a rail fence thirty yards from the river, they formed a line, and at a given signal clambered over, and with inspiring cries ran across the open field for the woods, in which the Rebels were posted, and out of which the well-aimed shots of our soldiers instantly drove them. In two hours from that moment a pontoon had been stretched across the stream, and a division had driven the Rebels across the peninsula to Broad River, which it is necessary to bridge before we can enter Columbia. General Logan promises he will have a brigade across Broad River and bridge the stream before morning.

General John A. Logan, a man who always fulfills his engagements, is well known throughout the land. His speech in Congress, when he declared that if the Rebels attempted to close the Mississippi River "the men of the Northwest would hew their way to the Gulf with their swords," will never be forgotten so long as the history of this war is read. Nor is any one likely to forget the General's personal appearance who has ever had an opportunity of seeing him. That lithe, active figure; that finely-cut face, with its heavy black mustache overhanging a sensitive mouth; that black piercing eye, that open brow, shaded by the long black hair—all make up a striking figure. Logan, too, is equally at home on the rostrum, leading the minds of men, or in the saddle, rallying his brave soldiers for the onset upon the foe. He possesses that mysterious magnetic power which calls forth the sublimest enthusiasm in men. On many of the battle-fields of this war he has ridden along the lines regardless of the storms of Rebel shell and bullets beating around him. He is a splendid representative of the Western men who have risen to high distinction by their energy, talents, and perseverance. He is a firm friend, a good hater, and an open fighter, and the pride of the famous fighting and marching 15th Corps.

The Saluda Factory, which is situated a few hundred yards above the pontoon bridge, is considered a place of sufficient note to be laid down on all the maps, new and old. The road leading to the factory buildings winds along the bank of the stream, which is prettily bordered with trees. When I visited the factory our skirmishers occupied the windows facing the river, and were exchanging shots with the Rebels, who lay concealed among the bushes and timber on the other side. This circumstance, however, did not hinder the operatives, all of whom were women, from hurrying through the building, tearing the cloth from the looms, and filling bags with bales of yarn, to be "toted" home, as they phrase it.

It must not be imagined that these Southern factory operatives are of the same class with the lively and intelligent workers of New-England. I remember that while reading descriptions of Saluda Factory, and discussing the probabilities of finding it in our line of march through South Carolina, many of our officers drew fanciful sketches of pretty, bright-eyed damsels, neatly clad, with a wealth of flowing ringlets, and engaging manners. Such factory-girls were visible in the great mills of Lowell, and the enthusiastic Northerners doomed to fight on Southern soil were excusable for drawing mental pictures of them. But when we came to see the reality at Saluda Factory, sensations of disgust and mirthfulness struggled for the mastery—disgust at the repulsive figures whom we encountered, and amusement at the chopfallen air of the gallant young staff-officers who were eager to pay their court to beauty and virtue. It would be difficult to find elsewhere than at this place a collection of two hundred and fifty women so unkempt, frowzy, ragged, dirty, and altogether ignorant and wretched. Some of them were chewing tobacco; others, more elegant in their tastes, smoked. Another set indulged in the practice of "dipping." Sights like these soon put to flight our rosy ideals.

The residences of these people accorded with their personal appearance. Dirty wooden shanties, built on the river bank a few hundred feet above the factory, were the places called homes—homes where doors hung shabbily by a single hinge, or were destitute of panels; where rotten steps led to foul and close passage-ways, filled with broken crockery, dirty pots and pans, and other accumulations of rubbish; where stagnant pools of water bred disease; where half a dozen persons occupied the same bed-chamber; where old women and ragged children lolled lazily in the sunshine; where even the gaunt fowls that went disconsolately about the premises partook of the prevailing character of misery and dirt. These were the operatives, and these the homes produced by the boasted civilization of the South.

The factory is a large stone building, filled with machinery for the manufacture of yarn and the variety of coarse cotton cloth known as Osnaburgs. The looms were dirty and rusty; the spindles were worn out by misuse; the spools appeared conscious that they had fulfilled their mission; the engine was out of joint and dirty. Filth and ignorance reigned over the entire business. As I left the premises and rode away down the glen, I passed a group of the degraded and unfortunate women already described toiling up the hill with back-loads of plunder. Some of our soldiers were helping them to carry their cloth and yarn.

In the old times it was a favorite argument of the slaveholders that their "peculiar institution" was a blessing to the negroes, and it was their habit to make comparisons between the condition of their slaves and that of our well-bred, intelligent factory operatives, asserting that the slaves were the higher and happier class of the two. We have seen what the slaves are; but here is a shocking exhibition of the disgrace and degradation which is visited upon white labor in the South. The visits we are paying our Southern brethren expose not a few of the shameless falsehoods and villanies of the slave oligarchy.

CHAPTER XVII.

OCCUPATION OF THE CAPITAL OF SOUTH CAROLINA—A TERRIBLE CONFLAGRATION.

Columbia, February 17*th*.—It is with a feeling of proud exultation that I write the date of Columbia. We have conquered and occupy the capital of the haughty state that instigated and forced forward the treason which has brought on this desolating war. The city which was to have been the capital of the Confederacy if Lee and the Rebel hosts had been driven from Richmond is now overrun by Northern soldiers. The beautiful capitol building bears the marks of Yankee shot and shell, and the old flag which the Rebels insulted at Sumter now floats freely in the air from the house-tops of the central city of South Carolina.

On our march hither we had the choice of Augusta or Columbia; and while many a brave man turned his indignant eyes toward Sumter and the sea, yet our General knew that this Holy of Holies to the Southern mind was of infinitely more importance than either of the other two cities, and he feels certain that Charleston is ours in any event. General Sherman also knew that, while he might capture Augusta, he could not be certain of reaching Columbia afterward, while with Columbia gained, Augusta was almost as easily won as in the commencement of the campaign.

The direct movement upon Columbia began at three o'clock this morning. General Logan kept his word. In the gray of the morning he bridged Broad River, and, in spite of fierce opposition from the Rebels, a brigade of infantry was pushed across, and gained a firm footing upon the eastern bank. Established there, our men drove the enemy back for a distance of two miles, and then, intrenching their position, awaited the arrival of re-enforcements over the pontoon bridge. Before this work was fairly accomplished, the Rebel forces retreated and the Mayor of Columbia came out to surrender the place. Of course, a surrender under such circumstances, as at Savannah, did not entitle the citizens to protection, for Beauregard had contested the possession of the city in its streets.

General Sherman and General Howard were the first to cross the bridge, and entered the city, followed by their staffs. A scene of shameful confusion met their eyes. On every side were evidences of disorder; bales of cotton scattered here and there; articles of household furniture and merchandise of every description cast pell-mell in every direction by the frightened inhabitants, who had escaped from a city which they supposed was doomed to destruction.

The skirmishers who had first entered the place gathered in groups and lustily cheered their much-loved chief, and the chorus was taken up by the negroes who lined the sidewalk and followed the column; so that the stranger looking on would have believed that this was the triumphal return to his home of some favorite hero, rather than the entry of the conqueror who had struck another blow at the heart of a people who hate him and his with the hatred of incarnate devils.

The welcome given to General Sherman by the negroes was singular and touching. They greeted his arrival with exclamations of unbounded joy. "Tank de Almighty God," they said, "Mister Sherman has come at last. We knew it; we prayed for de day, and de Lord Jesus heard our prayers. Mr. Sherman has come wid his company."

One fat old negro woman said to General Sherman, while shaking him by the hand—which he always gladly gives to these poor people—"I prayed dis long time for yer, and de blessing ob de Lord is on yer. But yesterday afternoon, when yer stopped trowing de shells into de town, and de soldiers run away from de hill ober dar, I thout dat General Burygar had driven you away, for dey said so; but here yer am dun gone. Bress de Lord, yer will hab a place in heaben; yer will go dar, sure."

In the main street the General was met by some of our prisoners, who had escaped before the removal consequent on our approach took place, and had been secreted in the town by the negroes. Not around the social board, not when meeting his dearest friends, not in that responsive moment of gladness when victory crowns our efforts, have I seen his face beam with such exultation and kindly greeting as when he took these poor fellows by the hand and welcomed them home—home to the army, to protection, to the arms of their brave comrades, to the dear old flag which had gone out of sight many months ago upon some well-remembered battle-field.

The outward appearance of Columbia is superior to that of most state capitals I have seen. The private residences are large and roomy, and are surrounded with gardens, which, even at this wintry season of the year, are filled with hedges, flowering shrubs, and bordered walks, all in summer green. The business streets lack that air of extensive commerce which marks Savannah; and in truth, although it has had a larger population than Savannah since the war, Columbia is not a commercial city. The excess of inhabitants has come from the refugees, who have sought what they supposed was a permanent and secure retreat from the hated Yankees.

The three or four days' notice of our approach enabled the government officials to remove most of the material belonging to the branch of the Treasury Department which was located at this point; yet large quantities of paper for printing Confederate notes and bonds, with type, printing-presses, etc., has fallen into our hands. This loss is irreparable to the Rebel government.

. The arsenal was found well stocked with shot, shell, fixed ammunition, powder, Enfield rifles, carbines, and other material of war. A full battery of four rifled English Blakely guns, which were in a battery commanding the bridge, was also taken, with caissons and other material. Connected with the arsenal are shops full of costly machinery for the manufacture of arms and ammunition, with founderies for all sorts of castings. A little way down the river there is a large powder-mill. All of this will be thoroughly destroyed.

In front of the arsenal barracks are fifteen light brass field-pieces, which have the crown of England marked upon the back, with the date of 1776. I could not but reflect upon the woeful truth how utterly these cowardly South Carolinians have lost all pride of nationality. Their teams and cars ran night and day to carry off cotton, but these glorious mementoes of the Revolution were kicked aside as valueless.

The store-houses are filled with all sorts of supplies—flour, meal, bacon, corn, harness, hardware, etc.—while cotton is found in every direction. As there is no treasury agent of our government to appropriate this costly material for somebody's benefit, I doubt if a very correct record of the quantity will be made before it is burned.

The capitol building is far from completion, but, if ever finished, it will be the most beautiful architectural creation in this country, as well as one of the most costly. It is very large, covering an open space in the high ridge which runs through the centre of the city. It is built of a light-colored granite, with the surface smooth from base to roof. The order of architecture, so far as it is completed, is pure Corinthian. The capitals of the columns, both upon the two wings north and south and the interior grand hall, are most delicately carved in the marble—the builders, with true artistic taste and good sense, rejecting all plaster and stucco imitations. These capitals, with a large amount of carved work for architraves, window-caps, and frames, are carefully housed in the numerous shops situated in the grounds around the building.

Although this great undertaking is not half completed, the work is sufficiently advanced to convey a fair idea of the intentions of its architects. To my mind, this order of architecture is the most beautiful of any for public buildings; and in this instance the artist has created a model of exquisite grace and harmonious proportions. If ever finished upon the present plan, it will be one of the finest works of art in this country or in the Old World. It is a thought of infinite pleasure to turn from these desolating scenes of war to this outgrowth of peace and plenty; and we study these graceful lines and noble contours with all the more satisfaction, mingled with sorrow, when we put them in contrast with the shocking architectural displays observable elsewhere in the country.

Brown, the sculptor, at great personal expense, has modeled and partially completed groups and *bas-reliefs* for this building, for which he has never received compensation. His work, yet unfinished, lies in some of the outbuildings.

I began to-day's record early in the evening, and while writing I noticed an unusual glare in the sky, and heard a sound of running to and fro in the streets, with the loud talk of servants that the horses must be removed to a safer place. Running out, I found, to my surprise and real sorrow, that the central part of the city, including the main business street, was in flames, while the wind, which had been blowing a hurricane all day, was driving the sparks and cinders in heavy masses over the eastern portion of the city, where the finest residences. are situated. These buildings, all wooden, were instantly ignited by the flying sparks. In half an hour the conflagration was raging in every direction, and but for a providential change of the wind to the south and west, the whole city would in a few hours have been laid in ashes.

As it is, several hundred buildings, including the old State House, one or two churches, most of the carved work stored in the sheds round about the new capitol, and a large number of public store-houses, have been destroyed. In some of the public buildings the Rebels had stored shot, shell, and other ammunition, and when the flames reached these magazines we had the Atlanta experience over again —the smothered boom, the huge columns of fire shooting heavenward, the red-hot iron flying here and there. But there was one feature, pitiable indeed, which we did not find at Atlanta. Groups of men, women, and children were gathered in the streets and squares, huddled together over a trunk, a mattress, or a bundle of clothes. Our soldiers were at work with a will, removing household goods from the dwellings which were in the track of the flames, and here and there extinguishing the fire when there was hope of saving a building. General Sherman and his officers worked with their own hands until long after midnight, trying to save life and property. The house taken for headquarters is now filled with old men, women, and children who have been driven from their homes by a more pitiless enemy than the detested "Yankees."

Various causes are assigned to explain the origin of the fire. I am quite sure that it originated in sparks flying from the hundreds of bales of cotton which the Rebels had placed along the middle of the main street, and fired as they left the city. Fire from a tightly-compressed bale of cotton is unlike that of a more open material, which burns itself out. The fire lies smouldering in a bale of cotton long after it appears to be extinguished; and in this instance, when our soldiers supposed they had extinguished the fire, it suddenly broke out again with the most disastrous effect.

There were fires, however, which must have been started independent of the above-named cause. The source of these is ascribed to the desire for revenge from some two hundred of our prisoners, who had escaped from the cars as they were being conveyed from this city to Charlotte, and, with the memories of long sufferings in the miserable pens I visited yesterday on the other side of the river, sought this means of retaliation. Again, it is said that the soldiers who first entered the town, intoxicated with success and a liberal supply of bad liquor, which was freely distributed among them by designing citizens, in an insanity of exhilaration set fire to unoccupied houses.

Whatever may have been the cause of the disaster, the direful result is deprecated by General Sherman most emphatically; for however heinous the crimes of this people against our common country, we do not war against women and children and helpless persons.

February 18*th*.—This morning the fires are all subdued, and the houseless people are provided with shelter, by General Sherman's order, in the residences deserted by their

COLUMBIA ON FIRE.

refugee owners. So far as it went, the fire made clean work; but there have been fewer dwelling-houses destroyed than was at first supposed, as the devastation was confined chiefly to the business part of the city.

Our occupation of Columbia has not retarded other movements. The 17th Corps has moved out in an easterly direction, while the 15th Corps and our engineer regiments are breaking railroad. The 20th Corps is crossing Broad River, and the 14th is moving north on the east bank of Saluda, where, in the vicinity of Germansville, Cheatham and Lee, of Hood's army, are attempting a passage, in the hope of damaging our rear and flank.

The exact number of this detachment from Hood we have not ascertained. It is probably not more than twelve thousand or fifteen thousand men, who have been kept at Augusta in anticipation of an attack upon that place. General Sherman's movements completely mystified and confused the Rebels. They thought the real objective was Augusta, with a view of opening up the navigation of the river; and I learn that, in consequence of this belief, all the public property of the enemy was removed from Augusta to a point far within the interior of Georgia. Sherman has a faculty for hoodwinking the enemy.

Columbia, February 19*th*.—General Sherman has given orders for the farther destruction of all public property in the city, excepting the new capitol, which will not be injured. I think the General saves this building more because it is such a beautiful work of art than for any other reason. The arsenal, railroad dépôts, store-houses, magazines, public property, and cotton to the amount of twenty thousand bales, are to-day destroyed. There is not a rail upon any of the roads within twenty miles of Columbia but

H

will be twisted into corkscrews before the sun sets, while upon two of the lines the work of destruction will be continued perhaps to their terminus.

This afternoon several loud explosions were heard in the direction of the river. I learn that, as the troops who were detailed for the purpose were depositing the shells and powder in the river, one of the former accidentally exploded, the fire communicating to other ammunition, and to a large pile of powder on the banks. The result was mournfully disastrous, for several men were killed, and twenty were wounded. The casting of this ammunition into the river was ordered by General Sherman, who preferred that mode of destroying it to an explosion of the magazine on the arsenal hill, where some one might have been injured. General Sherman was horrified upon hearing of the accident, and remarked that the life of one of his soldiers was of more value than all the arsenals and magazines in the South, or even the city of Columbia itself.

Columbia will have bitter cause to remember the visit of Sherman's army. Even if peace and prosperity soon return to the land, not in this generation nor the next—no, not for a century—can this city or the state recover from the deadly blow which has taken its life. It is not alone in the property that has been destroyed—the buildings, bridges, mills, railroads, material of every description—nor in the loss of the slaves, who, within the last few days, have joined us by hundreds and thousands—although this deprivation of the means by which they lived is of incalculable importance—that the most blasting, withering blow has fallen. It is in the crushing downfall of their inordinate vanity, their arrogant pride, that the rebels will feel the effects of the visit of our army. Their fancied unapproachable, invincible security has been ruthlessly overthrown. Their boastings, threatenings, and denunciations have passed by us like the idle wind. The feet of one hundred thousand abolitionists, hated and despised, have pressed heavily upon their sacred soil, and their spirit is broken. I know that thousands of South Carolina's sons are in the army of the rebellion; but she has already lost her best blood there. Those who remain have no homes. The Hamptons, Barnwells, Simses, Rhetts, Singletons, Prestons, have no homes. The ancient homesteads where were gathered sacred associations, the heritages of many generations, are swept away. When first these men became traitors they lost honor; to-day they have no local habitations; in the glorious future of this country they will have no name.

Another incident has occurred at Columbia which is illustrative of the soldierly patriotism of our troops. In the public square a beautiful monument had been erected in honor of the soldiers of a South Carolina regiment who had died in the war with Mexico. It was an iron palmetto-tree, placed upon a handsome pedestal. The names of the fallen brave were inscribed in brass letters upon tablets appropriately arranged at the base. One of our stragglers, while attempting to detach some of these letters, was at first warned, and, not desisting, was seized and severely handled by the soldiers for the commission of what they regarded as a sacrilegious crime.

By constantly improving many excellent opportunities for conversing with prominent citizens, I have unquestionable evidence of their desire to end the war by submitting to the national authority. While not disguising their belief in the sovereignty of a state, and scarcely concealing their hate for the Yankees, they acknowledge their powerlessness to contend against the might of the idea of nationality embodied in our armies and navies. A citizen, whose name may be found in the earliest annals of the state, and stands forth in high honor in the war of the Revolution, but whose sons are now in high office in the army of treason, said to me to-day:

"Sir, every life that is now lost in this war is murder; *murder*, sir. We have fought you bravely, but our strength is exhausted; we have no resources; we have no more men. The contest was unequal. You have conquered us, and it is best to submit and make wise use of the future. This is not my opinion because the Union flag is flying upon yonder capitol to-day, but it has been my conviction for many months past—a conviction more than confirmed by recent events. We could have peace, sir, but for that vain, obstinate, ambitious man, Jeff. Davis. I am not in excitement nor anger, sir, when I assure you that I know that a large majority of our people curse him, not only with their hearts, but their lips. His haughty ambition has been our ruin."

The words of this gentleman express the sentiments of nearly all the leading civilians I meet, excepting only that the expression is sometimes more vehement, while the conversation is occasionally interlarded with more violent objurgations against Jeff. Davis. Unhappy chief! failure has brought down upon him hatred and abuse. Were he in South Carolina now, no cheers would greet him, no friendly welcome would meet him; nothing but execrations would be showered upon his head.

Many prophecies and theories have been advanced as to the possible future of the slaves and their owners, but I never thought that the day would come to me when South Carolina slaveholders would beg me to take away their slaves—not because the negroes have been unfaithful, not that they would be unkind when we went away, for a lady bore witness, with tears in her eyes, to their attentions and kindness on the night of the fire; but, as she said:

"I know they wish to go with your army, and I beg of you to take them, for I have nothing for them to do, and can not feed them. We have scarcely food for our own mouths, much less theirs."

These requests are not isolated, but general. The motive which prompts them is visible wherever we march; but it is a singular development of the war that South Carolinians should petition us to give freedom to the slaves to retain whom in servitude they have sacrificed so much of the best life-blood of the land.

A characteristic feature of South Carolina chivalry, which has impressed itself upon all of us since we entered this state, had a marked illustration last night and this morning. I refer to a whining, helpless, craven spirit which shows itself whenever any of these people get hurt. In Georgia the sufferers said: "We expected to lose our cows, corn and poultry; war is a terrible thing at the best, and we must take it as it comes; so long as we are not injured in our persons we will not complain." But these fellows who were to "die in the last ditch," who would "welcome us with bloody hands to hospitable graves," are more cowardly than children, and whine like whipped school-boys. Ridiculously helpless, they sit and groan without making an effort to help themselves. There is not an officer or soldier in all our army who has not added to his dislike of the psuedo-chivalric negro-drivers the most supreme disgust and contempt.

CHAPTER XVIII.

THE MARCH RESUMED — CROSSING THE CATAWBA RIVER — NEWS OF THE FALL OF CHARLESTON — CAPTURE OF CAMDEN.

Winnsboro', February 21*st.*—This place is northwest of the Rebel capital, and the 17th Corps, which first reached it, has made the march from Columbia in two days, thoroughly destroying the track of the South Carolina Railroad as it moved. We have made wrecks of various lines of Rebel communication since the beginning of these campaigns, but in this instance the destruction has been made even more complete than usual. The rails used on the railroad to Charlotte are of different kinds, but chiefly strap-iron, which has been easily twisted into kinks, bows, and corkscrews, by the aid of the ties and telegraph poles found along the way. The Rebels are quite sure, by this time, that at least one object of our campaign is the destruction of this remaining artery connecting the East and West. In any event, they are not likely to be traveled, for the guage of this line from this point to Charlotte is narrower by four inches than the line which continues on to Danville and thence to Richmond; so that, whether or not we go to Charlotte, the material and running stock are rendered useless.

While the 17th Corps have approached this place by the direct road from Columbia, the left wing has made a detour, entering from the Broad River Road. The principal object of this diverging march is the desire to cover as much ground as possible for purposes of forage and supplies.

The 20th Corps arrived early this morning, just in time to prevent the spread of a conflagration which, starting in the central part of the city, threatened to destroy every thing in its path. Several regiments were engaged in this work, and especial efforts were successfully made to save the house of a brother of Governor Aiken. As it was, only a few buildings were burned, to the unbounded gratitude of the thousands of inhabitants, many of whom were refugees from Vicksburg, Nashville, Atlanta, Savannah, Charleston, and, later, Columbia. I am thus particular in mentioning the names of these places, for, as Mrs. Aiken told me, "They never expected a Yankee army would come here." Driven from one place to another, they sought this secluded, distant region of South Carolina for quiet and repose; but General Sherman, like an avenging Nemesis, has followed in their path, until they say, "We will go no farther; we submit."

We found here an untamed, impertinent fellow, who practices preaching for a living, one Lord, who formerly presided over an Episcopal church in the West. This individual, whose life and property had been preserved from the flames by our soldiers, took occasion to insult one of our officers by the utterance of the most treasonable sentiments. He richly deserved to be placed in the prisoners' gang, and marched along. The intercession of Mrs. Aiken, and his own insignificance, saved him the humiliation.

As I am writing, I hear the exquisite music of the band of the 33d Massachusetts regiment, who are serenading one of the general officers. This is the best band in the army, and the favorite of all of us. It is playing operatic and national airs. There was a time when Massachusetts men were not permitted in this chivalric state. The wretches who insulted Judge Hoar and his daughter have not, in this instance, been consulted in this matter. Those soul-stirring anthems of " John Brown" and " Rally Round the Flag" are now the familiar airs here, and when our troops marched into Columbia the other day, the bands began and ended with " Hail Columbia."

The region through which the army has lately marched is very barren. While not quite so sandy as the country below the Congaree, it is yet sterile in the extreme. Supplies are not found sufficient to furnish the army with its needs. We are promised richer fields and more fruitful harvests in a few days. The 15th Corps, which is upon our extreme right, has a better time. Kilpatrick hangs upon our extreme left, occasionally dashing off at some exposed points, to the confusion of the enemy, who continue to be at a loss to divine our intention.

The woods and fields in this vicinity are filled with rabbits, whose presence has been the cause of some excitement and a good deal of fun. After marching the prescribed distance for the day, one division after another will go into camp in the forests, the fields, and hill-sides, and if it is a corps detached from the main body of the army, they will extend eight miles, more or less, along the road. Last night, while quietly smoking after supper, we heard at a long distance the shouts of soldiers. As the sounds came nearer, we could distinguish the words, " Catch him, catch him; stop that rabbit," etc. Soon poor pussy came flying down the road, pursued by a throng of men, while the shouts were caught up and redoubled as she passed along. No one seemed disposed to injure the frightened animal, but every body enjoyed the fun of the chase. Probably that rabbit has become one of the pets which the soldiers love to attach to themselves in their long campaigns.

On the Banks of the Catawba, Rocky Mount Ferry, February 23*d.* — Our great leader has just made one of those sudden moves in the grand strategy of the campaign which must be so inexplicable to the enemy, and is not altogether clear to his own army. Day before yesterday the whole army was marching north up the peninsula formed by the Broad and Catawba, or, as it is called lower down, the Wateree River. It seemed as if we were making straight for Charlotte and Danville. Accordingly Beauregard withdrew his forces from our flanks, with the intention of contesting our advance into the hill country. But such was not the purpose of General Sherman. No doubt the Rebel general can find many strong positions between this and Charlotte where he could delay our columns a little while, but he can not find any such lines of defense as those made by the rivers which are in our path to the sea, for the sea we must reach before many days. There is a limit in these invasions beyond which an army can not go.

Yesterday morning Kilpatrick was sent to the extreme front with orders to occupy Chesterville, while the 14th Corps marched within supporting distance in his rear, destroying the railroad on its way. While the direction given to this column would seem to have been in confirmation of Beauregard's judgment, the 20th, 17th, and 15th Corps, who for days and weeks past had watched the sun rising over their right shoulder as the early morning found them in the column of march, now met its glorious rays face to face. The army is making a grand right wheel, and we are heading directly for the ocean.

Yesterday the 20th Corps made a march of twenty miles over a succession of horrible hills. For an army which for so long a time has traversed level roads, where the feet pressed gently in the yielding sand, mounting steep hills, descending into valleys upon hard clayey soil, is a change which results in stiffened muscles and sore feet. But we are all more than repaid for the fatigue and a late supper by having altogether outwitted the Rebels. Before four o'clock in the afternoon two regiments waded or swam across the stream, which, although three hundred feet wide, is shallow, and the Rebel cavalry, who dashed up to the ferry in the confident belief that they could offer an opposition which would delay our passage several hours, were met with a decided demonstration in the way of loyal lead flying about their ears, which was neither anticipated or especially entertaining, our skirmishers informing them, in jocose shouts, that it was only in celebration of the anniversary of the Father of our common country.

The Catawba, which becomes the Wateree River where the creek of that name enters the principal stream, does not abound with bridges, and we are obliged to cross the 20th and 14th Corps and Kilpatrick's cavalry at this place, while General Howard, with the 17th and 15th Corps, has laid a pontoon at Fay's Ferry, eight miles below us. The 20th Corps is very proud of its work yesterday, and with good reason. After making the toilsome march described above the men laid this pontoon, and before daybreak of this morning had passed over a division of troops and its trains. The task is all the more difficult because the road is not much used, and near the banks of the stream it is extremely precipitous, filled with huge boulders of granite rock and cut up with steep gulleys. The repairing of this road required more time than building the pontoon bridge.

In the early days of this campaign, when studying over the maps and speculating upon the objective points, the directions and roads we might traverse, we all saw that, wherever we went, there were natural obstructions in our way far exceeding those of the Georgia campaign, to say nothing of the possible transfer of Lee's army to the interior, which would have necessitated a change, perhaps, in General Sherman's plan, so far as the final objective is concerned. Indeed, I have reason to believe that the evacuation of Virginia by the Rebels was a contingency included in General Sherman's calculations. He repeated last evening what I heard him say at Savannah and during the march hither:

"If Lee is a soldier of genius, he will seek to transfer his army from Richmond to Raleigh or Columbia; if he is a man simply of detail, he will remain where he is, and his speedy defeat is sure. But I have little fear that he will be able to move; Grant will hold him as in a vice of iron."

Late last night we received what seems to be confirmatory news of the rumors among the citizens, both of Columbia and Winnsboro', that Charleston has been evacuated. Several negroes have come into our lines, who assert that they accompanied the Rebel soldiers when they left the city, and that they heard positively that the Yankees had entered the next day.

It is singular with what marvelous accuracy General Sherman's prophecies and combinations have resulted in splendid realities. At Savannah he was asked if he intended taking Charleston. He answered, "Yes; but I shall not sacrifice life in its capture. If I am able to reach certain vital points, Charleston will fall of itself. If the people remain there they must starve, that's all."

Three days ago, when the rumors of the evacuation of this proud city were reported to him, he said, "I have but little doubt of the truth of the story; I have already cut two of the great arteries which give them life; in a few days I will strike the Florence Railroad, and they must leave then, or they are gone up."

While there is no official verification of the fall of Charleston, so absolute is my faith in the genius of our commander, that I have no doubt whatever that the stars and stripes are at this moment waving over Fort Sumter. And, if it be true, what a sublime triumph is it for this army and its leader! Threatening three points of great value, in their confused, frantic efforts to save them all, the Rebels have lost one most cherished, and the other most vital, both in a military and political sense. But we will save our salvos until we are assured of the truth, and then we will have one good cheer for the old flag.

East of the Catawba, February 24*th*.—A storm, which has been gathering for several days, last night burst upon us, and has continued all day, with no prospect of clear weather. The rain patters upon the fly-tent over my head, and sputters in the fire, which, made from South Carolina rails, burns as brightly as it may under the circumstances. It sways to and fro in the fitful wind, now and then pouring into the open doorway (if a fly-tent can be said to have a doorway) a volume of smoke which is neither grateful to the eyes nor nostrils.

This is one of those northeast storms which we have at home; and I can almost imagine myself comfortably seated before a glowing coal-fire, with the evening paper to con over, and the cheerful faces of dear friends around, listening to the shaking of the windows and the rain dashing against the panes.

The reality differs somewhat from the fanciful picture, but the advantage, all things considered, is in favor of the former. I am as comfortably situated as the General commanding, and, with every soldier in the army, I am glad to share with him the deprivation, suffering, and honor, in the fulfillment of what we believe to be our duty to the country. These things considered, the sand-floor tent is better than the carpeted drawing-room.

In spite of the mud and a terrific hill upon this bank of the river, a portion of the '14th Corps have crossed the stream, and are in camp in the pine woods and upon the hill-sides. While the storm is likely to delay us for a day or more, it has its advantages in raising the rivers and preventing the crossing of the Rebel army, who have thrown themselves across what they supposed would be our path in the direction of Chesterville, and so on to Charlotte. Their troops can not cross the Catawba without ascending the stream some sixty miles, which will give us uninterrupted opportunity to complete our crossing.

Within the last week the Rebel cavalry have committed atrocities upon our foragers which make the horrors of a battle-field tender mercies in comparison. In one instance a courier was found hanged on the roadside, with a paper attached to his person bearing the words, "Death to all foragers." In another instance three men were found shot, with a similar notice upon their persons. Yesterday, our cavalry, in the direction of Chesterville, found in a ravine twenty-one of our infantry soldiers lying dead, with their throats cut, but with no notice given as a reason for the frightful murders. All of us understand that the reason assigned for these butcheries is a cruel farce, and that any one of us will meet the same fate if we fall into their bloody hands. There is but one course to be taken in this matter —retaliation, and that fourfold. General Sherman has given General Kilpatrick orders to hang and shoot prisoners who fall into his hands to any extent he considers necessary. Shame on Beauregard, and Hampton, and Butler! Has the blood of their patriot fathers become so corrupted that the sons are cowardly assassins? If this murderous game is continued by these fiends, they will bitterly rue the day it was begun.

The right wing was last night at Patterson's Cross Roads, and has made a light march of seven miles toward Flat Rock Post-office. Its route since the change of direction in our lines of operation has taken this part of the army through a region similar to that explored by the left wing, the hills being steep and the roads tortuous. The right wing, however, had the advantage of moving upon a shorter interior line, and thus was enabled to cross the river before the rains set in. It is not amiss to add that the corps and division commanders of the right wing have displayed great promptness, energy, and perseverance. The two wings of the army are now even in closer relation, if possible, than at any time since the crossing of the Salkahatchie. In truth, it seems as if the whole force is marching in solid column—a column widely extended certainly, but so admirably in hand that in the space of three hours all the troops could be placed in one grand line of battle. Daring beyond precedent in the grand strategy of this campaign, our leader is cautious and wily almost to a fault in the conduct of its detail.

Across the Catawba, February 25*th.*—The left wing has made but little progress since my last writing. Heavy rains have fallen, and the least movement of the trains cuts deep into the yielding mud until the roads become impassable. One division of the 14th Corps is across the river, and a portion of another. The greatest difficulty is experienced in surmounting the hill on this side, which is steep, and covered with three feet of mud, with here and there a hole. When a wagon once settles in one of these cavities it takes a final rest, for no effort of man or beast can extricate it from the tenacious grip of the mud. Thus the 14th Corps delays the movement of the left wing; not seriously, however, for until we have brighter skies, from five to ten miles a day is the limit of progress. General Sherman has issued an order to destroy two hundred superfluous wagons, now on the west side of the river, if they can not be brought over by to-morrow. A day's unnecessary delay may be of the greatest importance to the army. The adage that "delays are dangerous" must have had its origin in military operations, for in no circumstance of life have I seen more striking illustrations of the necessity of prompt action, when there is work to be done, than in the army.

Yesterday two divisions of the 15th Corps captured the towns of Kirkwood and Camden. General Corse, with the fourth division, had the advance. After some lively skirmishing, he drove the Rebel cavalry before him so rapidly as to save a number of our prisoners who had been removed to that place for safe keeping. Two thousand bales of cotton were burned by our troops, besides a large amount of tobacco. Kirkwood, which is a sort of suburb of Camden, is one of the most beautiful places in the South. The houses are large and finely built, and are surrounded by elegant gardens.

This neighborhood is rich in Revolutionary memories. Our army, night after night, has bivouacked upon the old camping-grounds and battle-fields of Gates and Cornwallis. The exact situation of these historic places is not indicated by monuments or other visible signs, and we are often obliged to trust to tradition; so that our patriotic veneration is not stimulated in any remarkable degree.

February 26th.—This morning opened with mists and

fog, obscuring the sun's rays, while now and then the humid atmosphere condensed into drops of rain. The horsemen dashing through the woods of low pine-trees shook off the moisture which had gathered upon the delicate spindles in beautiful drops of diamonds and pearls, and the gray mists swept over the hills and into the valleys, completely enveloping the long trains. Soldiers are taught, among other virtues, the cardinal one of patience; but three days' continuous rain, with its accompaniments of sticky mud, roads to be corduroyed, streams to be crossed, wet feet and clothes, and smouldering fires, we thought sufficient for one term; but, when every one was just preparing to be discontented, that generous old friend the sun, after a three-hours' struggle with the storm, won the fight, and shone out upon us all—upon bedraggled mule, upon toiling soldier, upon roads of mud, and upon the most picturesque landscape we have yet seen in South Carolina. The slopes are longer than the abrupt hills outside of Winnsboro', or else we are traveling upon a ridge, for we have moved along comfortably and rapidly, and go into camp at three P.M., after a march of ten miles—as long a march as we dare to make until we are certain the 14th Corps has well started on the road which it is to take a little way north of us.

This district of Lancaster is not only much more beautiful, in an artistic sense, than any we have seen in South Carolina—stretching away as it does for miles in gentle undulations, and dotted with the low pine-trees, which seem like spots of green upon a carpet of rich red and gold—but the land is more prolific. Wheat, corn, oats, cotton, and fruits grow in abundance, the barns and corn-ricks yielding a plentiful supply for all our needs. The surface of the country is mostly under cultivation; and not only is there a surfeit of rails, but some of the fences are built of boards, the first instance in our experience in this campaign of such extravagance in farm life. The soldiers, with a good taste which does them infinite credit, have appropriated the boards for building material. To be sure, it is only for a night, but one of the articles in a soldier's creed is to make himself comfortable while he can.

A fine house, surrounded by broad acres of rich lands, is near our camping-ground. "Who is the owner of this place?" I asked of a white man, seated among a group of negroes of all ages, sizes, and colors. The person to whom I addressed this question was decently dressed, but had a sickly complexion, and a dull gray eye. Turning to me, he answered:

"Colonel Jones, sir."

Continuing his speech, while he fondled a cunning specimen of ebony-colored humanity between his knees, he added,

"But he has gone away; he heard that your army was coming, so he drove off his cattle and horses toward Charlotte."

"To whom does that child belong?" I asked, pointing to the curly-headed little one in his arms.

"To master—to Colonel Jones."

"You don't understand me. I mean who is the father and mother of the child?"

"Well, I'm the father, and the mother is my wife—the black woman sitting yonder."

"Why did you marry a black woman? You said 'master' just now, in speaking of this Colonel Jones. You don't mean to say that you are a slave? You show no more indication of negro blood than any of the soldiers walking about here."

"No one takes me for a negro," he replied, "but I am Colonel Jones's slave notwithstanding. I was born and raised in my own father's house in Baltimore. Mr. —— it was, sir. He sold me down here several years ago. I don't know why he sold me, except that I was getting to resemble him too much!"

"Shall you go with the army?"

"Can I take my wife and these babies?" he answered. "If not, I shall remain behind; I will not leave them."

"You may try to bring them along, but it is against orders."

The woman had listened intently to this conversation, and, as I turned back after leaving the party, I saw that she had crept closer to her husband, and the white and black hands were intertwined.

This is a phase of Southern life!

To-night the army is in good spirits, for we have had confirmation of the reports that Charleston is evacuated, and in possession of our troops. Was ever a result of such magnitude obtained from causes geographically so far removed, but which were as direct and absolute as if General Sherman had environed the Rebel strong-hold as completely as he did Savannah? We have taken several prisoners who left Charleston at the time of its evacuation, and, supposing we had passed down the peninsula, thought they could escape us by taking this route north. One of these persons, a clergyman, said that some of General Sherman's friends of former days, who knew him when he was stationed at Charleston, had told him that they should remain there, confident that their old acquaintance would befriend them. Not only the citizens, but the military authorities believed —not hearing of the fall of Columbia—that the object of the campaign was Charleston. Knowing that if they remained in that city they would be captured, as the movement from Bull's Bay left them but one avenue of escape, they profited by that in time, and we have, as a glorious result, a grand yet bloodless victory.

CHAPTER XIX.

MARCHING UPON CHERAW — BRIDGES TAKEN — GENERAL SHERMAN AND THE NEGROES.

Twenty Miles from Chesterfield, March 1st.—When the army left Winnsboro', the orders to the army commanders were to move their troops in a direction which was indicated in general terms, but they were to concentrate at Cheraw, on the Pedee, at about the same time. The right wing in this movement had the base of a parabola, and, of course, the shortest route. I think it was the intention that General Howard's column should be a short distance in advance, but always within reach of support by the other column. The purpose seems to have been to gain the bridge crossing the Pedee at Cheraw—an object of great importance, for the swamps spread out for miles on either side of the river below that city. Meanwhile, the left wing, with Kilpatrick's cavalry, were to amuse the enemy with the idea that we were advancing on Charlotte.

As already stated, General Howard crossed the Catawba at Parry's Ferry, and immediately pushed forward with his usual energy, so that on the same day his advance was at Flat Rock. The left wing of the army was not so fortunate; for, although it made superb marches, and laid pontoon bridges with marvelous speed, it was found impossible to transfer the whole force across the Catawba before the heavy rains came on. Immediately afterward the roads became impassable, and the stream, whose current was dangerous at best, rose rapidly, bearing down upon its turbid bosom great masses of logs and drift-wood. For a while the guardians of this precious causeway were able to resist the torrent; but night came on, with more rain and high winds, and in spite of the greatest efforts eighteen of the frail canvas boats were torn to pieces in the centre, and the dissevered ends swung round to the opposite shores. This accident is serious, not only because it threatens to defeat the movement upon Cheraw, but also because it delays the progress of the campaign. Our twenty days' rations are nearly exhausted. The question of obtaining supplies is of vital importance. It requires an immense amount of food and forage to feed for even a day this army of 65,000 men and its 20,000 camp-followers. We can hold our own against the Rebels, but starvation is a foe we dread to encounter.

The bridge has been repaired, and last night the rest of the corps, with their trains, were on this side of the river, and we expect them to rejoin us in a day or two, as we are making easy marches for that purpose. The first order of march has been changed, however, by this accident. General Howard was halted for a day, but the bridge at Cheraw was too important a point to be gained, not to run some risk for it; the right wing has accordingly been pushed forward rapidly, regardless of the other columns.

At Lynch's Creek Howard's column has been seriously delayed. He is lower down the stream than we, and passes through the swamp country. Though often mentioned, it is next to impossible to give to one who has not floundered through these morasses a clear idea of the difficulties of progress. It is easy and speedy work to build a bridge of timbers across the stream, but the gulf of mud and water on either side, stretching for miles, seems fathomless. Sometimes the first layer of timbers placed across the road will

CORDUROYING AT LYNCH'S CREEK.

sink out of sight, and then the axmen and pioneers renew their work, cutting down large trees, sometimes separating them into four parts; these are again laid upon the road, with long timbers both above and beneath, placed parallel to the road, and pinned to the corduroy. A large part of Howard's troops for three days have been engaged in this wearisome work, in the effort to get through the swamp of Lynch's Creek.

Chesterfield, March 2d.—The foregoing prognostication had hardly been written, when news came from General Howard that the advance of the 17th Corps had arrived, at nine o'clock that morning, at a point thirteen miles from Cheraw, and had found the enemy intrenched in their front. It was said that Beauregard, Johnston, Hardee, and Hampton, with the garrisons of Charleston, Wilmington, and other points, were in Cheraw, and that a great battle was probable. The Rebels had certainly gathered an array of talent, in the way of generals, enough to appal this little army! The presence of all these men and any large force is doubtless an exaggeration, although there can be no question but the delays of the last few days have given the enemy an intimation of our plans, which they have improved by guarding the important outlet at Cheraw.

We were inclined to believe that the Rebels, not liking our society, would not interfere with our movements; indeed, that they would assist our passage through the country. The care with which they have laid in plentiful supplies of corn, fodder, hams, beef on the hoof, and other supplies, would have indicated this. Again, our infantry have hardly seen a Rebel soldier since we left Columbia until this morning. Our route from the Catawba crossed several creeks where there were valuable bridges uninjured, the destruction of any one of which would have delayed our column a day or more. Certainly we had every reason to suppose that the Rebels wished us a good riddance, and offered no objections to our speedy passage to the sea, or wherever we chose to go. Only one other hypothesis remained, and the presence of an enemy in our front to-night is a cogent argument in its favor. It is that the Rebel leaders did not divine the real movement until the last moment, and are now throwing obstacles in the way of our passage over the Pedee. We estimate that, without assistance from Virginia, they can not concentrate more than twenty-five thousand men in our front, and we will undertake to start that force in two or three days. Within that time we shall have brought up all our troops, and it will go hard with the Rebels, but we will have a pontoon floating quietly from either bank of the Pedee. Of course the hope of saving the bridge at Cheraw must be abandoned, and we must depend upon other resources.

Although for the last three days we have not seen the sun, and the rain has fallen now and then, the left wing has made some fine marches. The 14th Corps yesterday traveled over eighteen miles of the road which had already been used by the 20th Corps, and to-day the 20th Corps has marched twenty-one miles since daylight. Fortunately the route has led along the high ridges and through the pine barrens, where the soil is sandy, and better for the light fall of rain. Thus we were able to reach this place early in the afternoon, driving before us, at a good marching pace, Butler's, or rather Hampton's cavalry, who opposed the advance.

During the skirmishing, one of our men, a forager, was slightly wounded; but the most serious accident of the day occurred to a negro woman in a house where the Rebels had taken cover. When I saw this woman, who would not have been selected as the best type of South Carolina female beauty, the blood was streaming over her neck and bosom from a wound in the lobe of her ear, which the bullet had just clipped and passed by.

"What was it that struck you, aunty?" I asked.

"Lor bress me, massa, I dun know; I jus fell right down."

"Didn't you feel any thing, nor hear any sound?"

"Yes, now I 'member, I heerd a s-z-z-z-z, and den I jus knock down. I drap on de groun'. I'se so glad I not dead, for if I died den de Bad Man would git me, cos I dance lately a heap."

To-day is the first time within a week when I have seen a household where the women are neatly dressed and the children cleanly. The people who have inhabited the houses along the roads for fifty miles behind us are among the most degraded specimens of humanity I have ever seen. Many of the families I now refer to do not belong to the class known as the "poor whites" of the South, for these are large landowners, and holders of from ten to forty slaves.

The peasantry of France are uneducated, but they are usually cleanly in their habits. The serfs of Russia are ignorant, but they are semi-barbarous, and have, until lately, been slaves. A large proportion of the working classes in England are debased, but they work. But the people I have seen and talked to for several days past are not only disgustingly filthy in their houses and their persons, but are so provokingly lazy, or "shiftless," as Mrs. Stowe has it, that they appear more like corpses recalled to a momentary existence than live human beings, and I have felt like applying a galvanic battery to see if they could be made to move. Even the inroads of our foragers do not start them into life;

they loll about like sloths, and barely find energy enough to utter a whining lamentation that they will starve.

During this campaign I have seen terrible instances of the horrors of slavery. I have seen men and women as white as the purest type of the Anglo-Saxon race in our army, who had been bought and sold like animals. I have looked upon the mutilated forms of black men who had suffered torture at the caprice of their cruel masters, and I have heard tales of woe too horrible for belief; but in all these cases I have never been so impressed with the degrading, demoralizing influence of this curse of slavery as in the presence of these South Carolinians. The higher classes represent the scum, and the lower the dregs of civilization. They are South Carolinians, not Americans.

The clean people whom I met this afternoon were a refreshing spectacle. Several of the young ladies—the men ran away at our approach—were attending school at this place, where a seminary has been situated for many years. One of these girls, in reply to my question why she had not gone to her home, forty miles down the river, answered:

"What is the use? Your people go every where; you overrun the state; and I am as well off here as at my father's house."

I acknowledged the wisdom of her action, for there is no doubting the fact that our presence is quite sensibly felt.

March 3d.—This morning Jackson's division of the 20th Corps gained the bridge which, crossing Thompson's Creek, opens the road direct to Cheraw. A bridge above was taken from the Rebels last night by Hawley's brigade of the same division. When I say "the bridges were taken," I mean what there is left of them. The Rebels, when pursued by our skirmish line, are followed so closely that the burning of their bridges is sometimes their only salvation. They seem to comprehend in advance that they must work rapidly; so they place tar, oil, shell, and other combustibles upon these light wooden structures, and destruction almost instantly follows ignition.

I happened to be present this afternoon at one of those interviews which so often occur between General Sherman and the negroes. The conversation was piquant and interesting; not only characteristic of both parties, but the more significant because, on the part of the General, I believe it a fair expression of his feelings on the slavery question.

A party of ten or fifteen negroes had just found their way through the lines from Cheraw. Their owners had carried them from the vicinity of Columbia to the other side of the Pedee, with the mules and horses which they were running away from our army. The negroes had escaped, and were on their way back to find their families. A more ragged set of human beings could not have been found out of the slave states, or, perhaps, Italy. The negroes were of all ages, and had stopped in front of the General's tent, which was pitched a few feet back from the sidewalk of the main street.

Several officers of the army, among them General Slocum, were gathered round, interested in the scene. General Sherman said to them:

"Well, men, what can I do for you — where are you from?"

"We's jus come from Cheraw. Massa took us wid him to carry mules and horses away from youins."

"You thought we would get them; did you wish us to get the mules?"

"Oh yes, massa, dat's what I wanted. We knowed youins cumin, and I wanted you to hav dem mules; but no use; dey heard dat youuns on de road, and nuthin would stop 'em. Why, as we cum along, de cavalry run away from de Yanks as if dey fright to deth. Dey jumped into de river, and some of dem lost dere hosses. Dey frightened at de berry name ob Sherman."

Some one at this point said: "That is General Sherman who is talking to you."

"God bress me! Is you Mr. Sherman?"

"Yes, I am Mr. Sherman."

"Dat's him, su' nuff," said one.

"Is dat de grre-aat Mr. Sherman dat we'se heard ob so long?" said another.

"Why, dey so frightened at your berry name dat dey run right away," shouted a third.

"It is not me that they are afraid of," said the General; "the name of another man would have the same effect with them if he had this army. It is these soldiers that they run away from."

"Oh no," they all exclaimed, "it's de name ob Sherman, su'; and we hab wanted to see you so long while you trabbel all roun' jis whar you like to go. Dey said dat dey wanted to git you a little furder on, and den dey whip all your soldiers; but, God bress me! you keep cumin' and a cumin', an' dey allers git out."

"Dey mighty 'fraid ob you, sar; dey say you kill de colored men too," said an old man, who had not heretofore taken part in the conversation.

With much earnestness, General Sherman replied:

"Old man, and all of you, understand me. I desire that bad men should fear me, and the enemies of the government which we are all fighting for. Now we are your friends; you are now free ('Tank you, Massa Sherman,' was ejaculated by the group). You can go where you please; you can come with us or go home to your children. Wherever you go you are no longer slaves. You ought to be able to take care of yourselves. ('We is; we will.') You must earn your freedom, then you will be entitled to it, sure; you have a right to be all that you can be, but you must be industrious, and earn the right to be men. If you go back to your families, and I tell you again you can go with us if you wish, you must do the best you can. When you get a chance, go to Beaufort or Charleston, where you will have a little farm to work for yourselves."

The poor negroes were filled with gratitude and hope by these kind words, which the General uttered in the kindest manner, and they went away with thanks and blessings on their lips.

The important news reaches us that Johnston has been restored to command. I do not imagine for a moment that this change of Rebel commanders will influence General Sherman in his purposes, yet it will alter the *modus operandi*, for Johnston can not be treated with the contempt which Sherman shows for Beauregard. The Rebel citizens are delighted with Johnston's restoration, for they profess to think him the greatest general in the country. I have never heard but one expression of opinion among the Southerners relative to the respective merits of Johnston and Lee. Johnston is regarded as much superior to Lee, especially in a genius for strategy.

CHAPTER XX.

CAPTURE OF CHERAW—DESTRUCTION OF REBEL ARTILLERY AND SUPPLIES—THE ENEMY STILL BEFOGGED.

Cheraw, March 3d.—Yesterday the right wing of the army crossed Thompson's Creek. Corse's division of the 15th Corps, with two regiments of mounted infantry which are attached to the right wing, pushed on to the bridge crossing the creek upon the main road, and succeeded in saving it from the flames; so that the 17th Corps, which led the advance, was enabled to make a crossing.

The defense of Cheraw was not unexpected, for we knew that while the Rebels could not have had time to concentrate their scattered forces, yet the east bank of the stream was the strongest line they could have between this point and salt water. They must have been closely pressed, however, for the rapid march of the 20th Corps yesterday uncovered their right flank, and they were unable to get their guns over the bridge.

Cheraw is ours, with many cannon and bountiful supplies of stores.

March 4th.—The capture of Cheraw is of more value than we anticipated, although the force opposed to us was not so large as had been reported. The Rebel cavalry was a division of Hampton's men, and the infantry were those who had been brought up from Charleston. Their line was first formed at Thompson's Creek, which they were driven from instantly by the impetuosity of our troops, who did not give them time to reform, but drove the entire force through the town at the double-quick. Our soldiers were at one end of the bridge while the Rebels were leaving the other, but too late to save it from the flames. We captured twenty-five cannon which had been brought to this place from Charleston; they were Blakelys, twenty-pound Parrotts, and two of Rebel manufacture. All but the Blakelys have been destroyed. These guns, used so effectively upon our fleet at Charléston, will be carried to the sea-coast as trophies. General Mower fired them to-day in a salute in honor of the inauguration of Mr. Lincoln for his second term. Our honored President would have been as glad and proud as we, could he have heard the roaring of our cannon and our shouts of joy and victory. His first inauguration was not celebrated in South Carolina by loyal hearts and hands; but the glorification over the beginning of his second term goes to make up the deficiency.

The rebels appear to have made this place a grand dépôt for the munitions of war hurried away from Charleston in anticipation of attack. Besides the cannon, we have captured thousands of small-arms, a great quantity of fixed ammunition, and twenty tons of gunpowder, with commissary stores more than sufficient to fill all the wagons of the 17th Corps, and part of those of the 15th.

There can now be no doubt that the Rebels, after discovering their mistake in supposing our movement was upon Charleston, were united in their opinion that after the occupation of Columbia we would move at once upon Charlotte. All our subsequent operations seemed to indicate that point as our next objective; and, notwithstanding the delay in crossing the Catawba, the Rebels were not undeceived even up to the time of the appearance of the head of column of the 17th Corps approaching on the Camden road. Although they succeeded in burning the bridge, they have not prevented our crossing the river, for we pushed over a brigade this morning; and at the present moment our pontoons are in the water, and I can hear the scattering fire of the skirmishers of Mower's division, which marched over this afternoon.

It is foolish for the Rebels to destroy their valuable bridges when they do not defend the other bank, as in this instance; for, unless we were pursued by an enemy in the rear, many of them would be left standing by our army. When they do not prevent our laying pontoons by a more active opposition than we have yet encountered, the delay to us is merely a matter of a few hours, while the destruction of these bridges is a serious loss to the people.

It is incomprehensible to me that the Rebels do not make a more obstinate resistance to our passage of a stream like the Pedee, after they have destroyed a bridge; yet the truth is that the defense of South Carolina has been the most ridiculous farce of the war. The Georgians, with less of bombast, did much better. In South Carolina, there were several lines of infinite importance and great strength for a war of defense—first, the Salkahatchie, then the Edisto, Saluda, Broad, Catawba, and now the Pedee. At first we met with opposition, which delayed us with more or less of loss, but the passage of the others has been a work of comparative ease and safety.

The Rebels believed that Cheraw, at any rate, was a place of safety; Sherman and his army would not come here, wherever else he might try to go. So they not only sent hither their priceless field cannon and the powder, which is invaluable, but the people of Charleston gathered here with their household goods and valuables which could be easily transported. The statements of these people, with newspaper comments and prognostications, prove beyond a doubt that they are as much in the fog as ever as to General Sherman's plans.

The restoration of Johnston to command is said by the Rebels to be a reflection upon the management of Beauregard, which that haughty Gascon ought to resent. But he can not well help himself—nor, for that matter, can Jeff. Davis, for the appointment of Johnston has been forced upon him by the people of the central Southern States. Davis is cursed by every one I see with the utmost bitterness. To him they attribute all their misfortune. Johnston's removal, and the insults heaped upon that General, was the work of the Rebel chief; and from that act followed a train of dire results. Had Johnston remained in command, Sherman would never have come to Savannah, and, of course, would not have been able to march through South Carolina.

For our part, we should still have gone to Savannah, but might have been longer on the way. The only difference in the situation, to our minds, is, that while Davis's policy has scattered and broken up the Southwestern Rebel army, Johnston would have kept it nearly intact, and might have to-day re-enforced Lee with twenty-five thousand men. The Rebels hope that Johnston will be able to recall and reorganize that army; but no man living has that power. He might as well try to reclothe the naked limbs of those oak-trees yonder on the hill-side with last year's foliage of green; or, a task more impossible yet, restore to the Southern gentlemen their lost reputation for chivalry, honor, and manhood.

March 5th.—The sun shines brighter to-day, and the fresh wind blowing from the North gives us strength and new life. It is a promise of future health, dry roads, and long marches. I have been wandering through the town to-day, which is really pretty, with wide streets and avenues bordered with elm-trees, behind which, in the midst of beautiful gardens, are situated tastefully-built houses. A great many Scotchmen lived here. In the cemetery attached to the Episcopal Church, two out of three of the head-stones and monuments bear the prefix of "Mc." One of the wealthiest citizens in the place is a Mr. McFarland, whose interest in blockade running has, it is said, been very profitable to him. I hear that a liberal use has been made of his extensive collection of choice wines. Many a bumper was filled there yesterday to the health of Mr. Lincoln, and confusion to South Carolina.

Our ordnance officers have sometimes been puzzled in the effort to destroy the powder and fixed ammunition which we captured. The Rebels are criminally careless in the way they leave it about, stored in all sorts of places and in all kinds of buildings. Either in their extreme haste they packed it into any place which was handy, or they were determined to blow up the town. Thirty-six hundred barrels of this powder were just outside of the town, stored in a sort of arsenal; but another large lot was packed into a building near the dépôt, which the Rebels set on fire before we arrived. Trains of powder were laid from the dépôt to this store, and it seems wonderful that it was not ignited and hundreds of lives of non-combatants lost.

As at Columbia, our efforts to destroy this dangerous material without damage to the people resulted in a mournful accident, which cost us the lives of two men at least. A part of the powder was placed in a deep, wet ravine near the river, where all of it was to have been deposited, and then covered over with sand. Although it was carefully guarded, some reckless fellow managed to get a train in communication with the bulk of the powder. The instant the fire reached this sleeping monster it rose up with a most terrible roar, shaking and crushing to the ground several houses in its efforts to find air—space. For fifty rods around the ground was blackened, the trees begrimed and broken, and the hill-side torn up, while boxes of ammunition flew into fragments, the shell ascended far in the air, bursting at great distances from the scene of explosion. The danger was fearful, for more than twenty thousand men were standing within a quarter of a mile, waiting their turn to pass over the river.

Yesterday, as one of General Hazen's headquarters' wagons came into camp for the night, a little bright-eyed mulatto girl slipped off from the end of the tongue underneath the wagon, where she had been clinging for many a long hour, while the vehicle had made its devious journey over rocks into deep ruts, and through mud-holes and deep creeks.

"How long have you been there?" she was asked.

Turning her dusty, piteous face toward her kind interlocutor, she replied:

"Dunno; since de morning, I spec."

"Where did you come from?"

"Dunno; couldn't fine mammy nor sissy dis morning, so I jined the waggin."

The poor little waif was provided for by General Hazen, and perhaps it will be infinitely better for her future welfare that she lost her "mammy and sissy" in the march through South Carolina.

The lands along the Pedee are much richer than the country over which we have passed of late, and we have gathered in forage sufficient for many days. The transportation which came with the army from Savannah has grown lighter and lighter as we empty our wagons day after day of coffee, sugar, hard bread, etc., so that when we strike a rich place the empty wagons are filled to overflowing, and thus our noble horses, and those lovable, patient, hard-working little mules have good feed all the time. I have come to love that tough, untiring, much-abused animal, who is so often accused unjustly of obstinacy. One can not witness its faithful efforts, day after day, without a feeling of affection and admiration: the idea is absurd, no doubt, but I avow it unhesitatingly. A soldier who was astride a diminutive specimen of a jackass to-day, however, was not of my mind. He could easily have taken the jack under his arm and thrown him over the fence, but was trying to ride him, much to the long-eared donkey's horror and astonishment—subsequently, to his rage—for he made frantic, spasmodic, and successful efforts to relieve himself from the encumbrance, so that the blue jacket and trowsers of the soldier rapidly became yellow from frequent contact with the pools of mud in the road. After much hard work and coaxing, the wearied soldier jerked out the expostulatory remark: "Now Jack, go along quiet, and don't be mulish, will you?"

Nor are these the only peculiar incidents of our march. During the destructive fires at Columbia, Winnsboro,' Cheraw, and other places, our officers and men have been very active in their efforts to preserve private property. In many instances, whole families have been kept from want and suffering by the extinguishment of the flames in their dwellings, or the removal of valuable articles for household or personal use when it was impossible to prevent the destruction of a building. These people were naturally thankful for the kindnesses thus shown to them, and sometimes pressed upon our men the acceptance of some little gift as a

THE ARMY MULE.

token of their gratitude; so that it was not unusual to hear among the soldiers such conversations as this:

"Where did you get that splendid meerschaum?" or, "Did you bring that handsome cane along with you?"

"Oh," was the reply, "that was presented me by a lady in Columbia for saving her house from burning."

This style of answer, which was very satisfactory, soon became the common explanation of the possession of all sorts of property. An officer, taking his punch (they drink punch in the army when the coffee ration is exhausted) from an elegantly-chased silver cup, was saluted thus:

"Halloa, captain; that's a gem of a cup. No mark on it; why, where did you get it?"

"Y-e-e-s! that cup? Oh, that was given me by a lady in Columbia for saving her household gods from destruction."

An enterprising officer in charge of a foraging party would return to camp with a substantial family coach, well filled with hams, meal, etc.

"How are you, captain? Where did you pick up that carriage?"

"Elegant vehicle, is'nt it?" was the reply; "that was a gift from a lady out here whose mansion was in flames. Arrived at the nick of time—good thing—she said she didn't need the carriage any longer—answer for an ambulance one of these days!"

After a while this joke came to be repeated so often that it was dangerous for any one to exhibit a gold watch, a tobacco-box, any uncommon utensil of kitchen-ware, a new pipe, a guard-chain, or a ring, without being asked if "a lady at Columbia had presented that article to him for saving her house from burning."

This was one of the humors of the camp, and a soldier must have his joke.

CHAPTER XXI.

REFUGEE LOYALISTS—THE EMIGRANT TRAIN—CHARLESTON REBELS.

March 5th.—One of the most significant features of our journey through the South has been the frequent prayer and entreaty of the people that they might be permitted to join our column and march with us to the sea, or wherever we might go, so that they could leave this region of despotism to go any where out of the South and toward the pure air of freedom again. One is a mechanic, who was born and reared in the old Granite State. He came here four years ago as master mechanic in a railroad machine-shop. He has been able to avoid service in the Rebel army because his services were necessary in the shop. He will be taken with us, for he can be made useful.

Here is a little family, consisting of mother and daughter, whose limited means were long ago exhausted, and whose main stay, a brave lad, is a soldier in the Union army. The women wish to go to Connecticut, where relatives will gladly care for them, and where they can get news of their son and brother. Another is a poor Irish woman, whose husband was a conscript in the Rebel army, and is now a prisoner, sick in a Northern hospital.

At Columbia there were several families of wealth and position, who had always been suspected of loyal proclivities. Upon our occupation of that city, it became known to the Rebel inhabitants that these people had always assisted our prisoners, and, previous to our approach, had secreted a great many at imminent peril. It would be impossible to reject these generous, self-sacrificing friends. The fire had not spared their houses, and they were homeless, but we well knew that for them to remain after our visit would be certain death. Up to this time the want of means of transportation had necessitated a refusal of these requests. But some of the wagons were now empty; then there were a number of vehicles captured from the enemy; horses and mules we bring in every day, and again, not a few of the families asking our protection are able to furnish their own transportation.

General Howard was in command of the troops at Columbia, and these unfortunates did not appeal in vain to his generous, sympathetic heart, which never refuses to sympathize with those in distress.

With the approbation of General Sherman, General Howard at once organized an emigrant train, which was placed under guard of the escaped prisoners belonging to other commands. This train has since been separated, and apportioned to each division of the 15th and 17th Corps. The refugees are getting along famously. Ladies who have been always accustomed to the refinements of life seem to enjoy the journey as much as if it were a picnic. In truth, it is better than that; for, while they are not exposed to the dangers of war, they participate in its excitements. The column has a singularly *outré* appearance. First there will be a huge family coach containing ladies, with their personal baggage crowded about them; then an army wagon loaded with men, women, and children, comfortably seated upon such articles of household furniture as they are allowed to carry. Following this, will be a country cart filled with negro women—for the negroes come along also—and hosts of the little curly, bullet-headed youngsters gaze curiously upon the strange sights which meet their eyes.

General Hazen, whose name can never be mentioned but with inspiring recollections of the assault of Fort McAllister, tells me that the large number who accompany his division are but little trouble to him, and that they have so quickly learned to forage for themselves that they are no expense to the government. Two of the escaped officers, with a detachment of ten men, have charge of the train, which takes its assigned place in the column; a few tents, which are in excess or have been captured, are pitched when the column go into camp, and our little colony, with grateful hearts, go to their night's rest with the glad consciousness that they are, step by step, approaching a land of civilization and freedom.

In this life, so new and strange to the refugees, numbers of families become separated from each other. Portions of the army, who for days march upon separate roads, will at one time or another come together again, as at this place, for example, when three corps, which have been marching upon different roads, unite at Cheraw for the purpose of crossing the river. The troops and trains, although really distinct to the initiated eye, may be mistaken for one another. I have seen the negroes, especially, wandering about as completely lost as if they were in an uninhabited forest.

Last evening I had occasion to visit several families who had formerly resided at Charleston, and fled to this place to escape the danger of the bombardment. In the years gone by they were the leaders of the aristocracy of the state. First in the crime of treason, their sons and brothers had either been killed or were now in the Rebel armies; the young ladies were full of what they called patriotism and enthusiasm for the cause of liberty, which their lovers and friends were fighting for; although, when pressed to explain

REFUGEE TRAIN.

how their liberties had ever been endangered, they were unable to give any satisfactory answer.

The older men and women, in every instance, deprecated the war; they asked for peace upon any terms of reconstruction. They did not ask for the terms of peace—peace was all they demanded. They acknowledged the attempt at revolution to be without cause or reason, and showed that they were subdued and beaten without hope of recovery. This state of subjection was not a new experience to me, for we have met with little of bombast and rebellious puffiness from the more influential and wiser portion of the people we have seen in this state; but what strikes me most painfully, in my intercourse with these old families, is the evidence of intellectual decay. They are not only *pas en rapporte* with the age, but are so wanting in vitality and energy as to approach senility. In contrast with the soul-stirring spirit of our Northern soldiers and civilization, they appear to belong to a past day and a defunct nationality, with only a pretense of gentility remaining to show that they once laid claim to the leadership of society and fashion. The unceremonious usages of war shake rudely even that vestige of what once passed for refined hospitality.

In conversation, recently, with a young Southern lady who, with glowing eyes, informed me that her brothers and cousins were fighting in defense of the liberty of their country, I said:

"Please tell me what country? What do you mean by 'our country?'"

She replied: "The South, of course; South Carolina."

I continued: "Did I not see in the old church-yard yonder several monuments of brick without inscription, which seem to be falling to pieces? they are said to cover the dust of heroes who died in the old Revolutionary War. Is that true?"

"Yes; they fought under Greene against Cornwallis and Tarleton."

"What country did they die for? In defense of what cause did they suffer?"

"America, I suppose."

"You are right; and let me tell you that you South Carolinians have no claim to the honored remains of those martyred heroes. It is well that the stranger may not know who lies there, for their fame is your shame. To establish this grand American nationality, these men gave their life-blood. We are fighting to maintain that nationality in all its integrity."

While I do not for an instant suppose that this black-eyed Rebel was convinced of the error of her cause, she was somewhat astonished at the argument advanced, never having looked at the question in that way.

CHAPTER XXII.

CROSSING THE PEDEE RIVER — THE ARMY IN NORTH CAROLINA.

March 6th.—Although the left wing have placed pontoons on the river at Snedsboro', only the 14th Corps and Kilpatrick's cavalry will cross at that point; the right wing, which in the last movement was the advanced column, were by reason of that fact enabled to lay their pontoons and move over the two corps before noon this morning. To save time, the 20th Corps have marched down, and are expected to be in camp on the left bank by midnight.

With the safe transfer of the army to the east bank of the Pedee, there will probably be a change in the formation of our heads of column. The army was not properly together until the different corps arrived at the Salkahatchie. From that moment the form of our front was always concave. This tactical formation was no doubt deemed necessary, because the attack of the enemy was necessarily in front, our flanks being more or less protected. Obliged to cross several large rivers, which, according to all military rule and precedent, in the presence of an active enemy, were considered almost impassable, and which were adopted by the enemy with great wisdom as their strongest lines of defense, the passage was irresistibly forced by the two points of the concave, which were constantly thrust forward, first upon one side and then the other, or both at the same time, as General Sherman deemed best when threatening Augusta and Charleston.

These evolutions, planned with comprehensive wisdom, answered their purpose with the most perfect success, for in no instance did the central columns meet with serious opposition; and while the right wing was day by day fighting the enemy, suffering more in killed and wounded than either the left centre or extreme left, yet it was reasonable to suppose that we should have met with resistance upon our left flank, for we were sure that a portion of Hood's army were in that direction. These remarks apply only to the infantry of the army; and it should be clearly understood that General Kilpatrick's operations upon our extreme left and front unquestionably protected that wing of the army, and, in addition, deceived the enemy with the belief that we were moving upon Augusta.

In looking back upon the general features of this campaign, it can be seen with what geometrical precision this masterly conception of a concave front has been perfected, and its best proof is our presence here, without loss of men or material, with the fruits of victories in our hands realizing the most sanguine hopes.

This review is made at the present moment, because we are entering upon a new field, where the theatre of war changes its position, moving from front to flank. All our information goes to show that the Rebels have been falling back to concentrate at Charlotte, in the belief that we are advancing upon that place. Our movements within the last few days may open their eyes to the truth; and while the repeated lessons they have received may make them hesitate in attacking an exposed flank, yet the possibility that re-enforcements from the veteran troops in Virginia may be sent to impede our march to the sea, or the caution which is one of the marked characteristics of General Sherman, has induced him to change his front, so that the army has begun to assume a convex shape in place of the opposite form. Thus, moving forward his columns in *echelon* upon the centre, he can at any moment put more than one half his force in line of battle if attacked upon his left flank, which is most in danger.

The situation each moment deepens in interest. While there is but little fear that Grant will permit Lee to get away from Richmond, yet it is possible that a force may be detached to re-enforce Johnston. It is not wise to despise an enemy, especially when that enemy is so great a soldier as Joe Johnston.

March 7th.—The army is now all upon the east bank of the Pedee, marching upon roads leading due east. Kilpatrick covers the extreme left, and to-night is at Rockingham, where, yesterday evening, he came in contact with Butler's division of Hampton's Legion, which retreated with some loss before his spirited attack. The four grand columns of infantry are all south of Kilpatrick, covering a strip of country forty miles in width. All the corps commanders report abundance of forage and supplies, and the numerous streams which empty into the Pedee have excellent water-power, with flour-mills situated at points convenient for the army—a providential circumstance, for several divisions have exhausted their stores of hard bread. All these mills were in operation yesterday, and will not rest until this evening. They will grind corn enough to last for a week, when, perhaps, we shall have reached tide-water again.

To-day has been sunny and bright; the roads have been dry (in truth we have seen dust rising over the moving column for the first time since we left Savannah); the gentle wind from the east has come to us laden with fragrant per-

K

fume of pine and cedar, and all have journeyed on as happy and contented as mortals can be, and as glad as only men have a right to be who have plodded on so many dreary days through heavy mud and pitiless rain. The refugees, and especially the negroes, expand in this sunlight like flowers, if I may use such a simile when speaking of such dusky subjects. Their exuberant laughter may be heard for a long distance as they journey on, sometimes riding in their queer go-carts, with curious nondescript rigging, or puffing and sweating under a load of blankets, pots, etc.; or when, as in one instance under my observation to-day, three little girls were at the same time astride a patient, good-natured old mule.

At one point on the road to-day, where the column halted for a moment, I saw half a dozen three-year old "picaninnies," as their mothers called them, perched upon the top rail of a fence, and singing with all their might,

"I'm glad I'm in this army,"

an old Sabbath-school hymn, which they repeated, unconscious of its singular appropriateness at the time and place. The soldiers were delighted, and greeted them with shouts of approbation: "Go it, little one;" "Bully for you, curly-head;" "You're right there, little nig—we'll stick by you," etc.

To-night we went into camp in a magnificent grove of pines. The roots of the trees are buried in the spindles and burrs which have fallen undisturbed for centuries. The wind sings, or, rather, murmurs—for that is the sound—through the lofty tree-tops, while the air is filled with delicious fragrance. This evening the sun went down behind glowing bars of silver and purple, although now and then its bright rays would stream out, throwing long shadows across this

HEADQUARTERS OF GENERAL SHERMAN IN THE PINE WOODS.

great cathedral floor, transforming tree and bough into columns and arches of glittering gold. As I write, the campfires dance and flare upward; away out in the dark forest, strange, uncouth forms peer out from the shadows; while a distant band of music, mellowed by the distance, rounds in soothing cadences the restful tattoo. Ah! this is not the blood, the carnage, or the suffering of war; it is its delightful romance.

Laurel Hill, N. C., March 8*th.* — The central columns have advanced fourteen miles to-day, and, as was anticipated, without any opposition whatever. Whether or not the flanking column have seen any Rebels I do not as yet know; but it is probable there is nothing more than a light cavalry force upon our extreme left. A body of infantry is said to be in the neighborhood of Florence, on our right, but it will take good care not to approach within feeling distance of our columns. The rear I have never thought it worth while to speak of; for we have so frequently to cross rivers, taking with us the means of passage, that only a large and well-appointed army could annoy us in that direction.

The Charlotte and Raleigh papers afford us much amusement by their lugubrious guesses as to where Sherman will next strike a blow. They are all in the position of a group of men who hear a shell hurtling through the air coming in their direction: every one thinks he is the mark fired at. General Hoke, commanding at Charlotte, has issued an address to the people of the place, assuring them that when Sherman occupies the town he will protect the citizens and private property; he begs them to remain quietly at home, and trust to the generosity of the conqueror. The people of Charlotte will do well to accept the assurances of General Hoke until we get there.

The line which divides South from North Carolina was passed by the army this morning. It was not in our imagination alone that we could at once see the difference between the two states. The soil is not superior to that near Cheraw, but the farmers are a vastly different class of men. I had always supposed that South Carolina was agriculturally superior to its sister state. The loud pretensions of the chivalry had led me to believe that the scorn of these gentlemen was induced by the inferiority of the people of the Old North State, and that they were little better than "dirt-eaters;" but the strong Union sentiment which has always found utterance here should have taught me better.

The real difference between the two regions lies in the fact that the plantation owners work with their own hands, and do not think they degrade themselves thereby. For the first time since we bade farewell to salt water I have to-day seen an attempt to manure land. The army has passed through thirteen miles or more of splendidly-managed farms; the corn and cotton fields are nicely plowed and furrowed; the fences are in capital order; the barns are well built; the dwelling-houses are cleanly, and there is that air of thrift which shows that the owner takes a personal interest in the conduct of affairs.

The conduct of the soldiers is perceptibly changed. I have seen no evidence of plundering; the men keep their ranks closely; and, more remarkable yet, not a single column of the fire or smoke which a few days ago marked the positions of heads of column, can be seen upon the horizon. Our men seem to understand that they are entering a state which has suffered for its Union sentiment, and whose inhabitants would gladly embrace the old flag again if they can have the opportunity, which we mean to give them, or I am mistaken as to our future campaigns.

Rain has fallen all day with a most disagreeable pertinacity. A more striking and unromantic contrast to the beautiful scenes of yesterday one does not care to imagine, much less experience. Pitching camp in the mud, with a torrent of water drenching every thing about you, and especially yourself, is not the most cheerful business that any person, civilian or soldier, can engage in. There is no help for it, and I am painfully conscious that the impertinent floods of water will deluge me before morning, and even waterproof blankets will not save me. I'll to bed, and try to bear it with patience. The camp is still as a grave-yard, except that I have never heard that dead men snore, and our quartermaster (a quiet, good-hearted man when his eyes are open) is snorting under the adjoining fly like a locomotive getting up steam. Now for the blankets and a good sleep!

CHAPTER XXIII.

MARCHING UPON FAYETTEVILLE—DELUGE—AN ADVENTURE IN THE WOODS—A PERILOUS ROAD.

Bethel Church, March 10*th.* — Yesterday our four columns, with the cavalry, crossed the Little Pedee River, or, as it is called near its source, "Lumber Creek." The 14th Corps passed Love's Bridge, on the extreme left, in good condition, and moved over rapidly, so that its head of column last night must have been within fifteen or twenty miles of Fayetteville. The 17th Corps, the flanking column on the right, was equally fortunate, and moved along with so much rapidity that it was necessary to check it, in order that the left wing might first move north of Fayetteville. The government property, consisting of valuable machinery and material, which was moved to this place from Harper's Ferry, it is desirable to recover, if possible. Farther than this, and perhaps more important yet, if the Rebels make the stand they threaten at Fayetteville, a force between them and their Southern communications would endanger their safety. With a line of bayonets extending to the Cape Fear River, they must inevitably be captured.

To return to our present pósition. The two central columns were not so fortunate as their companions. The bridges on both roads—Gilchrist's and McFarland's—had been destroyed, and our troops were obliged to build bridges. The 15th Corps, at the former place, put down pontoons, but the crossing at McFarland's was not so easy. On both sides of the stream there grew a forest of small water-oaks, which had become partially submerged by the flood of water. It would have been easy to span the stream proper with three or four pontoon boats; but one of the conditions in laying these canvas boats is a clean bottom. If one of them rests upon a root or tree-stump, not only is the boat injured, but there may be hours of delay, involving serious consequences. So General Robinson detailed a sufficient number of men at daylight yesterday morning, and by four o'clock in the afternoon a strong bridge one hundred feet in length was completed, ready for the passage of the column.

The successful completion of these bridges proved to be important in the highest degree; for about five o'clock in the afternoon there descended from the heavens a deluge of rain. "Deluge" is the only expressive word to use; for so large a quantity of rain fell in so short a space of time, that by nightfall the surface of the country was one entire sheet of water. It was my fortune to be separated from my canvas home some fifteen miles, and, with a party of couriers, attempted to cross the country. The way led through pine forests, where roads, if dependence can be placed in the state maps, existed several years ago. The rain fell in torrents, blinding riders and horses, and drenching every one to the skin. Waterproofs were not proof against this floodwater, which seemed to have a power and penetration peculiarly its own. The road soon became less marked; a mile farther it degenerated into a single path; and, finally, it disappeared from sight altogether. Investigations to the right and left and before us gave no clew to the lost track. Halting under the tall pines, we held a council of war. It was but an hour before nightfall, and, supposing we had come thus far in the right direction, there were yet ten miles between us and our destination.

Consulting my pocket-compass, we ascertained that the general direction was correct; yet we hesitated to push blindly through an enemy's country so far in advance of the army, and with so wide a space between the columns, but the darkening sky and sullen thunder warned us to push on in some direction. If there had been a plantation near, or any indication of human existence, we could speedily have settled the difficulty; but for miles around nothing was visible but the solemn woods and sandy plains. So again we applied the spur, and splashed through the wet grass, keeping to the south as before. Another half hour of hard riding ended in another consultation, which had the same conclusion.

Some of the party became confused, and insisted we were going north; others thought we were traveling straight toward Fayetteville. There were those who lost faith in the pocket-compass. One or two believed in the little instrument. Every body argued that he was soaked through; no one was cross or discouraged, but, on the contrary, jocose and jolly, in spite of the prospect of a night out of doors without food or fire. Most of us had been in precisely that predicament before, and knew very well that the situation would not improve by swearing at it. So we jogged on for a while, and then, gradually looming up in the rain, we descried a blue coat and a white-eared mule approaching.

"Halloa, stranger, where are we? where did you come from, and where are we going?" were the inquiries addressed the new-comer.

"Well, I should say that we were in a d—d hard rainstorm. I came from the 20th Corps, 'bout quarter mile back. I'm looking for forage in this cussed sand country. Now, where you're going you ought to know best."

The time and occasion were not conducive to long conversation; so we pushed ahead, found the 20th Corps, obtained farther information, struck a new road which did not run out of sight, but did lead into the main road, and, finally, after rousing up a goodly number of people at camp-fires that did not burn, and in negro huts which were filled with white soldiers, we got some of the localities of our objective —reaching it about midnight, rather moist, to be sure, but quite contented that we were not hugging the bark of a pine log away off there in the dark forest.

But this was not the end of the adventures of the night in this wild and uncivilized region. Another journey had to be performed; and it is somewhat difficult to say which was the worst—the woods in which a party of us got lost, or the road which duty required me to travel alone. The distance next to be traversed was about three miles, and I was warned on all sides that it would be "the death of me;" that there were holes in the road which were bottomless; that there was no escape by taking to the swamp on either side, for there a man would be drowned, without the benefit of burial, which the road afforded, and more to the same effect.

All day I had ridden a horse, which, though a steady old fellow, is neither of a lively temper nor in his best condition, so I gladly accepted the kind offer of a gray nag from a brother officer, who assured me of his many noble qualities. When I got into the saddle, Prince (for that was the animal's name) turned his head toward me, shaking it wisely, as if to say, "I don't like this night trip in the pelting rain, and, besides, I don't know you." A shake of the rein, and a light touch of the spur, convinced him, however, that there was but one mind in the matter, and that he must go ahead. Not having been over the road before, I had no comprehension of the serious task I had undertaken. The first five rods of the way lay through, or, rather, into a bog, where the mud was knee-deep; at any rate, Prince managed not to sink much lower than that depth, avoiding the catastrophe by a series of plunges which were any thing but pleasant or satisfactory to his rider. This was succeeded by a small lake, through which the road was indicated by a sort of bridge of rails, which had, no doubt, been laid upon comparatively dry ground before the flood. Prince tumbled over and through them in the most delightful manner, stepping high and occasionally twitching his head around in an expostulatory way, as if he had come to the conclusion that we had gone far enough. To which I replied, "No, Prince; we must keep on to the end of the journey;" and as, at that moment, I involuntarily pressed his flank with the spur, he leaped forward, with decided earnestness, into another sea of mud, which he swam through with creditable facility.

At last we found dry land—that is to say, bits of hard ground occurred here and there in the middle of the road and on both sides of the wheel tracks. But wherever the wagon wheels had gone, there the anxious inquirer could have found a hopeless abyss. Neither was it safe to step outside the narrow roadway, for the original builder of this road had dug ditches on both sides for the purpose of carrying off the water. As this was the best part of the road, it may readily be imagined that nobody would have selected this locality for a pleasure jaunt.

After a while we (*i. e.*, Prince and I) found a string of wagons and ambulances in every imaginable condition of helplessness. Some of them lay entirely upon one side, buried in the mud; another stood very nearly on end, as if it was about to descend out of sight headforemost; while upon the little hillocks in the swamp the drivers and guards had built fires, around which the contents of the wagons had been placed, pending a desperate effort to rescue the wearied horses. I met several of these luckless teamsters, and, if my memory serves me, they were swearing, although I am told there is a depth of wretchedness, an extreme point of misery, befalling travelers upon that route, where even profane drivers find themselves unable to do justice to the subject.

A few rods farther I discovered a row of tents, which were relieved from the pitchy darkness by several glowing camp-fires; around these were seated groups of officers. The temptation was too great for Prince and his rider; both halted. "How are you?" "where are you going?" "get down and stay here to-night;" "we've only been out of the water about an hour; the flood is running off, and this is a North Carolina crevasse." These and other exclamations were addressed to me by my good friends, who insisted that I should go no farther. "A few rods beyond them were scores of mud-holes absolutely impassable. It was dangerous."

Prince, who stood near and heard the conversation, shook his head in approval; but it was useless. The dispatches must be delivered that night, and away we started, over a cruel piece of corduroy, into the mud-holes again, through several creeks, and once again on a bit of firm ground, where I found the General, stretched at full length asleep on the floor in the pulpit of a church.

It was nearly midnight when I again mounted the noble gray to retrace my steps, which I had resolved upon, notwithstanding the kind offer made me of a vacant pew for a bed-chamber. To a man who has ridden fifty miles in wet clothes, three miles in addition, even over such a road as this, is nothing, in view of a dry shirt and a nice five-hours' sleep between comfortable blankets. So off we started again. By careful watching we were able to navigate through the dangers of the road, until we reached our friends upon Ararat, who were more than astonished at the success of the journey. It is to be feared that either Prince or his rider, when the road was again taken, had become unduly elevated with well-deserved praises; for, as the latter was enjoying the comfort of a well-filled pipe, he became suddenly conscious of a violent motion, by which, in the first instance, he found himself embracing the neck of his good steed, and the next moment sliding, in spite of himself, into a very wide and reasonably deep pool of mud. Prince floundered out of the mud to a strip of firm ground, and there waited with magnanimous patience while I groped about for cap and cherished meerschaum.

As we neared the blind pathway which turned off through the forest to the wagons, I gave Prince the rein to see if he would remember the way, not because I questioned Prince's intelligence, but that I desired to show the noble fellow how thoroughly I trusted him who had carried me so safely through such a wretched, dangerous journey as that just passed. We said good-night to each other as I left him munching a good supper of corn and oats. Good, faithful Prince! He should have had my bed, had he needed it more than I.

March 11*th*. — The sun shone out again this morning bright and cheerful, making glad the hearts of all of us, and of none more than the soldiers and teamsters who have been laboring night and day through these wretched swamps.

What a noble army we have here! Every day produces fresh and striking illustrations of the men's cheerful acceptance of all the discouraging circumstances of the situation. For instance: a wagon, painfully toiling along the road, suddenly careens; the wheels are submerged in a quicksand;

HEROES WHO ARE NOT GAZETTED.

every effort of the mules or horses to "pull out" only buries the unfortunate vehicle deeper in the mire, and very soon the animals have dug for themselves a pit, out of which many are never extricated alive. The driver sees at once that it is useless to whip and swear; so he dismounts. Then the train guard, who have been resting upon their muskets watching the proceedings, quietly stack their weapons, and at once plunge into the mud. A dozen of them are at work with shoulders at the wheels and body of the wagon, and finally they lift it out of the hole upon firmer ground. One or two wagons "stuck" in this way show at once that the road must be corduroyed. Then, with many a jest and an untiring flow of good humor, the men wade into the neighboring swamp, cut down and split the trees, and soon bridge over these impassable places. A few rods farther on the head of column arrives at a creek, which in ordinary seasons is ten feet wide, and has a few inches of water running over a hard sandy bottom. Now the water is four or six feet in depth, and spreads out to a width of sixty feet, encroaching upon the softer earth. A bridge must be built. Into the water dash our men without hesitation, for they know the work must be done at once. Waist deep, throat deep, not a dry spot about them. "No matter for that," they say; "we shall be in camp by-and-by, and then, before our roaring fires, we will rehearse the incidents of the day."

Thus these good, brave soldiers endure every hardship, shrink at no exposure of life or limb; not only without grumbling, but with a good humor and merriment which no hardship dampens and no risk discourages. Old officers of the army, who have served in Florida and Mexico, continually remark this peculiar feature of Sherman's army. It does not belong to any particular corps or regiment, but all the soldiers share it alike, and at all times.

It has been said that a soldier has one right, which is always conceded and reserved—the right to grumble; but our men do not claim it. They are jolly and contented under circumstances which test a man to the utmost. I have never tried to analyze this fact, nor reason upon it, having been too happy in witnessing its beneficial results.

CHAPTER XXIV.

CAPTURE OF FAYETTEVILLE—THE UNITED STATES ARSENAL RETAKEN—TALKS WITH THE SLAVES—WADE HAMPTON—"BUMMERS" AND THEIR PECULIARITIES.

Fayetteville, March 12*th.*—This morning, the two flanking corps of the grand army, who had not seen each other for six weeks, met in the streets of Fayetteville. They met as soldiers love best to meet brave comrades, on a battle-field; for the Rebels, with foolish pertinacity, refused to give up the place without a fight, and they had their hands full of the work; for the extreme right and left of our army came together upon concentrating roads, like a well-bent bow in the strong archer's hands, whose arrow, charged with fire, sped swiftly, causing death, reaping victory.

Again we have made a capture of much greater importance than was at first supposed. The magnificent arsenal which our government built here contains millions of dollars' worth of machinery and material. The Rebels have used the work-shops in this city for the manufacture of guns, fixed ammunition, gun-carriages, etc., to a much larger extent than was supposed by any one outside the Rebel states; always excepting General Sherman, who seems to know every thing of this nature. Here are stored vast amounts of well-seasoned woods, weapons in all stages of completion, thousands of muskets; in short, every description of machinery and tools requisite for the manufacture and repairs of material of war. The Rebels tried to remove the most valuable part, but it was too bulky for easy transportation, and we came forward so quickly that they had hardly time to save their own worthless bodies. We take possession of this property by a double right. It was originally the property of the United States, paid for by the general government, and was stolen from us; and again it is ours by right of conquest. We shall destroy it utterly. There is not a piece of this costly machinery but will be broken in fragments; not a stick of timber that will not be burned to ashes; not one stone or brick of these beautiful buildings will be left standing upon another. By Monday night that which should have been the pride and honor of the state and the country will be a shapeless mass of ruins.

The city of Fayetteville is beautiful. The arsenal buildings are situated upon a commanding eminence at the west end of the city, and from every point they present an exceedingly picturesque appearance; and, taken together with the old buildings buried among the trees, which are just putting on their livery of green, give to the place the romantic air of some of the old towns in the vicinity of Paris. An ancient market-house, of very tasteful architecture, stands in the centre of the main street, which is a wide avenue, lined on either side with substantial stores and dwelling-houses. Toward the river there are mills and manufactories, and on its banks strongly-constructed steamboat piers, all showing evidences of the trade and commerce belonging to river navigation, although there is not depth of water sufficient for any but light-draught steamers, except at certain seasons of the year.

The people generally are of the better class. They do not all profess to have been original Unionists, but they do not disguise their hostility to Jeff. Davis and his despotism. The slave population is not large, and is composed chiefly of women and children. As in other parts of the South which we have visited, the masters have run away, taking with them all the able-bodied slaves; but the negroes who were able escaped, and have returned to join our column. It is generally understood among these colored men that the Rebel Government intend to put them in the army to fight against the "Yankees." The infatuation of the slaveholders upon this point seems to me one of the most singular of all their self-deceptions; for, among the hundreds of blacks with whom I have conversed during the progress of this campaign, I do not remember one who did not possess a better understanding of the merits of the questions at issue than the master who claimed to own him. While the masters still have faith that the slaves will fight for them, and offer the additional inducement of their freedom if they come safe out of battle, the slaves distrust them, and underderstand that their own bondage was one of the principal questions involved in the rebellion.

An intelligent old quadroon woman, whose mother, eighty-six years of age, sat near, and who was surrounded by her daughters and grandchildren—four generations in one group—said to me to-day:

"There, sir, are my two sons-in-law. Yesterday morning their master tried to take them away, offering them their freedom if they would go into the army voluntarily; but they know better than that. They never would fire a gun against the Federals."

"No," interposed one of the young men; "I would not fight for the man who is my master and my father at the same time. If they had forced me into the army, I would have shot the officer they put over me the first time I got a chance."

The old grandmother, who, with her family, spoke with no trace of the negro dialect, continued:

"No, sir; the slaves know too well what it means; they'd never put muskets in the slaves' hands if they were not afeared that their cause was gone up. They are going to be whipped; they are whipped now. Supposing they do free the colored men who fight for them, what is to become of us, their mothers, wives, and children at home? We are to remain slaves, of course."

She continued in the same strain:

"Didn't a Charleston newspaper say the other day that to offer freedom to the slaves was to acknowledge freedom to be better than slavery, and that we were property, like horses and mules; and that the proper way was that our boys should be put into the army just as horses and cattle are put there? I heard tell that the Congress at Richmond have talked about giving the negroes their freedom when the war is over. Doesn't that mean that we are entitled to our freedom? All the time my master and mistress in the house there, and the preacher we hear of a Sunday, tells us that the Bible says it is right we should be slaves!"

The old woman said all this in an impassioned manner, her eyes burning like living coals.

I said to her: "But you have been well treated. You have told me that you were married in your master's parlor, and that those girls have been brought up almost as if they were the daughters of their master. Ought you to complain?"

"You don't understand it," she replied. "Our advantages make it all the worse. We had better have been ignorant plantation slaves. There are three of my daughters, sir; but they have been kept here with me because they breed well. If they didn't have children every year, they would have been sold away as poor Hannah was, my second child. She was sickly, sir, and could not or would not breed children, and they sold her away on a plantation. All my girls, sir, are married but one. As soon as the grandchildren are old enough to do any kind of work they are put away—sometimes sold. I have near me five daughters and three sons grown up; all that they earn goes into the hands of master and mistress."

I said: "Do you wish to leave your master? There will probably be means to go down to Wilmington."

"Indeed, sir," they all broke out with one accord, "if we can only get to any place where we can be free, and able to work for ourselves, we shall be thankful."

It is my impression that their prayer will be granted.

Instances of Rebel inhumanity are not rare here. In the hospital, where there are several hundred sick and wounded Rebel soldiers, I found some of our men, who had been wounded in the attack upon this city. One of these men, who showed me a ghastly wound in his shoulder-blade, was not injured in battle. He had been taken prisoner a few days before, and belonged to Kilpatrick's cavalry. As he was dragged along the main street of the town with his comrades, a Rebel, one of Hampton's cavalry, rode up to the procession, and, pointing a pistol at his breast, said, with an oath, "I want to kill another d—d. Yankee." Just as he pulled the trigger the helpless prisoner moved a little, and the ball passed through his shoulder instead of his heart, at which it was aimed. With a shout of exultation, the cowardly assassin rode down the streets.

The poor sufferer told me the story just as I had heard it from several citizens who witnessed the shameful sight. Generals Wade Hampton and Hardee were in the town, and knew of the occurrence, but no action was taken; nor has the would-be murderer been sent to us. This dastardly act is a significant commentary upon the correspondence which took place between Generals Sherman and Hampton upon this very subject of shooting unarmed and defenseless prisoners. Hampton, in his letter, denies that his men have committed such murders; and, with an ingenuity which would do credit to a pettifogging lawyer, but is too small for a greater mind, plays upon the word "murderer" in reply to General Sherman's threat to "retaliate in kind."

Hampton has also taken the excellent opportunity afforded him to issue one of his furious addresses to the people. He charges us with house-burning and all sorts of outrages upon women and children, and raves in the Billingsgate style; but, as usual, his fulminations have very little foundation in truth. Houses have, unquestionably, been burned during our march, but they were the property of notorious Rebels, who were fortunate in escaping so easily; while I have yet to hear of a single instance of outrage offered to a woman or a child by any soldier of our army.

A characteristic incident of the capture of Fayetteville properly finds place here, and gives an opportunity to describe that odd but very useful class in the army who are popularly denominated "Bummers."

The origin of this nickname is unknown. No English dictionary contains it; only the "bummers" themselves know exactly what it means, except, perhaps, inferentially. Probably the word originated among themselves; they are certainly not ashamed of it.

If it be asked what a bummer is, the reply is easy. He is a raider on his own account—a man who temporarily deserts his place in the ranks while the army is on the march, and starts out upon an independent foraging expedition. Sometimes he is absent for a few days only, occasionally he disappears for weeks together. An officer whose duty requires him to pass from one column to another, or a private soldier sent out upon a scout in the forest or on the flank of the army, not unfrequently stumbles suddenly upon an encampment of bummers in the woods, or finds a party of them at a house by the wayside. This party bears all the outward aspect of an authorized and perfectly legitimate foraging party: the capacious wagons are there, with caparisoned mules; blooded horses stand tethered within reach of their apparent owners; the camp-fires burn brightly; a sumptuous meal is ready. But if one of these men be accosted with some such question as this, "To what command do you belong?" the answer comes thus:

"Well, we don't answer for any body in particular—'bout every corps in the army; eh, Bill, ain't that so?"

"Bill" says "Reckon!" and thinks it a huge joke, and then every body except the interlocutor laughs.

"How long have you been away from your regiment?"

At this question the bummer rises upon his feet, and replies, rather more respectfully:

"A week or ten days, cap'n."

"Have you any authority for foraging?"

"No, sir."

"What use or benefit are you to the service, to say nothing of the criminality of your absence without leave? Now, you belong to a class which has brought discredit upon your comrades. You ought to be ashamed of yourselves, all of you."

The dozen muscular and daring fellows who heard this little speech seemed to fail to see the point of it. One of them replied:

"See hyar, cap'n; we ain't so bad after all. We keep ahead of the skirmish line allers. We let's 'em know when an enemy's a-comin'; and then we ain't allers away from the regiment. We turns over all we don't want ourselves, and we can lick five times as many Rebs as we are, any day. Ain't that so, boys?"

"Lick 'em! d—n 'em, yes."—"Why, of course!" were the instant replies of the "boys."

"Rather shoot Rebs than hogs, any day!" roared another.

It may be readily imagined that high moral precepts are lost upon these men, and that conversations with them upon the general impropriety of their conduct are decidedly useless. They are the Bohemians of the camp, and they act upon this consolatory reflection.

A "bummer" may once have been a foot-soldier, but I never saw one who was not mounted on some sort of an animal. Sometimes he bestrides a superb blooded horse, which is the envy of every general in the army; more frequently he rides a broken-down nag that is able to hobble along sufficiently fast for its owner's purposes; but the favorite is the mule. There may be little or no actual poetry in a mule —although I profess an unwillingness to admit any slur upon that much-abused beast—yet it would be difficult to find a more hardy, long-winded, strong-legged, uncomplaining, and altogether lovable creature for the use of man than the mule. The "bummer" appreciates his good qualities, and hence the favoritism.

Sometimes we see the "bummer" approaching the camp from a piece of woods with a wagon which he has overloaded with good things. The scene is frequently exhilarating. The "bummer," coming in on horseback, holding the bridle in his teeth, clasps under one arm a basket of fresh eggs, and under the other a pailful of delicious honey, while a brace of fat sheep, hams, chickens, or geese, lie across the saddle in front and rear, and the carcass of a hog, firmly tied to the mule's tail, is dragged along the road. The "bummer" himself is probably clothed in an irregular sack-coat of linen, with a ridiculously unmilitary hat perched on one side of his head, and, as he approaches, his face beams with smiles of recognition, tempered by a half-suppressed apprehension lest his bounteous supplies should not be accepted as a peace-offering for his delinquencies.

Aside from the freedom from control which gives bad men opportunities to commit wanton deeds of violence, these wanderers from the ranks are often of great benefit to the army. Better flankers can not be found. Spreading out from the marching column, they are the first to scent danger, and the last to leave the field, unless actually forced back. They understand the art of squad-fighting to perfection. Parties of them, without officers, will join together to resist an onset of Rebel cavalry, or to make an attack upon the enemy, and they are almost always the victors in a skirmish.

When the army remains in camp for any length of time the "bummer" becomes absorbed in the great mass of the army.

But to the incident I was about to relate.

During the skirmish in front of Fayetteville, one of our captains, who was in advance of his men, crept, in a citizen's coat, up to a fence, in order to get a better look at the enemy, who were retreating, but firing rapidly. Suddenly he was confronted by a ragged and barefooted fellow, whom he instantly recognized as one of the "bummers." The recognition, however, was not reciprocal; for the "bummer" exulted in the thought that he had caught a Rebel, and proceeded to salute him thus:

"Halloa! just stop right thar," surveying his extremities. "I say, come up out o' them boots."

"I couldn't think of it," was the reply; "they are a fine pair of boots, and they are mine."

"You needn't say another d—d word. Come out o' them boots. P'raps you've got a watch about your breeches-pocket; just pull her out. No nonsense now; I'm in a hurry to get arter them Rebs."

"Perhaps you would like a horse?"

"A horse?" (the bummer's eyes sparkled). "A horse? Well, now, you jes come up out o' them boots, and we'll discuss that ar' hoss question sudden. Where is the hoss?"

"Oh, he is right near by, in charge of my orderly."

"Thunder! are you an officer of our army? I thought you was a Reb."

And then the "bummer" went to the rear under arrest, disgusted beyond measure.

THE "BUMMER."

CHAPTER XXV.

A FIGHT BETWEEN KILPATRICK AND HAMPTON—THE ARMY IN COMMUNICATION WITH WILMINGTON—DESTRUCTION OF THE FAYETTEVILLE ARSENAL—THE ARMY ACROSS CAPE FEAR RIVER—REFUGEES SENT TO WILMINGTON.

WE have just received news of a sharp fight between Kilpatrick and Hampton, at a place called Solomon's Grove. It appears that, by the movement of our left wing, the Rebel cavalry under Hampton and Wheeler were cut off from Fayetteville, the only point for sixty miles where they can cross the Cape Fear River. By one of those circumstances which speak more for Kilpatrick's courage and energy than for his caution, he had pushed a brigade of his command across an ugly swamp to an intersecting cross-road, and a highly important position. Hampton, with two divisions of cavalry, arrived by a side-road, to find his bold enemy across his path. There was nothing to be done but a reckless dash through the lines, and at it they went with courage, and, at first, with success; for, riding over the pickets before a shot was fired, they were in front of Kilpatrick's headquarters, captured the few men on guard, and nearly caught the General, who rode through them, it is said, not in full uniform. Hampton at once put a guard over the house, in which were several officers; but this success did not last five minutes. The little brigade had collected together in the swamp, and from that vantage-ground killed off the Rebels as rapidly as they could fire at them. Then, charging upon them, they recaptured their six-pounders and turned them upon the bold raiders.

Kilpatrick's men must have fought with terrible earnestness, for they had been surprised and driven out of their camps. Something besides their horses—their honor—was at stake.

The attack was made at daylight. The sun was two hours high before the Rebels had left the ground, with about one hundred and fifty prisoners and several horses as the only fruits of their venture. Seventy-six of their dead remained upon the field. It is sufficient evidence of the desperate defense of our soldiers, that the Rebels had no time to enter the house, so that the officers there were not captured.

It is not remarkable that an assault like this was partially successful, when the Rebels are familiar with every foot of the ground, and we strangers in the country. But it is the highest honor to our brave men that they so gallantly regained what was lost, and that in the face of thrice their own numbers. The fight cost us fifteen men killed and thirty wounded; but defeat was bravely turned into victory.

If one could have believed all the stories published in the Rebel papers during the late campaigns, our brave and dashing cavalry General would have appeared to be the spirit of some ancient hero, permitted to revisit the earth at will; for those remarkable journals have reported him killed, and his bold raiders vanquished, a hundred times. The best evidence that Kilpatrick is a gallant soldier and a competent commander, may be found in the fact that, since the moment we left Atlanta, he has so perfectly guarded and protected the flanks of the army, that in no instance has an infantry column been broken in upon by the enemy's cavalry.

In personal appearance General Kilpatrick is of slight stature, but broad-chested and wiry-limbed. His face is expressive of determination and daring. A firm chin, earnest mouth, prominent nose, clear gray eyes, and expansive forehead, make up a striking physiognomy. His beard is reduced to side-whiskers. He is an excellent, if not a graceful horseman. In conversation he speaks earnestly and rapidly, and has the great merit of placing the full value upon the services of his troopers, insisting upon their claim to all the honor due to their daring deeds. His officers and men have too often followed him in the wild charge not to repose perfect faith in him, or regard him with an enthusiastic affection.

Kilpatrick is a faithful, intelligent, and brave soldier; and in Major Estes he has an adjutant who is as gallant and chivalric a gentleman as ever drew sabre.

March 13*th*.—The army is now in full communication with Generals Terry and Schofield at Wilmington, by way of the Cape Fear River. A little army tug, which courageously ascended the river to this point, returned last night with a freight of newspaper correspondents, refugees, and a mail for our Northern friends. The arrival of this boat, with its attendant circumstances, was one of the thrilling episodes in the annals of war which recall the story of chivalric deeds done by brave men in mediæval days. The history runs thus:

On Wednesday morning of last week—five days ago—a scout started from our army to carry through a dispatch to General Terry, at Wilmington. He must have ridden fast, and without intermission, for the dispatch, which promised that we would be in Fayetteville on the Saturday following, was received by Terry on Friday night. It seemed as if

General Sherman's promise was believed to be as certain of fulfillment as if the event had already occurred, for the little tug and its gallant crew at once steamed up the river, a distance of ninety miles, to find us in possession of the town, which we had taken only six hours before; while in the distance across the river might be heard the cannon of the retreating foe. We are proud that men have such grand faith in the valor of the army and the word of our chief.

As the little steamer last evening sped swiftly down the stream with the glorious red, white, and blue showing against the green banks of the river, and its living freight springing to their feet, waving their hats, and cheering for their loved General, who stood watching them, I felt that choking sensation in the throat which makes tearful eyes. We of the army are not much given to weeping, but there was a moment then when I was not ashamed of a tear or two.

This morning a gun-boat came to anchor opposite the town, and again we welcome the blue jackets of the navy. I ought to say, however, that the officers of the navy arrived here last night. They had traveled on foot from Wilmington, taking the swamps and by-roads, and were sometimes in great danger of capture; but they bravely pushed on, and struck our column some ten miles from this place, in the rear. They are brave men; for that which would have been a comparatively easy task for one of our couriers, accustomed to the words and the tricks of the Rebels, was a difficult feat for these navigators of the sea.

To-night we expect the arrival of a number of transports with supplies. They will not detain us, for we shall unload them into the wagons rapidly, and then we must be up and away. For that matter, the larger part of the army is already on the northern side of the Cape Fear. Two pontoon bridges were finished the afternoon of the day we arrived here, and the troops at once commenced passing the stream.

We hear all sorts of rumors of the movements of the enemy, but pay little heed to them. One report is that either Hardee or Johnston intends to make a stand at Goldsboro'; another, that Lee is evacuating Richmond in order to throw his army into North Carolina; still another, that there is a large Rebel force in our rear. These stories, which float about among the citizens, give the army subjects for jest; the fact being that we know all that is necessary for us to know of Rebel movements. Beyond that we bother ourselves but little. Sufficient for us are our strong hands and our well-aimed muskets.

March 14*th.*—Last evening the transfer of our army to the left bank of the Cape Fear River was completed. The passage has been made easily, for a kindly sunlight has glowed upon us, and 'for once we have not laboured up steep banks nor through oceans of mud. We have left the town pretty much as we found it. Several public buildings, factories, and mills have been destroyed, but private property has been respected to a degree which is remarkable, when it is considered that the Rebels defended the town, killing our soldiers in the streets, and, in truth, shelling the place from the other side of the river after they had been driven out.

The destruction of the arsenal buildings was thorough. The splendid quarters for the officers, the machine-shops, armories, foundries, and stables, covering some twenty acres of ground, were in the first instance leveled by battering-rams, and then fired; so that there is not even a foundation left to build upon, should any disinterested individual ever desire to make an investment in public institutions in that locality. It was impossible to avoid a feeling of regret when these beautiful buildings were destroyed; but the stern behests of war must be obeyed.

Several transports arrived yesterday from Wilmington, bringing supplies for the army. They returned laden with our sick and wounded soldiers, and as many refugees as they could carry. We have also taken this opportunity to disencumber the army of the host of negroes who have joined us day by day from the hour we left the sea-coast. By order of General Sherman, all of these people have been gathered together from the different corps into one camp; and now, under the direction of a competent officer, with a sufficient guard and ample supplies, they are to march to Wilmington.

While the refugees were scattered throughout the command, it was not easy to ascertain their number. We can now arrive at an approximation. Upon our arrival at Fayetteville, there could not have been less than twenty-five thousand non-combatants who had joined our columns since our departure from Savannah. A very large proportion are negroes, chiefly women and children. As I look back upon the extraordinary march we have made, and reflect upon the stupendous difficulties which have been in the way of the successful transit of even so large an army as this, the fact of its accomplishment with twenty-five thousand useless, helpless human beings, devouring food, and clogging every step onward, will remain one of the marvels of military operations.

God help the poor creatures! They have endured exposure and suffering in pursuit of freedom, and they have attained the boon at last.

Thus far we have been altogether disappointed in looking for the Union sentiment in North Carolina, about which so much has been said. Our experience is decidedly in favor of its sister state; for we found more persons in Columbia who had proved their fealty to the Union cause by their friendliness to our prisoners than all in this state put together. The city of Fayetteville was offensively rebellious; and it has been a matter of surprise that our soldiers, who are quick to understand the distinction, have not made the citizens feel it in one way or another. Perhaps it is partially due to the fact that the 14th Corps has guarded the city, that such strict order has been maintained. This corps has had its share of the hard work, and but little of the perquisites of the campaign. Occupying the extreme left of the army, it has had more marching, being on the outside of the parabola, and harder work than any other corps, and has never had the fortune to capture a city, the central column generally striking important positions. But in this instance the left wing, in order to enter the town first, was swung round (as was the right, but withheld by orders from garrisoning the town). For these reasons, I suppose, the men of the 14th Corps wished to show the rest of the army how orderly they could behave, and they have succeeded remarkably well.

The army has not moved far to-day, probably not more than ten miles. It is curious to see how quickly the soldiers become conscious of the presence of an enemy—as upon a summer's day, opening fair and bright, one finds the presage of a storm, though there are but few clouds in the sky, floating lazily upon the edge of the horizon, while bees are humming, birds singing, and a gentle breeze rustling the leaves. There may be no marked indications of change, yet you feel an indefinable sense of a coming tempest. As I passed, to-day, our front of last night, I noticed a light breast-work thrown up, as if the soldiers had determined that a surprise should not find them unprepared.

CHAPTER XXVI.

THE BATTLE OF AVERYSBORO'.

March 15*th.*—The order of march has been changed. The larger part of our trains are thrown over to the right, and two thirds of the army are moving forward unencumbered with wagons. The truth is, we expect to meet the Rebels in all the force they can concentrate in our front by to-morrow or next day. Kilpatrick, who has the advance, ran into a strong body of Rebel infantry this afternoon, and skirmished with them until night came on. He captured several prisoners, among them Colonel Rhett, son of the noted Robert Barnwell Rhett, one of the "first family" names of which South Carolina is so proud. From the conversation of this Rebel colonel, I judge him to be quite as impracticable a person as any of his class. He seemed most troubled about the way in which he was captured. Some of Kilpatrick's fast riders got inside his skirmish line, and one of them, without any sort of regard for the feelings of a South Carolina aristocrat, put a pistol to the colonel's head and informed him, in a quiet but very decided manner, that "if he didn't come along he'd make a hole through him!" The colonel came; but he is a disgusted man. From what I know of the sentiments of Kilpatrick's men, I make no doubt that they would have had but little scruple in cutting off one branch of the family tree of the Rhetts if the surrender had not been prompt.

About the middle of this afternoon a heavy shower came up, with thunder and lightning; but no harm was done, except the discomfort of a wet camp and wet clothes, for we had made all the distance required for to-day. To-morrow we would prefer to see the sunlight; for, although we have a supreme contempt for the threats and evil prophecies of the Rebel newspapers that "North Carolina mud" is to stop an army which has built several hundred miles of corduroy roads within the last two months, yet we had rather march over dry ways when we can.

I have said that the order of march is changed with reference to the wagon trains. This refers more especially to the 20th and 14th Corps and Kilpatrick's cavalry, all of which are marching on the Cape Fear River Road—a route passing through Averysboro' direct to Raleigh. The right wing moves on roads leading more to the east, but within supporting distance, in order to be prepared for any immediate necessity of concentration. The Goldsboro' and Wilmington Railroad is threatened, and our movements mean the capture of Goldsboro' or Raleigh, or both. One division of the 20th Corps is detached, with the trains, on the right of the left wing.

March 16th.—The indications which induced the precautions of yesterday were not groundless. The storm has come. The blood of patriot hearts has again watered Southern soil; brave souls have passed into the spirit world; maimed and bleeding bodies lie suffering to-night.

Our troops have been fighting all day. The Rebels were found strongly posted, and in greater numbers than we anticipated; but, amid heavy showers of rain and powerful gusts of wind, our soldiers dashed bravely into the battle, one division after another; and the first day's fight is a victory to our arms in what will be known in history as the battle of Averysboro'!

The first infantry troops engaged were two divisions of the 20th Corps, who went forward to support the cavalry, which had found the enemy strongly intrenched behind earth-works upon the brow of a hill, skirted by a ravine and creek. After three or four hours' sharp fighting, in which our artillery, at four hundred yards' distance, silenced the Rebel guns in position, a brigade crossed their front, and went in with a rush upon their flank, while our entire line was advanced. The Rebels ran away as fast as they could, leaving in our hands three pieces of artillery—light twelve-pounders—and two hundred prisoners. They were closely followed by the victorious soldiers for half a mile, when they came upon another and more thoroughly built line of works, behind which it soon became evident the Rebels lay in great strength.

A division of the 14th Corps came up about noon, and were put in on our left. We then ascertained that the Rebel line of works stretched from Black Creek to the Cape Fear River, which at this point makes a bend to the east. Wherever we felt the Rebels' front we found the active presence of their infantry. Their force was composed of three divisions—commanded respectively by Butler, Rhett, and McLaws—amounting in all to ten thousand men, made up of the Charleston garrison of heavy artillery, and a portion of Hood's old command. In addition to this, Hampton and Wheeler, with their cavalry, were posted on our extreme right, covering the left flank of the enemy.

Although the engagement lasted all day, and into the night, the fight, after all, can scarcely be termed a battle. Six hundred men will probably be the whole number of our killed and wounded. The greatest loss sustained by our forces was that of the third division of the 20th Corps, under command of General Jackson. Captain Grafton, of this division (Second Massachusetts regiment), was among the killed. He was a gallant officer and a courteous gentleman. Twice dangerously wounded in Virginia, he has found a soldier's grave under the lofty pines of a Southern forest. He could not have found a nobler death, nor could we have lost a nobler soul. Colonel Morse, of the same regiment, was wounded later in the day, a ball piercing his arm above the elbow, but happily not touching the bone.

The Second and Thirty-third Massachusetts regiments are the only representatives of the glorious Bay State in our army. A nobler record of heroic deeds may never be found than in the history of the Second, which has suffered so severely to-day. On its roll of fame may be found among the names of those dead in honorable battle, Shaw, Dwight, Savage, Lowell, Grafton, Storrow, and others; and to-day the living heroes are models of chivalric soldiers, the pride of their comrades.

As night came on there was heavy musketry firing along the lines, especially near the main road. Many wounded were borne to the rear; many dead were left where they fell. Now and then the Rebel cannon would belch forth grape and canister. Above all this sound of battle could be heard the wild wind singing among the pine-tops; while the rain swept down in passionate, fitful showers upon true patriot and false traitor alike. God will care for those who have gone to Him this day. In the hospital yonder lie several hundred suffering ones: may He remember them in his infinite compassion!

March 17*th*. — The early morning found the Rebel intrenchments evacuated, and their former occupants in full flight toward Averysboro'. They escaped in the night, leaving their picket posts to fall into our hands; for a neglect to remember those who are placed in front to cover their movements is quite common among these chivalric Southern gentlemen when they wish to save themselves by running away. It is evident that the enemy suffered severely yesterday; although it is fair to suppose that our losses in wounded are greater than theirs. Their killed, however, probably outnumbers ours, on account of the short range of our artillery in the early part of the day, and their loss in prisoners, whom we captured whenever we pressed forward, we know to be heavy. We have already buried forty Rebels, and have one hundred wounded in our hospitals. We find the wounded scattered all along the line of the enemy's retreat to Averysboro'.

The regiment of Charleston heavy artillery, which is made up of the best blood of South Carolina, was in our immediate front during this fight. It fought well, and suffered severely both in officers and men. Although veterans in the service, this was its first field experience, and a very unpleasant experience it must have seemed.

A larger proportion of officers were wounded in this fight than in any I have known. In the latter part of the day there was very little artillery used upon our side. Our line was pushed up to within one hundred yards of the Rebel works. The swampy nature of the ground did not admit of the use of our batteries. Besides this, General Sherman did not wish to sacrifice unnecessarily any lives. He knew that General Howard, with the right wing, would, by noon of to-day, reach the road leading toward Goldsboro', which the Rebels were trying to hold. One division of the 20th Corps were on roads to the right, with the supply trains. This reduced our numbers nearly equal to the Rebels, with the advantage of position upon their side. We ascertained during the day that the principal object of the Rebels in holding this position was not so much to prevent our march to Raleigh as to give time for the crossing of their trains at the ferry near by on the Cape Fear River. These trains had been run up to this point from Fayetteville, and had not been ferried over.

The Rebels have shown more pluck than we have seen in them since Atlanta. To be sure, they were behind strong breast-works, and fully equaled us in numbers actually engaged, but they supposed the whole army would come up, which was half the battle to us in its moral effect upon them.

CHAPTER XXVII.

THE BATTLE OF BENTONVILLE—RETREAT OF JOHNSTON.

March 17*th, Evening.*—The left wing, with the exception of the cavalry and a division of infantry, has made a right wheel, and is marching in the direction of Smithfield and Bentonville. Until to-day our movement has been in the direction of Raleigh, and the evidence goes to show that the Rebels believed it to be General Sherman's intention again to gratify his taste for taking capitals. It is possible that our flank march of to-day will undeceive, although the cavalry and infantry which are thrust forward upon the Smithfield Road may continue to mislead them. The main body of the army is making for Goldsboro', but upon parallel roads so near together that musketry fire can be heard from one to the other.

We find the Rebel cavalry upon almost every road leading north. They generally have a section of artillery with them, which does little execution, for they fall back before the foraging parties, who band together whenever they meet the Rebel pickets, and, as they say, "pitch in for the fun of it."

The last two days have been sunny, and the air deliciously pleasant, full of the balmy influences of spring. The trees feel it, for the peach and apple are full of their delicate pink and white blossoms. Their delightful fragrance floats in the air, greeting us with Nature's tenderest offerings. We are passing through a well-cultivated country, with rich farm lands skirting the roadside. The houses are well built, the granaries are full of oats and corn, and our animals are getting their fill—much to their satisfaction, no doubt, for they have been on short rations for a day or two. The right wing has been very fortunate, for it has marched upon public roads, and has found more forage than it could bring away.

March 19*th*.—The headquarters' camp was pitched last night in the midst of the soldiers. Artillery, infantry, and cavalry surrounded us upon all sides, and we were lulled to rest by a hundred bugle-calls. This morning, before the dawn, I was aroused from sleep by a brigade band playing the tune of "Old Hundred," a grand old anthem, which never sounded to me more sweetly solemn than then, for with its strains came thoughts of home and dear ones there. I got up to find that it was Sunday, and with that knowledge came a longing for rest such as the soldier dares to indulge in but for a moment. It is a long campaign we have had, marching for sixty days over four hundred miles of an enemy's country, and repose would be welcome.

March 20*th*.—The extreme danger of a flank march was strikingly illustrated yesterday. By pushing on rapidly, without trains, and with but little artillery, Johnston was able to concentrate upon our left flank all the troops at his command, including Hood's old army and the sea-coast garrisons from Savannah to Wilmington. If we could have moved our trains at the ordinary pace, we should have passed this point and avoided a battle; but, as it was, General Slocum found the enemy in great force in his front. They did not give him much time to form his line, but attacked furiously, in the hope of beating his advanced divisions before the other columns could come up to his support.

In order to understand the situation, it is necessary to describe the order of march for the day.

Our first object was to reach Goldsboro', and all the heads of columns were pointed in that general direction. The 17th Corps was in the vicinity of Mount Olive, guarding the trains; the 15th Corps was on the direct road from Lee's Store to Cox's Bridge; the 14th and 20th Corps were on the Bentonville or Smithfield Road, which diverges to the right about five miles from Bentonville, forming a junction with a road leading to Cox's Bridge. It was at this crossroad, where the Rebels met our head of column, that the fight took place.

It should here be stated that the maps of North Carolina are old, none of them bearing a date later than the year 1854, and are therefore unsafe guides to follow. They misled some of our commanders in this instance. On the 17th of the month our advance had skirmished with the Rebel cavalry, driving them back and occupying the cross-road; but the reconnoissance which was made by our forces on the night of the 17th and the morning of the 18th did not develop the existence of any other road leading north to Bentonville. General Sherman had concentrated the heads of column of three corps at this point, as the last and perhaps the most dangerous where an enemy could strike our flank. The Rebels, in retreating before our left advance, had burned the bridges over what was supposed to be the only avenue to Bentonville and Smithfield, leading us most naturally to suppose that they had fallen back toward Raleigh.

Johnston, however, was well informed of what it was impossible for us to know, and took advantage of this new road to surprise our flanking column. In the morning, the 14th Corps, which was in advance, found cavalry in their front, which were driven back as usual; and it was not until a later hour that the presence of infantry was discerned behind hastily-constructed works. Some of these works were carried by an impetuous attack of our troops, but the two leading brigades soon found themselves environed by a largely superior force of infantry, and were forced back, leaving two guns mired in the swamp, which were not recovered.

By this time other brigades came up, and a line was formed, upon which the Rebels made three furious assaults, but they were repulsed by our artillery and musketry. The enemy finally retired from the field, leaving hundreds of dead, wounded, and prisoners in our hands.

At nightfall General Slocum had withdrawn his right and left wings, and this morning he is in a strong position, which the Rebels are not likely to attempt to force. It was not known in the right wing that any serious engagement was going on until late in the afternoon, when officers arrived with reports of the fight.

The events of yesterday may be summed up with the statement that Johnston hoped to catch our left wing and ruin it, and that he has been repulsed with a severe loss. Our casualties may all be included in a list of fifteen hundred men killed and wounded. The enemy's loss can not be less than three thousand killed and wounded. Meanwhile new dispositions are in active progress, and Johnston will find cause to repent most bitterly the manœuvre he has made.

March 20th, Evening. — Last night the detachments guarding the trains of the 14th and 20th Corps were all moved up to General Slocum's line. Hazen's division, which was yet on the road from Lee's Store, was marched back and put in position upon Slocum's right. The 17th Corps left the trains to the care of General Terry (who is coming up from Wilmington, and is now at Mount Olive), and, starting at midnight, arrived at Cox's Bridge, in the rear of two divisions of the 15th Corps. This column, at early dawn, was upon the road leading from Cox's Bridge to the cross-road where Johnston first struck our troops. As I have said, this was the road by which Slocum was to have passed to join the other portion of the army—intending to cover our left flank until we had reached the Neuse River. It will be seen, therefore, that the advance of the 15th and 17th Corps upon this road to-day took Johnston in the rear. Our troops moved rapidly forward, although many of them had marched a distance of twenty-five miles with empty stomachs. Brave fellows! rations are the last thing they think of when there is a foe to meet and beat.

During this advance the Rebels skirmished with the head of our column all the way until within half a mile of the cross-road. At this point our men found a strong force posted behind temporary intrenchments; but these were carried by assault, with a determination which astonished the enemy, who could not have anticipated the speedy approach of so large a force on their flank and rear, or, more properly, on their left flank. Each of our divisions, as soon as it came up, was placed in line. That old veteran and brave soldier, General Wood, was ordered to the left, with orders to make a junction with General Hazen on the right of General Slocum. Wood had a hard fight for the position, but he gained it before night; so that, while I am writing, there is a line of battle extending from Kilpatrick's station upon General Slocum's extreme left, beyond the Smithfield Road, to Mill Creek on the right. This creek empties into the Cape Fear River. The general direction of the line is northwest and southeast, corresponding to the Rebel line, which is refused upon each flank. The Rebel line is across the new Bentonville or Smithfield Road, which must be Johnston's line of supplies.

The afternoon has been spent upon our side in reconnoitring the enemy's position and firmly establishing our lines. The Rebels are evidently in great doubt as to our intentions, for by this time they must be aware that a large portion of the army is coming into position. They have greeted some of our more daring skirmishers, who crept too near their main line, with volley firing, which, however, does very little harm, while it shows that the enemy are perturbed.

March 21*st.*—During the whole of to-day there has been skirmishing and hard fighting from extreme right to extreme left. Wood, Corse, Hazen, and Smith, who are on the right, have pushed forward their line of battle until the skirmishers are within three hundred and fifty yards of Johnston's principal intrenchment, and now there is one unceasing roll of musketry. Every few minutes the artillery in position in the rear of Corse and Wood opens fire, and the forest re-echoes the loud, sharp report, with terrible grandeur. Repeatedly the Rebels dash out of their works, making frantic attempts to retake the rifle-pits out of which they have been driven; but they are as often forced back, leaving their dead and wounded to mark the scene of their discomfiture. On our left, General Davis has assaulted and captured a battery, but the men were driven back before they could bring it off, or the triumph be sustained by adequate support.

As we continue to develop the position of the enemy, we find the line, semicircular in form, refused upon the left quite sharply. This part of the Rebel line has been found

M

since our right wing swung in from Cox's Bridge. For some reason which does not yet appear, the Rebels contest every foot of ground with extraordinary pertinacity; more tenaciously than the occasion seems to require. Johnston has his entire force concentrated here. We have already captured men from the commands of Hoke, Hardee, and all the old corps of Hood's army. It is now evident that Johnston did not divine our flank movement from Fayetteville until we withdrew from Averysboro'. He had undoubtedly concentrated his forces at Smithfield, with the intention of striking us in flank if we moved upon Raleigh. On the 17th or 18th he heard of our advance upon Goldsboro', and made forced night marches for Bentonville, hoping to strike the 14th Corps in flank as it passed toward Cox's Bridge. On the afternoon of the 18th we knew there was nothing but cavalry upon that road, for our foragers and cavalry were as far advanced as the position now held by our right wing.

Johnston moved his army forward without wagons and but little artillery. He was thus able to get his troops into position faster than we could do, for our 20th Corps was covering the rear of this column, and, of course, had all its wagons in advance. Before nightfall, however, our troops were in position; and the Rebels, thinking they had a certain victory in prospect, made these repeated assaults, which were repulsed with a fearful loss to them. At every discharge, our artillery swept away the heads of their charging columns.

It appears certain that the line of battle now held by the Rebels is a new formation, intended for the attack of our right wing, which they are forced to guard against upon their flank and rear.

Evening.—This afternoon General Mower made a decided demonstration upon the extreme right. He pushed his division past General Smith, who was previously upon our extreme right. Advancing through forest and swamp, he carried two extensive lines of intrenchments, and then, after a hard fight, took a breast-work, which appeared to be the Rebel main line, half or three quarters of a mile in advance of Corse and Smith.

At this point our troops encountered a determined resistance from a large Rebel force, which attacked Mower at once in front and on both flanks. General Sherman gave directions to advance our entire line if the right wing should become engaged, but he did not desire to bring on a general fight. Mower was accordingly withdrawn, with a loss of about one hundred men killed and wounded; but not before he had disturbed the quiet of a Rebel battery in position, and destroyed one of its caissons. Mower's advance has evidently created a serious commotion in the ranks of the enemy, for the fire has broken out with renewed vigor from right to left. General Sherman thinks that our batteries are enfilading the Rebel lines.

It has not been an agreeable day for fighting. This morning the clouds gathered dark and threatening, and all the afternoon the rain has fallen, sometimes in fierce torrents. This is annoying to every one, and must be especially uncomfortable to the brave fellows in the advanced skirmish line, who can not be relieved until night sets in. Meanwhile the musketry rattles, and our cannon are hurling shot and shell into the Rebel camp.

General Sherman has anticipated the possibility of a few days' delay at this point, and already long trains of wagons are on their way to Kinston, to return speedily with supplies for the army. This responsible labor is under the charge of Colonel Garber, a gentleman of large heart and fertile brain, who has acted as chief quartermaster for the army during this campaign.

March 22*d*.—Victory! Johnston last night began to draw off his discouraged and defeated troops, leaving the field to us. It must be said to his credit that he made a bold effort, but it came near being his ruin. We have driven him beyond Mill Creek with our infantry, capturing hundreds of prisoners at every point. He has only saved his army by burning the bridges behind him.

Mower's reconnoissance of yesterday was perhaps the immediate cause of Johnston's speedy retreat. We know now how that movement must have carried consternation into the Rebel ranks. We have found the bodies of some of Mower's skirmishers within fifty yards of Johnston's headquarters; they were killed there and near the bridge, which was their principal line of retreat, and extending in the rear of the Rebel position. When Mower was ordered to move on our right, it was not supposed that he would advance so far; had that movement been intended, he would have had the support of the other divisions of the 17th Corps. With fifteen thousand such veterans as those of the glorious 17th Corps intrenched on Johnston's line of retreat, an attack along the entire line would have insured the total destruction of the Rebel army. Many noble men would have been lost who are now rejoicing in the fruits of a less bloody victory; but there would no longer have been the Rebel Army of the South. It is better as it is; for, although it may be for the good of future generations that this Rebel horde should be swept from the earth, yet this destruction carries death to many a true patriot who should live to enjoy the fruits of peace.

In truth, there never was a moment in history when the

A REBEL ASSAULT AT THE BATTLE OF BENTONVILLE.

grand strategy of war becomes so humane, so powerful as now. It is almost impossible in this contest for either one side or the other to catch his opponent unprepared. Both parties, in a wonderfully short space of time, will throw up defenses which can not be carried without a disastrous loss to the assaulting party.

War means bloodshed; yet there are ways of conquering a peace without excessive destruction of human life, and it is in this light that General Sherman's grand campaign looms up in magnificent proportions, equaling the most splendid achievements of the world's greatest captains.

The battle of Bentonville was General Slocum's fight. While his name is most honorably associated with almost every great battle of this war from Bull Run to Gettysburg in the East, and since that of Missionary Ridge in the West, the bloody combat at Bentonville was peculiarly his own affair, out of which he has come with fresh laurels. The unexpected attack, the fierce assaults, several times repeated, called for all the resources of a brave, cool, experienced soldier; but Slocum was more than equal to the necessities of the hour, for he was victorious, and his success justified General Sherman's selection of him as the commander of the left wing of the army.

General Slocum enjoys the reputation of a thoroughly accomplished soldier. It is probably owing to his complete mastery of all the details of his profession, his keen sense of order and discipline, and his energetic and magnetic manner, that the 20th Corps, which he commanded for a long time, has gained its splendid reputation. He is a native of New York, and is as proud of his state as his state is proud of him. His personal appearance is prepossessing. Long, wavy brown hair, brushed back behind his ears, sparkling brown eyes, a heavy brown mustache, a height above the medium, and a manner which inspires faith and confidence, make up a most attractive figure. He seems to know precisely what he has to do, and to be perfectly sure that he can do it. It is very certain that he is one of those rare men who has made no mistakes. He should thank Heaven and be happy.

There are other commanders who have been prominent in this battle.

General Morgan's division of the 14th Corps received the first shock of conflict. A younger soldier than General Morgan, or one less brave and not so cool, would have been appalled at the furious onset; but he gathered his scattered forces well in hand, and awaited the arrival of assistance, but the Rebels became too numerous for him to resist successfully. Speaking of this fight, he said: "For the first time in my experience, I was attacked in flank and rear, and was obliged to form my line outside my own breastworks." Morgan, who is a man of small and wiry figure, is an earnest, modest, and conscientious soldier.

In this battle, also, General Jeff. C. Davis displayed those admirable soldierly qualities which have distinguished him. It was said at the beginning of the war that General Davis had a leaning of strong sympathy toward the Rebels. If the rapid formation of a line temporarily driven back, and the concentration of half a dozen batteries of artillery to belch forth grape and canister upon the Rebel charging column, shows any affinity for rebellion, then he has it. General Davis is a prompt, energetic, hard-working soldier, who understands his profession, and does his whole duty faithfully and conscientiously. He has an earnest way in conversation, like most men of decided opinions; but his earnestness is rather of speech than of manner.

General Charles Wood, one of the best fighting men in

the Western army, is an officer but little known in the East. His service has been chiefly on the border, and in the armies of the West. He is familiarly designated by the officers of the old army as "Susan" Wood. I should not mention this feminine title if it were ever used in any disrespectful sense; for no man who has ever met this stanch, loyal soldier in the line of service can think of him except with courteous admiration. He commands the first division of the 15th Corps. What he is, and what they are, may best be told in the history of every campaign, and almost every battle fought west of the Alleghanies. When their skirmish line advances, somebody must give way; and when they get their feet once planted, there is a line of battle which they hold with a tenacity that can not well be imagined by any one who has never experienced that peculiar sensation of the whiz of a score or more of bullets. In a battle, I know of no safer position than behind Wood's division, for it never falls back without extraordinary cause. What is said of the division is said of Wood: soldiers take their spirit from their commander.

General Wood is a tall, and not altogether graceful man, with a quiet, blunt manner. He is honest, large-hearted, and brave.

M 2

CHAPTER XXVIII.

ENTERING GOLDSBORO'.

Goldsboro', March 22d.—The army has entered Goldsboro'. Its march has been delayed seventy hours by Johnston's operations, but the interruption has not materially interfered with the plans of our General. Yesterday General Terry moved up to Cox's Bridge, laid a pontoon, and crossed a part of his troops. General Schofield is in Goldsboro'. Our army will at once be moved into position in the vicinity of this place to refit for the next campaign; not only to be reclothed, but to gain the repose it needs. Mind, as well as body, requires rest after the fatigues of rapid campaigns like these. These ragged, bareheaded, shoeless, brave, jolly fellows of Sherman's legions, too, want covering for their naked limbs.

Yet, with all the hardships of the campaign, the surgeons' returns show the wonderfully healthy condition of the army. Only two per cent. of sick are in hospital. A much larger proportion of the army would be in hospital had we remained quietly in camp during the past two months. The great majority of the soldiers are strong, healthy, cheerful, confident. The mental strain, however, is visible in the general air of lassitude in the army. Relief from active duty for a few days will restore the balance, and remedy this evil.

The explanation of this psychological phenomenon is found in other causes than bodily conditions. When the army cut loose from the sea-coast, and began the invasion of South Carolina, there were but few of its soldiers who did not comprehend the precarious and dangerous nature of the undertaking. They were confident in their own strength; they had a proud, sublime faith in the genius of their leader; they trusted, without knowledge of his plans or his combinations, that they would come out safe somewhere; yet there was constantly before them a shadowy future, and a possibility of impending and unseen danger: thoughts of the great distance from a base, and from safe anchorage ground; pictures of wide and swollen streams, bays, and marshes; images of gloomy forests and arid desert lands, which were to be traversed by night and day. The presence of the foe, or the roar of artillery and the rattle of musketry, have few terrors for the veteran soldier, but no man can avoid the influence of a mysterious, unknown danger; and to him whose heart and soul are bound up in the nation's honor, the thought of possible disaster to the cause adds to his anxiety.

Therefore, we are all glad that we have reached a place of rest. With a few days of quiet for animals and men, rehabilitated mentally and physically, and equipped with supplies for future wants, we will soon be ready to strike another blow for our nationality.

March 24*th*.—The army is marching through the city to the designated camping-ground, where it will for the present remain. As the troops passed through, we found food for infinite merriment in the motley crowd of "bummers." These fellows were mounted upon all sorts of animals, and were clad in every description of costume; while many were so scantily dressed that they would hardly have been permitted to proceed up Broadway without interruption. Hundreds of wagons, of patterns not recognized in army regulations, carts, buggies, barouches, hacks, wheel-barrows, all sorts of vehicles, were loaded down with bacon, meal, corn, oats, and fodder, all gathered in the rich country through which the "bummers" had marched during the day. Quartermaster General Meigs should have been here to see the funny additions made to his department.

As a barefooted soldier here and there appeared in the ranks, it was difficult to repress an expression of sympathy for them, although the brave fellows themselves are the last to complain of any thing. One of them said to me, a day or two ago:

"My shoes gave out eleven days ago, sir; but I don't care. My feet are getting used to it, but the corduroy is awful hard to travel over."

As brigade, division, and corps, with measured tread, marched into the city, every man seemed to bear himself with conscious pride. The fresh breeze displayed each flag and banner, and one might have read there the historic names of "Fort Donelson," "Shiloh," "New Orleans," "Port Republic," "Vicksburg," "Malvern Hills," and "Atlanta," and many another field of battle. How the heart thrills at these words!

But few trophies were brought along with the army. There were two twenty-pounder Rebel Parrott guns, captured by the first division of the 17th Corps; a Blakely, English gun, presented to the State of South Carolina by one of her citizens abroad; and two forty-two-inch shell, thrown into Charleston by the monitors, and presented to the Columbia Arsenal by Beauregard. These relics will be sent North by General Hazen, of the 15th Corps.

It is a proud moment for General Sherman and his two lieutenants, Howard and Slocum, to watch this brave army as it moves along—safe, after ten months of ceaseless marching, working, and fighting, with its *morale* and its organization, to the last regiment and the last company, intact as when it left Savannah. The consciousness of this great achievement, and the knowledge that a grateful nation greets them and their army with glad pæans, are more than compensation or reward.

The army has indeed accomplished a great work, and gained important ends. Let us look for a moment at the results.

In the record of great wars we read of vast armies marching through an enemy's country, carrying death and destruction in their path; of villages burned, cities pillaged, a tribe or a nation swept out of existence. The deeds of Alexander's conquering legions, the conflicts of the Roman and the Gaul, have passed into history, and are almost shadowy myths; but war, with its terrible consequences, remains nearly the same now as then. There are ameliorations introduced by the agencies of modern civilization; but the Minié bullet and the bursting shell take human life even more mercilessly than the ancient spear and battle-ax. History, however, will be searched in vain for a parallel to the scathing and destructive effect of the Invasion of the Carolinas. The immediate disasters to the Rebel cause, the cities captured, arsenals and munitions of war destroyed, the communications severed, will be appreciated by the military mind in Europe, as well as by our own army and people. But, putting aside the mere military question for a moment, there are considerations which, overleaping the present generation, affect the future existence of the section of country through which our army has marched.

Over a region forty miles in width, stretching from Savannah and Port Royal through South Carolina, to Goldsboro', in North Carolina, agriculture and commerce, even if peace come speedily, can not be fully revived in our day.

The greater and more prolific portion of the Carolinas is of a swampy nature. The rivers, rising in the mountains of Tennessee, descend into the plains, gliding sluggishly, in parallel lines, to the sea. Commerce has justified the building of but few lines of railways, which, widely separated, traverse these states. Thus the means of communication between the people, the towns and cities, has been upon the highways. Over the numerous rivers and creeks bridges have been built at enormous expense. Upon our approach, hundreds of these costly causeways have been burned by the Rebel military authorities, in spite of the protests and prayers of the inhabitants. Often they were burned apparently from a petty feeling of spite, as, for instance, in the vicinity of Columbia, and on the Big and Little Salkahatchie, the Upper and Lower Edisto, the Congaree, Saluda, Broad, Wateree, Santee, Pedee, Cape Fear, and Neuse Rivers. Over all of these streams, bridge after bridge has been devoured by the flames. All this is a minor incident in the record of devastation. Day by day our legions of armed men surged over the land, destroying its substance. Cattle were gathered into increasing droves; fresh horses and mules were taken to replace the lame and feeble animals; ricks, granaries, and store-houses were stripped of corn, fodder, meal, and flour; cotton-gins, presses, factories, and mills, were burned to the ground; on every side, the head, centre, and rear of our column might be traced by columns of smoke by day, and the glare of fires by night. Injury to private dwellings was forbidden, and food for present necessities was often left for the women and children; but, in all the length and breadth of that broad pathway, the burning hand of war pressed heavily, blasting and withering where it fell. It was the penalty of rebellion.

But some will say, "The land is still there, and with the

return of peace agriculture and commerce will revive." Perhaps so—if the laborers yet remain whose hard hands tilled the soil, and gathered the corn and cotton, and cut the timber for the bridges. The swarthy slave, however, the sweat of whose brow enriched the lord of the soil, has turned his back upon the master. He has joined the army of the Union, and to-day he is earning the bread he eats, and the freedom he has gained is in his hand. No! the labor which was once the life of this country has gone out of it. The South must hereafter live a new life.

In the campaign of the Carolinas the future historian will find ample material for the illustration of all the great principles known in the art of war, even if he does not discover precedents which are not established in the books of the present day. Among the infinite details included in the daily operations of so large an army, there are pre-eminent considerations which it may be well to note here. It has already been said that, when our columns pushed up from the sea-coast, Beauregard's strongest line of defense was the Salkahatchie; but his earlier steps were fatal to his cause, and insured the success of our movement toward our first objective—Columbia—if not to the final triumph of our campaign. Beauregard committed the gross error of attempting to defend cities which possessed no strategic value, neglecting, or having been ignorant of the truth, that the surest road to a successful system of defense was the concentration of all his forces upon the line of the Salkahatchie, and the abandonment of Charleston, Augusta, and all other garrisoned places. Although it would have been no easy task, we will suppose that Sherman had outflanked and forced this line. By moving upon converging lines, the Rebel leader could always have had the choice of a central position, which he could have occupied sooner than our army, obliged as it would have been to cross the river encumbered with trains. Such a point was Branchville, on our right; and another was Augusta, on the left. The advantage of either of these positions would have been that, if our objective had been Charleston, with the Rebel army at Branchville, even though we had succeeded subsequently in crossing the Edisto, the enemy would have been in our front or flank. Had Augusta been our objective, the enemy could have thrown a dangerous force in our rear. Again: if Beauregard had fallen back to Augusta, and our objective had been either that place or Charleston, the same logic would have held good. The Rebel army would have been as near Columbia as ours, with greater facilities for reaching the capital before us, had we marched in that direction.

Of the three defensive positions here indicated, unquestionably that of Orangeburg was the best; for, while it possessed all the advantages of the other two, it left open a safe line of retreat toward the Rebel army in the East, while a retreat upon Charleston might have resulted in the hemming in and capturing of their entire force at that place.

Johnston executed precisely the manœuvre thus indicated after we crossed the Cape Fear River. No doubt he would have disputed the passage of that stream, and, indeed, that of the Pedee at Cheraw, but that he labored under grave disadvantages. Sherman was moving upon interior lines with singular directness and rapidity. Johnston had but just assumed command of the Rebel troops, which had been scattered by his predecessor; and a concentration of these detachments was Johnston's first aim. He chose the position of Smithfield because it was at a convenient distance from Kinston, where Schofield stood watching and waiting for the commands of Sherman. Smithfield also covered Raleigh; while, in the event of disaster, there was a wide door open in his rear toward the Danville Railroad.

The great error in Johnston's calculation lay in the supposition that Sherman's objective was Raleigh. His discovery of the change made in the direction of our columns came too late to be of practical advantage to him; and, indeed, he was fortunate, after the battle of the 19th, to get away without the loss of his entire army.

I have thus detailed the late movement of Johnston at the risk of repetition, because it signally illustrates the wisdom of his strategical combinations, as opposed to the ruinous policy of Beauregard, who, by attempting to hold widely separated posts in order to prevent invasion, gave Sherman easy access by the line which he had chosen in the beginning. As in the Georgia campaign, Sherman had alternatives to which he would have turned had physical or other causes barred his way; yet, in view of the natural obstacles overcome, and the victories of Averysboro' and Bentonville, he would be a presumptuous critic who could suggest the idea of failure in that campaign which has culminated so gloriously at Goldsboro'.

There is another incident affecting General Sherman's immediate operations which finds a place here. Shortly after we left Savannah, one or more of the newspapers at the North published the information that Sherman had changed his base of supplies from Hilton Head to Morehead City. This statement was eagerly copied by the Rebel papers. Johnston at once saw that Wilmington was not our objective. He made a show of opposition at Fayetteville, while he exerted every means in his power to concentrate his army between the Cape Fear and Neuse Rivers: the battles of Averysboro' and Bentonville, with their carnage and death, were the result. Upon whose head rests that shedding of blood?

It should be added that there were co-operative movements which distracted the attention of the enemy from our intended line of march. General Foster, in command of the Department of the South, was instructed to continue his demonstrations upon Charleston, both from the direction of Pocotaligo and upon James Island. At the same time, Admiral Dahlgren moved a large fleet into Bull Bay, and succeeded in making a landing of one thousand men. To the enemy these operations seemed to indicate Charleston or Georgetown as the objective of Sherman. While these demonstrations were made from the sea, Stoneman, a brave and capable cavalry officer, had moved down the valley of the Tennessee in the direction of the passage in the mountains known as Broad Gap. His instructions were to endeavor, as far as was prudent, to join Sherman's command; but to use his force in such a manner as to give the enemy the impression that an army corps was approaching. Stoneman found it impracticable to push through to Sherman's army, but he succeeded most admirably in convincing Lee that an army corps was actually descending from the mountains upon the most useful line of the Rebel communications.

Still another expedition was in progress. Schofield, detached from Thomas, had transported a considerable portion of the Army of the Ohio by land and sea to Newbern, North Carolina. This was the most important movement of all. More than a mere demonstration, its success was directly co-operative, as the result proved; for, while Schofield's advance upon Kinston did not prevent a concentration of the Rebels in front of Sherman, it delayed that event until Sherman and Schofield were within supporting distance of each other.

There were two incidents—one of omission and the other of commission—which were properly within the scope of Sherman's operations. It is generally understood that Thomas was ordered to advance into Alabama simultaneously with the movement across the Carolinas. The bad condition of the roads is the reason assigned for the delay, or, rather, for the failure to move. It may be thought that a descent upon Montgomery and Selma might be too distant, geographically, to influence Sherman's march; but it is fair to suppose that such an expedition would have retained at those points the fragments of Hood's army, which subsequently fought us at Averysboro' and Bentonville. This was the act of omission. The act of commission is so inextricably and most unfortunately connected with political considerations that it is hardly proper for it to find a place here. For several reasons the capture of Fort Fisher and the city of Wilmington was supposed to be of immediate importance; yet every military mind can see at a glance that the occupation of Fayetteville involved the evacuation of Wilmington, or the surrender of its garrison without any sacrifice of life. At the same time, Wilmington was of use to Sherman when he arrived at Fayetteville; but the Cape Fear River was not necessary to the successful completion of the campaign.

In reviewing this campaign, with its captured cities; its trophies of cannon and munitions of war; its destruction of arsenals, magazines, subsistence, and railroads; its splendid tactical combinations; its still grander strategic features; its victories over apparently insurmountable obstacles, both natural and artificial; its final arrival at the pre-arranged objective point intact, after defeating the concentrated Rebel armies of the South, I can not look upon it as a unit, but rather as a part, like the campaigns of Atlanta,

Georgia, the Carolinas, and the march yet to be made; all forming a harmonious whole.

Goldsboro', April 8*th.*—The period of the army's stay at Goldsboro' is short, but marked by extraordinary activity in every department. General Sherman has given the command until the 10th of April to rest and refit. The day of the entrance of the army witnessed the arrival of the first train of cars from Newbern, the soldiers replying to the well-remembered scream of the locomotive whistle with vociferous shouts of welcome.

It is marvelous to see with what energy and promptitude the army is supplied with ammunition, quartermaster's, and commissary stores. Quartermaster General Meigs is again among us, giving his personal attention to the requirements of his department. In fourteen days twenty thousand men have been furnished with shoes, to replace those which had been worn out in the late march; one hundred thousand men have been supplied with clothing, etc., the necessities of a campaign for thirty days. What an interesting, valuable history will one day be written of the herculean task performed by these branches of the service!

Meanwhile the army has quietly settled into its camps about the city, upon the hill-sides, and in the sweet-scented pine forests. Water is found in plenty every where, and its liberal use has an excellent sanitary effect upon the soldiers.

During the fortnight just passed, General Sherman made a visit to City Point, where he met President Lincoln, Lieutenant General Grant, and other generals of the Eastern army, and a plan for future operations was agreed upon. During our march from Savannah, the Army of the Potomac had been preparing for a movement in the direction of

Dinwiddie Court-house. General Sherman received his orders for a co-operative movement, which would have placed his army in junction with the Army of the Potomac. Upon his return to Goldsboro', all things had been made ready; the new order of march was issued, which directed the army to move toward Weldon and the line of the Roanoke, when the thrilling, glorious news reached us of the splendid victories in front of Petersburg, the capture of that city, and the retreat of Lee's army. Certainly, in all the land, there were no prouder or more exultant hearts than in this army. With one accord they said:

"These grand successes, this overthrow of Lee's army, are the legitimate fruits of the bloody battle-fields in Virginia. They are reaping the reward of their suffering and bravery. This victory belongs to them, and we are glad they won it for and by themselves."

General Grant's overwhelming success at once caused a change of direction in the movement of this army. The situation has changed somewhat from that of the campaign just ended. Then our objective was a designated point on the sea-coast, or in the interior. The chief purpose aimed at was prospective rather than immediate: we were not eager to fight great battles. Now the only objective is the Rebel General Johnston and his host, and such remnants of Lee's army as may escape General Grant's hot pursuit.

While the army has been resting and refitting, its organization has undergone important changes. The right and left wings are retained as before, with their old commanders, Generals Howard and Slocum; the left wing, however, has the additional designation of the "Army of Georgia."

The organization has been made complete by the formation of a central column. The 23d Corps, under command of General Cox; the 10th Corps, and portions of the 24th Corps, commanded by General Terry, now constitute a central column under the direction of General Schofield.

Kilpatrick reports, as before, directly to General Sherman, and his command is increased by a regiment of Pennsylvania cavalry which has hitherto been attached to General Terry.

There is one characteristic of this noble army which I mention here proudly and gladly. I do not believe there ever was an army where there is so little petty jealousy among the officers generally, or between the different corps and their commanders. There is worthy emulation, such as becomes brave men fighting in a common cause; but the various organizations work together in harmonious co-operation, insuring success and bringing honor to all.

The army has occasion again to be grateful for the prompt manner with which the mails have been forwarded. One of the first persons who met General Sherman when he descended the Ogeechee River the night of the capture of Fort McAllister, was Colonel Markland, known throughout the army as the chief army mail agent. The day following he landed several tons of mail matter, and now he has performed the same thankful office here. Colonel Markland is a gentleman of great efficiency, energy, and capacity.

A few words concerning the general officers not already named will not be inappropriate, in connection with the reorganization of the army, in closing this part of our record.

General Mower has been relieved from the command of a division in the 17th Corps, and appointed to the command of the 20th Corps. The 17th has lost a favorite officer, and the 20th has gained a noble chief. Few officers in the service have distinguished themselves like Mower; for, while there may be some who possess more military genius, none are more absolutely indifferent to personal danger than he. At Vicksburg he led a charge up a road which was exposed to the fire of two batteries. He lost half his men, and failed in an attempt which would never have been made but for the representation of a general officer who has since left the service. Mower has been on the skirmish line and in the very front of battle ever since. It is said in the army that "three successive sets of his staff officers are in Heaven;" but, strange to say, the chief of these braves has never been hit. His manner in social life is exceedingly courteous, reserved, and unobtrusive. He is almost painfully reticent in conversation, but under fire his presence of mind and gallantry incite to great deeds. He is always confident in battle, and would be termed rash, but that he usually succeeds in what he attempts.

Mower is a man of athletic frame, tall and well proportioned; his rich brown hair is long and thick; his beard is of the same tint, and very full; a large Roman nose makes a wide separation between his large brown eyes; and a broad, expansive forehead crowns a face which belongs decidedly to the antique. He is one of General Sherman's favorites, has few enemies, is in the regular army, and is not a West Pointer.

General Williams, one of the oldest officers of high rank in the army, has had a singular experience. Before the appointment of General Mower to the 20th Corps, he held temporary command of that part of the force, succeeding General Slocum by virtue of rank. He was a division commander at Bull Run and Fredericksburg, and a corps commander at Chancellorsville. At Gettysburg he was in command of the 12th Corps, but went back to a division again' when the 11th and 12th Corps were united in the 20th; afterward became corps commander again; and, now that General Mower has been appointed to the command of that corps by order of the President, he once more returns to his division. This shifting and changing is a part of the fortune of war, and not the fault of Williams, for it is universally conceded that he is one of the best officers in the service. He has been in many trying positions, and no charge of blunder or failure lies at his door. A favorite with officers and men, he is delightfully hospitable, possesses an unfailing fund of good humor, is thoroughly subordinate, unenvious, unselfish, and as cool and self-possessed in the battle-field as at his quarters. In person, he is heavily built, about the medium height, with a large beard and still larger mustache, which lend a peculiar expression to the face—an expression, however, which is forgotten when the genial, kindly eyes light up in conversation.

It is not pleasant to go back to a division when an officer has commanded a corps; but Williams has received the warmest thanks of his brigade commanders (and the thanks of such brave soldiers as Hawley, Selfridge, and Robinson are worth having) for acceding so cheerfully to their request to resume command of his old division.

General Schofield is a gentleman of fine address and elegant manners. There is nothing of the plausible sycophant either in his words or his actions. He listens well, talks but little, and appears to reflect and carefully weigh both what he hears and says. At the first view of his round and well-developed head, his resolute mouth, and calm, reflective eyes, one is impressed with the idea that he is in the presence of a statesman rather than a soldier. Perhaps Schofield partakes of the character of both. His brilliant military history proves him to be a superior soldier. When General Sherman detached the 23d Corps from Rome with Schofield to join Thomas, he knew that he was sending back one of the most trusty generals of his army. The battle of Franklin justified that act, and later, when Schofield was intrusted with that most important of all the co-operative movements of the late campaign, the advance from Newbern, Sherman was positive that Schofield would march into Goldsboro', if it lay within the power of man to accomplish the task. Schofield was there at the appointed day.

General Schofield not only possesses will and purpose, but he is perfectly versed in that technical knowledge of his profession without which will is almost valueless. While he may not be gifted with that dash and spirit which characterize other commanders, he has a calm assurance and a sober judgment which are never disturbed, even in the hour of repulse or disaster, and which is quick to seize the moment when success, wrung from doubt, carries victory. Such is the commander of the Army of the Ohio.

The 23d Corps is under the command of General Cox— a tall man, with small and finely-marked features, expressive of earnestness and manliness. Cox wears his hair cut closely to his head, and his full beard is neatly trimmed. He is always well dressed, and he has the manners of a well-poised gentleman. He has served during the greater part of the war as a brigadier general, always doing his duty well. Promptitude is one of his great merits. When General Sherman was in pursuit of Hood, he stood one evening upon the top of Pine Knob, eagerly watching the western horizon for indications of the presence of an army. Cox had just arrived upon the ground with his head of column, by a detour round the eastern base of Kenesaw. Welcoming him, General Sherman pointed in the direction of the Allatoona and Dallas Road, and said: "General Cox, I wish you to push out upon that road until you strike the Dallas Road. Let me know the position of your head of column by a flame and smoke. Burn barns, houses, any thing; but let me see from this point where you are."

General Cox instantly departed. In a few moments a blue column of smoke rose up into the still air, and then another, and yet again another—stretching out and winding among the hills and valleys, creeping up out of the forest, and gradually lost in the gray and purple twilight. No sound of cannon disturbed the exquisite beauty of the scene, and these silent witnesses of the forward steps of our soldiers told us that no enemy was near. Cox's merit in this movement was that of prompt and vigorous action at the right moment.

Goldsboro', April 10*th*.—The grand army which begins a new campaign to-day is perhaps the finest organization in numbers and material that has ever taken the field in this country. The men are not raw recruits, hastily gathered together and pushed into the service to fill up a gap in wasted battalions, nor are they troops so long used to garrison life as to render them unserviceable for active work, but a grand army of veterans, who have marched and fought over one half the continent.

They set out under many favorable auspices; led by one of the Captains of the age, whose face and form have become familiarized by his presence upon a hundred battle-fields, the plaudits of the nation are yet ringing in their ears in praise of their splendid campaigns and battles in Georgia and the Carolinas. Lee's shattered columns are flying before the heroic soldiers of the Army of the Potomac.

The army is complete in all respects, and starts full of life and in the grandest of spirits. We hope to see the rebellion fully extinguished before the autumn leaves begin to fall.

PART III.

THE SURRENDER AND THE END:

CHAPTER XXIX.

SMITHFIELD—THE BEGINNING OF THE END.

Smithfield, April 12*th.*—Last night, the army, which had drawn out of Goldsboro' during the day, camped at a point ten miles from that place, on the main road leading toward Smithfield. The 20th Corps had the advance, on the road nearest the Neuse River, the 23d Corps following in the rear. The 14th Corps marched, four miles to the right, upon what is known as the Little River Road. In this movement our extreme right wing consists of the Army of the Tennessee, composed of the 15th and 17th Corps. We skirmished actively with Rebel cavalry all the way to this place, losing perhaps twenty men killed and wounded.

The country which we have traversed is rich in corn and fodder, notwithstanding its recent occupation by the Rebel armies. Handsome two-story houses are the homes of the owners of the most prolific farms in the Southern country. We see wheat-fields once more, and the yield of cereals is more like that of Ohio and Wisconsin. The people are intelligent, and profess a sort of half-way Unionism—*i. e.*, they want the war closed.

Johnston left this place on the 10th, moving toward Raleigh. A part of his force crossed at the bridge here, while the main body moved up to Battle's Bridge, thirteen miles above. As usual, the Rebels destroyed the bridges behind them; gaining but little, however, even in point of time, by that act, for our pontoons are already laid across the stream, and the army will move over in the morning.

The Rebel newspapers assert that Wilson's cavalry has taken Selma and destroyed it. If this report is true, the success of the movement will have a most important bearing upon the closing of the war. Thomas is reported to be coming down the valley of the Tennessee, while Stoneman is represented to be at or near Charlotte. The net is fast closing about the remnant of the Rebel army.

Smithfield, an ancient city, but neither wealthy nor beautiful, was captured yesterday by the 14th Corps, which had been in possession for two hours when the 20th Corps entered the place. The enemy made a desperate effort at defense, fighting stubbornly in the streets, erecting barricades, shooting at our men as they advanced, and frightening the women and children, but fortunately none of the latter were injured. Our troops pressed steadily forward and took the town.

The court-house and jail stand in the public square; and that relic of the past, the public stocks, stood by the side of the jail until our progressive soldiers cut down the machine and burned it. The River Neuse winds around the edges of the town; its steep banks lined with beautiful flowering shrubs, and clothed with the fresh green of spring.

We found a few citizens, who seemed to be undemonstrative Union men. The ladies are about equally divided; that is, we again meet with the same experience which is found throughout the South. When a woman has a lover or a near relative in the Rebel army her sympathy is naturally with the Confederate cause; yet all we meet are anxious for the return of peace.

April 13*th*.—In the order of march described yesterday the army has moved upon Raleigh. The central column and left wing crossed the river at Smithfield, the right wing going over at Battle's Bridge, fifteen miles farther up. The information we have received seems to indicate that Johnston will not fight until he reaches the Danville and Charlotte Road.

This morning news of the surrender of Lee reached us. Our army went wild with excitement when this glorious result was announced, and blessings were showered upon the grand old Army of the Potomac, which, after so many mortifying failures, is thus crowned by Grant's genius with magnificent laurels. Our troops gave cheer after cheer to express their joy, and then, when cheers became too feeble an expression, uttered yell upon yell until they waked the echoes for miles around. Then the bands burst forth in swelling strains of patriotic melody, which the soldiers caught up and re-echoed with their voices. Every body was proud and glad. In the language of our noble General, "Glory to God and our glorious country!"

With light step and eager hearts the soldiers have filed out upon the roads all day, marching with the elation of victory. The heads of columns have had some skirmishing with Rebel cavalry during the day; but every thing has been so quiet in the rear of the advanced guard, that no one would have supposed there had been any fighting at the front but for the occasional sound of booming cannon. Along the ranks the soldier shouted to his comrade, "We must push Johnston now!" Whenever Johnston makes a stand, there will be one of the quickest and most effective battles known in history. Our men are all ready for a furious onslaught upon any foe that may choose to meet them.

To-night the army has halted some fourteen miles from

Raleigh. Kilpatrick, who this afternoon passed ahead of our extreme left wing, came upon Hampton's cavalry in force, and is reported to have whipped the Rebels handsomely. At any rate, he captured a train of railroad cars which were returning to Raleigh. It appears that several citizens, including ex-Governors Swain and Graham, had received permission to go to General Sherman with a letter from Governor Vance, containing propositions which should protect the state from ravage and destruction. This permission was afterward countermanded by Hardee, who probably acted under the orders of Jeff. Davis, who has continued his journey southward, and is now at Greensboro'. Unfortunately, Kilpatrick interfered with authority which, for the moment, was superior to that of Hardee—the authority of several thousands of strong arms wielding good sabres. Kilpatrick, getting into Hampton's rear, drove three of his brigades from their position, scattering them in every direction, and capturing a large number of prisoners. The train containing the embassy was also cut off and taken. The passengers were prisoners, so far as civilians could be prisoners of war, for they had been turned back by Johnston's authority from the fulfillment of their mission. They were brought thence to the army, to receive General Sherman's response to Vance's letter. What this answer will be remains to be seen.

A few days ago Vance was fearfully belligerent and valiant in his threats to demolish this army; but affairs have suddenly changed.

The envoys from Raleigh say that the railroad between Greensboro' and Danville is cut, so that the dashing Stoneman is probably on the track. If we can reach the railroad first, Johnston will be in precisely the same situation that Lee was in on the Appomattox, and the result will most likely be the same.

CHAPTER XXX.

THE CAPITAL OF NORTH CAROLINA—ITS SURRENDER.

Raleigh, April 14*th.*—The capital of North Carolina was yesterday occupied by General Sherman. The victory was bloodless, with a single exception. A Rebel fired upon General Kilpatrick as he entered the public street, after the place had been surrendered by Hampton; and although the poor wretch harmed no one, he was hanged at once for his attempted assassination.

The movement of the army upon Raleigh was continued in the manner already described, with the difference that the right wing was divided—the 15th Corps crossing Battle's Bridge, while the 17th Corps proceeded farther, passing the Neuse River at Neuse Mills, directly opposite Raleigh. By this last movement, the city would have been approached from the northeast by one of our columns without impeding the march of the other, which advanced more directly from the east and south. The event, however, proved that there was but little need of caution in the advance upon the city, for Johnston did not intend making a fight here. The envoys who came to General Sherman on the night of the 13th were sent back, and arrived here just before the entrance of Kilpatrick, carrying the assurance of our commanding General that the persons and property of the state officers and citizens of Raleigh should be respected, provided no resistance was offered to our occupation of the city.

Raleigh, the City of Oaks, is a beautiful place. Situated

near the geographical centre of the State of North Carolina, and encircled by the range of hills which mark the first rise of land above the level fields and swamps which sweep down with the rivers to the ocean, its position is admirable, and its natural attractions striking. It is the place of residence of the oldest and best familes of the state — families whose names go back beyond the settlement of this country, and some of noble blood, who found their way across the waters with the great Earl. The memory of these family lineages and traditions are cherished by their descendants, and the stranger meets with much of the stately manners and courteous receptions of the olden time.

There is a large proportion of highly educated and refined people in the vicinity of Raleigh. We see little of that painful ostentation which is met in Charleston, Columbia, and other cities of the South, but a genuine civilization, marked by taste. The evidence of wealth and refinement impresses itself upon the eye of the stranger when he first enters this city, especially if it be his good fortune to wander through its wide streets in that season of the year when Nature puts forth her countless glories. The houses, which are large and of neat architecture, are surrounded by ample gardens, filled with flowers of every variety. The lawns, with their close-cropped carpets of green, remind one of an English country place; the walks are bordered with fragrant rose-bushes; and overshadowing the dwellings, along the drives and roadways, magnificent oak and elm trees stand. So great is the profusion of foliage, that the whole city can not be seen from any one point of view. The houses, peering out from their exquisite surroundings, present a thousand pictures of enchanting beauty.

The most prominent building in the city is the Statehouse, which stands in a central position, from which the broad avenues and streets diverge at right angles. This building is constructed of a light granite similar to that at Columbia. A happy mingling of the Corinthian and Doric orders of architecture, with an imposing dome and cupola, give the structure an air of grace and dignity befitting the halls of legislation. Unfortunately, the crime of disunion has debased its noble proportions to other uses. When the city was occupied by the Federal troops, several Fresnel lanterns, stolen from United States light-houses on the coast, were found there, packed away; but when General Meigs, our faithful and watchful quartermaster general, visited the army upon one of his frequent tours of supervision and inspection, this property was carefully boxed up and sent to the Naval Department at Washington.

The State Library of North Carolina we found to be small and of modern selection. Several years ago it contained thousands of rare and valuable works, nearly all of which were then destroyed by fire.

In the chambers of the Senate and House of Representatives in the capitol hang several fine portraits. One of Washington, painted by Stuart, represents the Father of his Country in the attitude of guarding the national flag—the immortal figure making a significant reproach of those who daily enacted treason under its benignant eye. A bronze statue of Washington stands upon a pedestal in the courtyard. It is a copy from Houdon's statue in the Boston State-house and at Richmond.

There are several pretty churches in Raleigh, one of them, of Gothic architecture, built of brown freestone, and exceedingly elegant and modest, standing in the capitol square. At the foot of the avenue fronting south from the State-house, stands the governor's mansion, a musty old brick building, which, in derision, has been called the "Palace." When the frightened Rebel Governor Vance ran away, he managed to carry off all the furniture of this "palace" with him, so that, uncomfortable at any time, it was almost uninhabitable when General Sherman took possession and established his headquarters there.

A building of more pretension, and with little or no claim to beauty, is the Insane Asylum, situated upon a high hill in the outskirts of the city. I walked through the wards where the inmates of both sexes were confined, and thought they seemed more idiotic than insane. One of the few who showed evidences of intellect, even if it was a disordered one, I heard demanding his papers of General Sherman. This poor victim declared that he had remained there long enough; he "wanted his walking papers."

The General spoke kindly to him in these words:

"When the papers come up to me in regular shape I will attend to them. Meanwhile you must be quiet, and put your faith in God."

"In God?" answered the man, fixing his keen gray eye upon the face of his interlocutor.

"Yes, in God; you certainly believe in Him, and His power to take care of all of us."

The old man, who had been born and reared in Massachusetts, hitched his body a little upon one side, but did not remove his fixed gaze from the General's face as he rejoined:

"In God? Well, I think I do believe in a sort of Divine Providence; but when it comes to the question of power, it strikes me that for a man who has been walking about over the country whipping these cursed Rebels, you have a d—d sight more power than any body I know of!"

After this the General turned away.

There are a few other public buildings in Raleigh. A seminary for young ladies, called St. Mary's Hall, and an asylum for deaf and dumb, are prominent institutions; but they have no pretension to consideration aside from the work they are intended to assist.

The beauty of Raleigh is in its elegant private residences. It was fortunate that our troops entered the city so speedily as they did; for Wheeler's cavalry had begun the work of pillage and outrage which have marked their infamous career at every city we have captured. They seem to make no distinction between friend and foe where plunder is possible. All through Georgia and South Carolina, and now in the capital of the old North State, the same scenes of lawlessness have been witnessed. They broke open the stores and entered the houses, robbing their own people of every thing they could get their hands upon, adding to theft such acts of personal violence as would have been shameful cowardice, if visited even upon an enemy.

The Federal troops at once restored order. General Walcott's division garrisoned the town, and in a few moments patrols marched through the streets, stationing guards at the proper points. No violence or disorder occurred from that moment, and the secession sympathizers, who had trembled with fear of Sherman's army, opened their eyes to the fact that these long-dreaded Vandals, as they had been taught to believe them, were Christian gentlemen, if they did make earnest war.

To the Union people who remained in Raleigh during these four long years of despotism, the raising of the old flag upon the capitol building was an event of prayerful joy. Until the army entered Raleigh, the Union sentiment, which was said to have existed in the state, had manifested itself in a very limited way. Here there could be no doubt about it. It may appear inconsistent for men to profess to have been loyal to the government all this while, in spite of the fact that many of them, in accepting magistracies and other state offices, took oaths to sustain the Confederate government. All men will hail with unbounded honor those heroic patriots in the South who gave up home and property, and took up arms for the defense of our nationality; but at this hour of victory, when the beautiful Angel of Peace hovers over these blood-stained fields, let us be charitable to the men who have believed they could best serve the great cause by staying with their people, even at the expense of apparent disloyalty to the national government.

There can be no doubt that the presence of men like Holden, Warren, and Badger has been an element of great strength, to the injury of the Richmond despotism. The State of North Carolina has been as much under the influence of military terrorism as was ever Hungary or Poland; and, now that the Rebel bayonet is removed from the throats of the people, they will reassert their loyalty to the national government with more vehemence and unanimity than did Maryland or Missouri.

Upon the question of slavery there is but one opinion. The secessionists gave up the principle that they were originally fighting for, when they made soldiers of their negroes. This question was discussed just long enough, and sufficient action was taken by Davis and his friends to commit themselves thoroughly, and they do not hesitate to acknowledge the fact. As for those who have always been inimical to slavery, they seem to recognize in the President's proclamation a binding obligation to do away with slavery. Whether or not that grandest deed of all time was effective, except as a war measure, is sometimes questioned; but the people of the South have accepted it as a fixed and irrevocable fact that the slaves are no longer property, but FREE.

CHAPTER XXXI.

A TALK WITH A REBEL COLONEL.

In one of the private residences in Raleigh I found the colonel of a Georgia Rebel regiment lying weak and helpless from the effects of a bullet wound in the leg, received in one of the desperate charges on our works at the battle of Bentonville, on the 19th of April. A Rebel surgeon, who had been left in charge of this officer, asked me to go and see him, "to cheer him up," and I went.

The colonel was the representative of a large class of young Southerners who entered into the war with all the passion and vigor of their enthusiastic tropical natures. A strong feeling of sympathy moved me as I gazed upon that handsome face, pale with suffering. The long black hair was tossed back from a high and intellectual forehead; the eyes glowing with an unnatural light; the smooth, white face and sensitive mouth, contracted with pain—all told the story of the war. The same type of the Southern race I have seen upon many a battle-field, lying cold and stiff in death.

The colonel said to me that it was a relief to him to talk, adding that he was glad to see me, and inviting me to take a seat. He then offered me a pipe which, he said, he had carried through the battles in Virginia, and pointed to some Southern tobacco of excellent quality. So we fell into a pleasant conversation about the war, and one engagement after another was fought over again.

"You might have broken up our army at Antietam," said the colonel. "I took in one hundred and ninety-five men, and brought out twenty. The rest were either killed or wounded. But we should have followed you up at Chancellorsville. We could have driven Hooker's army into the river, sir."

Soon afterward he said:

"The South lost its greatest General in Jackson's death."

Presently the conversation turned upon the cause of the war.

"I never believed that the Constitution recognized the right of secession," remarked the colonel. "I took up arms, sir, upon a broader ground—the right of revolution. We were wronged. Our property and liberties were about to be taken from us. It was a sacred duty to rebel."

"But," I answered, "supposing for an instant that you were wronged, or were about to have all those outrages committed upon you (which, of course, I deny), was there justification in taking up arms against a good government in anticipation of some wrong yet to be inflicted? Farther than this: you are an intelligent, and, I believe, a conscientious man. You say you were a Democrat in politics; how can there be justification for revolution under a government where there is universal suffrage? It is as much as to say that three men shall coerce five. Surely that is not democracy?"

"I must say that I never saw that point before," he replied. "Yet surely you do not mean to say that there might not have been acts committed by the North which would have justified revolution?"

"No," I rejoined; "the North could not have so wronged the South as to justify a revolution and the bloody scenes we have witnessed within the last four years. Minorities have their rights; but it is not one of them to rule majorities."

The colonel said his mother had a large number of slaves, some of them old men and women, and many more little children, adding: "It makes my heart bleed, sir, when I think of what is to be their fate under this proclamation of emancipation. What is to become of them? Where are they to go? I love them, and they love their mistress and me. They must not be turned out upon the world to starve."

I suggested, in reply, that probably the government would provide some measures which would remove his apprehensions; and that, in the mean time, he could adopt a system of compensated labor and education for these people, which would anticipate the action of the government; adding that, at the same time, he would probably find himself more than repaid by the results.

"But," replied the colonel, "it is easy for you to suggest methods, you who have not the fearful responsibility upon your conscience as we have. Besides, these negroes are ignorant; they yearn for liberty, no doubt, but they do not really comprehend what liberty means. I shudder at the thought of the future of the South."

I answered: "Ignorance as to the meaning of the word 'liberty' is not confined to the negroes. I am not surprised that you anticipate serious troubles at the South, but they may be avoided if *you* will but recognize what liberty really is. If you attempt to exercise upon these people, who know they are free, the spirit of the mastership, you will find that they will assert themselves to the point of bloodshed."

"God help us!" sighed the colonel.

"God will help you; for, as you said a moment since, this

is all His work. But you must fully accept the equality of man before Him before you can take the first onward step."

Since the people of the South have become convinced that the rebellion is a failure, and that the power of the national government is to be maintained, they have begun to agitate this question among themselves. They fully acknowledge the fact that slavery is dead, and that the colored race are free; but they are utterly at a loss to understand how the Emancipation Act is to be put into practical operation.

I parted from the wounded colonel with the assurance that in this, as in all questions relating to reconstruction, there would be the wisest and most careful legislation.

CHAPTER XXXII.

THE CONSTRUCTION CORPS OF THE ARMY.

THE interruption of the narrative of the march gives me an opportunity to speak of the Construction Corps of the army—a corps which has performed vast labors during these campaigns, and merits particular mention.

There is a story in the army, that one day in the Rebel camp there was great exultation and shouting because Forrest had injured a tunnel on our line of railway; whereupon an intelligent Georgian growled out:

"Oh, stop your noise.; s'posin' Forrest has broken in the tunnil—Sherman's got a duplicate of it, and it's fixed up 'fore this time!"

This was a rough way of saying a good thing; for the Georgia soldier was nearer the truth than he thought. Officers of high rank in the Rebel service, as well as our own, have paid deserved compliments to the ingenuity and celerity of the men of our Construction Corps.

During our march this corps has been under the direction and management of Colonel Wright, who is one of the remarkable men developed by the war. His clear comprehension, ingenuity, energy, and forethought have been of vast service to us. He has employed a larger or smaller body of men as the exigency required. In the Atlanta campaign a large force was needed to repair the railroads, the lines of which were advanced, in running order, as fast as the troops marched. Colonel Wright performed almost as great a feat in this state. True to his promise to General Sherman, he ran a locomotive into Goldsboro' on the day of the arrival of the army there; whereupon the soldiers shouted with delight, for they saw visions of supplies, shoes, etc. And again, three days had not elapsed after our occupation of Raleigh, when a train of letter-bags and forage arrived from Newbern. In order to accomplish the last feat two bridges were built, one of them across the wide Neuse River, and eight miles of the railroad track were entirely relaid. Laying a rail-track at that place and time was no small matter; for it was necessary to cut the sleepers from the forest and take them to the road-bed, and rails were transported from below to take the place of those which had been removed by the Rebels.

To describe the work accomplished by this corps alone would be to tell the history of the Atlanta campaign. The bridge thrown across the Chattahoochee—more than one thousand feet in length, and one hundred feet in height—entirely made from timber freshly cut, was put up and a train of cars running over it in less than four days. One morning a freshet came down the always turbulent stream, and swept away some fifty feet of the bridge, disjointing the remainder; but within twenty-four hours a duplicate of the structure was up, and the trains again ran over it. And so, away back to Chattanooga and Nashville, across many a river, and creek, and ravine, these bridges and their duplicates were always ready to repair the devastation caused by Rebel raids.

Brave men are these of the Construction Corps. Often their labors are interrupted by the dash of Rebel cavalry, but they fight and work on. Night and day are alike to them. Their homes are upon the platform-cars; their food is taken as best they can; they work fast, and they work well, for they know that upon their efforts hangs the fate of armies. Colonel Wright is a quiet man in appearance; not large, but rather thick-set, with a well-proportioned face, black eyes, full beard, and plenty of hair—all jet black. He never makes a promise without knowing exactly what he has to do, and his word never fails.

CHAPTER XXXIII.

PURSUIT OF JOHNSTON — CONFERENCE BETWEEN SHERMAN AND JOHNSTON — A TRUCE.

Raleigh, April 19*th.*—Orders have been issued for a new movement of the army in pursuit of Johnston. Under the directions for this march, the right wing moved upon Morrisville and Durham's Station, along the railroad; the central column going more directly west, to the south of Chapel Hill, and the left wing advancing upon roads yet farther to the south. The first objective was the town of Ashboro', situated about sixty miles south by west from Raleigh, and thirty miles directly south of Greensboro', the point of junction of the Raleigh and Danville Railroads.

As the prospect of another arduous campaign loomed up before the soldiers, who had looked forward to North Carolina or Virginia as the final battle-fields of the war, there were some expressions of discontent; but when the different corps got fairly under way the grumbling ceased, and the men thought only of outmarching, outmanœuvring, outfighting, and beating the Rebels. There is an old saying that a "stern chase is a long one," and the army had a distinct recollection of Johnston's facility in falling back. That capable commander certainly displays masterly ability in the conduct of retreats, and our soldiers were not to be blamed for expecting a long run on the track of the Rebels. The condition of affairs on this march, however, was not that of the Atlanta campaign, so far as our army was concerned, although Johnston's situation was similar to what it had been. The differences in our favor probably inspired General Sherman with the hope of bringing Johnston to bay; the promise of success in this effort lying in the fact that the Rebel forces could not leave the line of the railroad and subsist. Not only was Johnston forced to depend upon the railroad to supply his infantry, but Hampton's large cavalry command obtained its forage chiefly by the same means.

It will be seen, therefore, that General Sherman's proposed line of march to Ashboro', and thence probably to Salisbury, marked out a line which was nearly straight; while Johnston, moving upon the arc of a semicircle, would inevitably have been intercepted before crossing the Yadkin River, even with two days' start, and making no allowance for our own advantages in the ability to leave our trains in the rear, or, indeed, to have marched faster on any line than the disorganized and dispirited soldiers of the Rebel army could have done.

The new movement had begun; the faces of our soldiers had again been turned southward, and we were once more about to undertake a pilgrimage which, to say the least, was of uncertain end, when an unexpected event instantly arrested our progress. It was the dawn of PEACE.

On the 15th of April General Sherman received a letter from General Johnston, asking if some arrangement could not be effected which should prevent the farther useless effusion of blood. On the day following General Sherman's reply reached General Johnston. It was to the effect that he would gladly receive any propositions looking toward a cessation of hostilities; intimating, also, that he could offer terms of the tenor of those agreed upon between Generals Grant and Lee.

General Johnston answered this communication by proposing a personal interview with General Sherman, to be held on the next day, at a designated point situated between the lines of the opposing armies. This proposition was at once accepted by General Sherman, with the single alteration of the time of meeting from ten o'clock in the morning to the hour of noon.

The day of this conference—Monday, April 17th—will be memorable in the history of the war. The fratricidal struggle of four long and weary years virtually ended on the day when two great men came together in the heart of the State of North Carolina, intent, with true nobility of soul and in the highest interests of humanity, upon putting a stop to the needless sacrifice of life. This conference was not held after days of bloody battle, when the heavens had been rent with the roar of artillery, the scream of shell, and the rattle and crash of musketry, but under better auspices than these. As General Sherman rode past his picket line upon that sunny spring morning, the ear was not pained by the moans and cries of mangled men, but the fresh breeze came laden with the fragrance of the pines, of apple blossoms, of lilacs, roses, and violets. The eye rested upon a thousand forms of beauty; for the rains and warm sun had quickened into life countless buds and flowering plants, until the hill-sides, and glens and bushes were brilliant in their robes of delicate green. Here and there in the forest, the deep-toned evergreen of some sturdy old pine or cedar was displayed in dark relief against the fresher verdure; but the prevailing tone of earth and sky was pregnant with the loving promise of spring. The scene was symbolic of the new era of peace then just beginning to dawn upon the nation.

The two Generals met upon the road, warmly greeting each other with extended hands. On the brow of a hill a few yards farther on there was a small farm-house, to which they repaired for consultation, while the general officers and staffs who accompanied their respective chiefs fell, after a few moments, into amicable conversation. Kilpatrick and Wade Hampton soon got to fighting their cavalry battles over again, contented this time with making it only a war of words.

On this occasion I had my first view of the Confederate Generals. The study of their manners and personal appearance was a decided pleasure, for we had heard so much of their characteristics that curiosity had become whetted.

Wade Hampton, a large and powerful man, gave but little opportunity for a critical examination of the graces of his person; for during the morning he lay stretched, in an indifferent manner, upon an old carpenter's bench by the side of the house; and when he afterward followed his superior out of the inclosure, dangling after him an immense sword which must have been imported for the occasion, either nature or his tailor, or both, gave him an appearance of vulgarity and clumsiness which surprised those who had been educated to believe that a South Carolinian who owned many slaves was necessarily an elegant and refined gentleman. It should be said of Hampton's face—that is, what could be seen of it behind a beard which was unnaturally black for a man fifty years of age—that it seemed bold even beyond arrogance; and this expression was, if possible, intensified by the boastful fanfaronade which he continued during the whole period of the conference.

General Johnston, whom we had an opportunity of observing later in the day, is a man of medium height and striking appearance. He was dressed in a neat, gray uniform, which harmonized gracefully with a full beard and mustache of silvery whiteness, partly concealing a genial and generous mouth, that must have become habituated to a kindly smile. His eyes, dark brown in color, varied in expression—now intense and sparkling, and then soft with tenderness, or twinkling with humor. The nose was Roman, and the forehead full and prominent. The general cast of the features gave an expression of goodness and manliness, mingling a fine nature with the decision and energy of the capable soldier. These were my impressions of General Joe Johnston, as I saw him, now assenting to some propositions of General Sherman, put forth in his acute, energetic manner, or when in conversation with a brother officer of the old army, General Barry, met here for the first time in many years; and these impressions are justified in the acts of the man, if we put aside his first offense against the state. As a soldier, he has been open and manly; and now, at this crisis in the fate of the cause he espoused, while his own army may not be said to be *in extremis*, he courageously steps forward and proposes to end the unnatural struggle by honorable capitulation of all foes in arms against the United States Government.

Such was the general nature of the propositions made by General Johnston in the first day's interview. General Sherman assented to the proposition to treat with General Johnston for the disarmament of belligerents besides those within his immediate command, but would not consent to a delay of four days, which was asked for in order, as Johnston said, that he might consult with others. The next day, and the same hour, were then fixed upon for another meeting.

On the 18th, with a proper degree of ceremony, the two Generals again met. Precisely at the hour of noon, Sherman and Johnston, with their staffs, rode to the top of the eminence opposite to the little farm-house already referred to, and the brilliantly-costumed crowd of staff officers, in full uniform, paused for a moment, as their chiefs rode forward

CONFERENCE BETWEEN GENERAL SHERMAN AND GENERAL JOHNSTON.

into the open space, lifting their hats courteously, and then, grasping each other by the hand, Sherman and Johnston dismounted and passed into the house. In a few moments one of the Rebel officers dashed off down the road in the direction of the escort which had accompanied General Johnston, and in a short time a tall gentlemen rode up, and, hurrying through the crowd of officers, quickly entered the house where the two Generals were in conference. Almost every person present recognized in the new-comer John C. Breckinridge, the Confederate Secretary of War.

The proceedings of the conference which ensued may only be known by the results which are before the world. In the negotiation, General Sherman refused to recognize any such authority as the "Confederate States," treating with Johnston and Breckinridge simply as insurgent generals. At the same time, the conditions agreed upon by the Rebels were understood to have been approved by Jeff. Davis.

As these terms embraced a settlement of the entire question at issue, involving responsibilities which General Sherman considered were not within the scope of his powers, an armistice was concluded, to last until an officer could be sent to Washington to obtain the approval of the President.

Large numbers of two newspapers published in Raleigh, the *Standard* and the *Progress*, were brought along in the cars with General Sherman's party, and distributed along the route. They contained a lecture by the Rev. Henry Ward Beecher delivered before the people of his church. The conciliatory, generous sentiments toward the humiliated South expressed in this discourse were received with surprise by both our army and the Rebel officers, who have mistakenly supposed Mr. Beecher to be an unreasoning fanatic. These charitable expressions of feeling were received with marked approbation by both our soldiers and the Rebels, coming as they did at a critical moment, and from one who represented in a great measure the radical element in the North.

On the second day of these proceedings an indescribable gloom was cast over us by the terrible tidings of the assassination of President Lincoln. It is but just to say that the Union officers could not have expressed more horror and detestation at that dastardly act than did General Johnston and his friends. They seemed to understand that in Mr. Lincoln the South had, after all, lost the best friend it had in the government and at the North.

The conference ended, and the parties separated, to meet again so soon as an answer was received from Washington. Meanwhile the two armies were to remain in the same relative positions; that is to say, the line was to be kept inviolate, extending from Bennet's house, where the conference was held, southward to Chapel Hill. The Union army, as conquerors of the soil, were to forage upon the neighboring country, but not to encroach upon the line designated. Throughout the negotiation General Johnston appeared sincerely desirous to put a stop to the terrible incursions of our troops upon the houses. Indeed, several officers who returned from Lee's army since the surrender aver that the principal cause of the demoralization of that army at the time of the last fatal and decisive battles was, aside from the knowledge that Sherman's great host was marching upon their flank, that they were tortured with anxiety to know the fate of their families, whose homes lay in the track of our march in Georgia and the Carolinas. We saw then, as we never did before, how effective, in a moral sense, had been the terrible influence of these campaigns through the heart of the enemy's country. In that experience, too, the South has learned a lesson which will not be forgotten in this century.

CHAPTER XXXIV.

THE END.

Raleigh, April 25th.—Lieutenant General Grant has arrived, with an answer to the terms of settlement arranged between Generals Sherman and Johnston. The terms have been rejected. It is not my province, nor is this the proper place to discuss the propriety of the action of the government in this matter, or the wisdom of General Sherman's agreement with Johnston. It is painfully evident that that agreement has been misunderstood or misconstrued; and I may add, from personal knowledge of some of the circumstances attending the conference, that General Sherman had reasons for his action which he regarded as cogent and convincing.*

It is essential to the truth of history, however, that some of the principal reasons for this armistice and agreement should be briefly stated in this connection.

General Sherman knew that he could reach Johnston's army at any time; and, while it might have been impossible to bring the enemy again to bay as an organized force, it was certain that the Rebels would have been scattered by our attack. They would then have spread over the country in the form of many small commands, imposing upon us the fatiguing task of chasing squads. This duty would have

---

* General Sherman's own explanation of his course, as given in his official report of the conference with Johnston, is given in the Appendix to this volume.

required the constant employment of a large force, a farther sacrifice of life, and an enormous expense to the nation.

In a military point of view the armistice was favorable to us, and to Johnston's disadvantage. Wilson was marching north, working disaster to the Rebels, capturing their cities, and destroying their bridges and munitions of war. Stoneman also could join this command, when his cavalry would have been of great service in the event of the resumption of hostilities. He has done all the harm to the enemy that he can do in his present position.

April 26*th*.—The notice of forty-eight hours which was to be given by either party who chose to resume hostilities was yesterday evening sent to General Johnston, with the information that the government had refused to ratify the agreement proposed at the former conference. The truce was thus to terminate at noon of the 26th.

It is useless to deny that the officers and men of the army were chagrined and disappointed at this result; orders were at once issued to the troops to return to the camps, which had been temporarily abandoned. Orders were also given out to the entire army to hold itself in readiness to march, while the 17th Corps received directions to move to Jones's Cross-roads.

Yesterday evening a message was received from General Johnston, asking for another meeting with General Sherman, to take place at noon of to-day, and the latter has this morning gone to the front, while General Grant remains at headquarters awaiting the result of the re-opened negotiations. That there will be a surrender of Johnston's army there can be no doubt, for the Rebels are not in a condition to fight a battle. Johnston is as anxious as we to put his army in such a position that they will not break up into predatory bands to maraud and desolate the country; nor do we desire to undertake a pursuit which would involve continued expenditure of means with no compensating results.

An odd question arose during the armistice just closed. As General Sherman foresaw, Wilson continued his operations, and, while Johnston withheld the troops which possibly might have gone to the rescue of Macon, Wilson rides forward and captures the city. The authorities, however, surrendered under protest, and with them Johnston demands that Macon, with Cobb and other prisoners, be released, on the ground that during the armistice war could not be waged within the limits of Sherman's command. This raised a nice point for discussion; but meanwhile Sherman refused to order Wilson from Macon, although he gave directions to release Cobb and the rest, as they remained in Macon, and were captured while under the impression that the armistice covered and protected them.

It is understood that this order was given by General Sherman in obedience to instructions received from the Secretary of War.

April 27th.—Yesterday the curtain of peace fell upon the closing act of this great tragedy of war which has been enacted during these eventful four years. Generals Sherman and Johnston again came together at the place of former conference, and the articles of capitulation were signed which surrenders all the Rebel forces in arms between this point and the Chattahoochee River, which includes Johnston's command. The terms of capitulation are the same as those arranged between Generals Grant and Lee. The officers are to retain their side-arms; the men are to be paroled until exchanged, and in the mean time not to take up arms against the United States Government. All material of war is to be turned over to officers to be designated.

The evidence goes to show that Johnston has been induced to surrender quite as much by the discontent and threats of his own soldiers as by the Federal force in his rear. The Rebel troops see the utter folly of farther resistance, and refuse to fight longer. Johnston has pursued the only wise course left open to him.

It is to be presumed that there are those in the North who will ask why an unconditional surrender has not been demanded by Generals Grant and Sherman; but such persons can not reason so fairly, nor judge as wisely as those who have seen the utter desolation and humiliation of the South, even if it were not fearfully expensive, and almost impracticable, to hold as prisoners of war such large bodies of men.

The war is practically over. The South is crushed almost beyond hope of speedy resurrection. Its armies are destroyed; its manufactures ruined; its work-shops and public buildings in ashes; its commerce and agriculture swept away. For us and for them a new era begins. A great work is to be accomplished in the rehabilitation of a wasted region.

April 28*th*.—The orders are issued for the return of the army home. The 23d and 10th Corps, with Kilpatrick's gallant troopers, remain here to garrison the country. The rest—the faithful, patient 14th; the swift, tireless, heroic 15th; the tried veterans of the 17th; the noble, war-worn heroes of the 20th—companions of many a wearisome march and hasty bivouac—comrades upon many a battle-field—never defeated, always victorious, brothers always—are going to their homes, to be welcomed by the loving embrace of wife, mother, and sister—to meet the warm grasp of a brother's hand—to receive from the Nation the high honors she gladly and proudly pays to her gallant defenders.

Yet, in these hours of parting, let us not forget the brave and noble Dead! The companions of our journey who sleep in obscure but honorable graves, merit the meed of our profound and earnest homage. The memory of our dead is their noblest monument. Thousands of gallant spirits, whose remains are lying in the valley of the Tennessee, on the banks of the Oostanaula, by the Allatoona Pass, at Atlanta, and in the swamps of the Carolinas, live with us to-day. They shall never be forgotten while our hearts beat or the nation lives. The army pays them that tribute of respect which can only be given truly by the soldier who has stood side by side with the departed, hour by hour, day by day, year after year, in storm and sunshine, on the march or in the cloud of battle, in the bivouac or at the moment of sudden death. Peace to their ashes! May their memory be green, and our thought of them in coming years be that of love and pride!

GOING HOME.

On the 24th of May, Sherman's Army passed in review before the President of the United States in Washington. It was the last act in the rapid and wonderful Drama of the four gallant corps. With banners proudly flying, ranks in close and magnificent array, under the eye of their beloved Chief, and amid the thundering plaudits of countless thousands of enthusiastic spectators, the noble army of seventy thousand veterans paid their marching salute to the President of the Nation they had helped to preserve in its integrity—and then broke ranks, and set their faces toward Home. This was the farewell of Sherman's Army! So, too, ends the STORY OF THE GREAT MARCH.

APPENDIX.

I.

General Sherman Report of the Georgia Campaign.

Headquarters of the Military Division of the Mississippi,
in the Field, Savannah, Georgia, January 1st, 1865.

Major General H. W. Halleck, Chief of Staff, Washington City, D. C.:

GENERAL,—I have the honor to offer my report of the operations of the armies under my command, since the occupation of Atlanta in the early part of September last, up to the present date.

As heretofore reported, in the month of September the Army of the Cumberland, Major General Thomas commanding, held the city of Atlanta; the Army of the Tennessee, Major General Howard commanding, was grouped about East Point; and the Army of the Ohio, Major General Schofield commanding, held Decatur. Many changes occurred in the composition of these armies, in consequence of the expiration of the time of service of many of the regiments. The opportunity was given to us to consolidate the fragments, reclothe and equip the men, and make preparations for the future campaign. I also availed myself of the occasion to strengthen the garrisons to our rear, to make our communications more secure, and sent Wagner's division of the 4th Corps and Morgan's division of the 14th Corps back to Chattanooga, and Corse's division of the 15th Corps to Rome. Also a thorough reconnoissance was made of Atlanta, and a new line of works begun, which required a smaller garrison to hold.

During this month, the enemy, whom we had left at Lovejoy's Station, moved westward toward the Chattahoochee, taking position facing us, and covering the West Point Railroad about Palmetto Station. He also threw a pontoon bridge across the Chattahoochee, and sent cavalry detachments to the west, in the direction of Carrolton and Powder Springs. About the same time President Davis visited Macon and his army at Palmetto, and made harangues referring to an active campaign against us. Hood still remained in command of the Confederate forces, with Cheatham, S. D. Lee, and Stewart commanding his three corps, and Wheeler in command of his cavalry, which had been largely re-enforced.

My cavalry consisted of two divisions; one was stationed at Decatur, under command of Brigadier General Garrard; the other, commanded by Brigadier General Kilpatrick, was posted near Sandtown, with a pontoon bridge over the Chattahoochee, from which he could watch any movement of the enemy toward the west.

As soon as I became convinced that the enemy intended to assume the offensive, namely, September 28th, I sent Major General Thomas, second in command, to Nashville, to organize the new troops expected to arrive, and to make preliminary preparations to meet such an event.

About the 1st of October, some of the enemy's cavalry made their appearance on the west of the Chattahoochee, and one of his infantry corps was reported near Powder Springs; and I received authentic intelligence that the rest of his infantry was crossing to the west of the Chattahoochee. I at once made my orders that Atlanta and the Chattahoochee Railroad bridge should be held by the 20th Corps, Major General Slocum, and on the 4th of October put in motion the 15th and 17th Corps, and the 4th, 14th, and 23d Corps, to Smyrna camp-ground; and on the 5th moved to the strong position about Kenesaw. The enemy's cavalry had, by a rapid movement, got upon our railroad at Big Shanty, and broken the line of telegraph and railroad; and with a division of infantry (French's) had moved against Allatoona, where were stored about a million of rations. Its redoubts were garrisoned by three small regiments under Colonel Tourtellotte, 4th Minnesota.

I had anticipated this movement, and had, by signal and telegraph, ordered General Corse to re-enforce that post from Rome.

General Corse had reached Allatoona with a brigade during the night of the 4th, just in time to meet the attack by French's division on the morning of the 5th. In person I reached Kenesaw Mountain about ten A.M. of the 5th, and could see the smoke of battle and hear the faint sounds of artillery. The distance, eighteen miles, was too great for me to make in time to share in the battle, but I directed the 23d Corps, Brigadier General Cox commanding, to move rapidly from the base of Kenesaw due west, aiming to reach the road from Allatoona to Dallas, threatening the rear of the forces attacking Allatoona. I succeeded in getting a signal message to General Corse during his fight, notifying him of my presence. The defense of Allatoona by General Corse was admirably conducted, and the enemy repulsed with heavy slaughter. His description of the defense is so graphic, that it leaves nothing for me to add; and the movement of General Cox had the desired effect of causing the withdrawal of French's division rapidly in the direction of Dallas.

On the 6th and 7th I pushed my cavalry well toward Burnt Hickory and Dallas, and discovered that the enemy had moved westward, and inferred that he would attempt to break our railroad again in the neighborhood of Kingston. Accordingly, on the morning of the 8th, I put the army in motion through Allatoona Pass to Kingston, reaching that point on the 10th. There I learned that the enemy had feigned on Rome, and was passing the Coosa River on a pontoon bridge about eleven miles below Rome. I therefore, on the 11th, moved to Rome, and pushed Garrard's cavalry and the 23d Corps, under General Cox, across the Oostenaula, to threaten the flanks of the enemy passing north. Garrard's cavalry drove a cavalry brigade of the enemy to and beyond the Narrows, leading into the valley of the Chattooga, capturing two field-pieces and taking some prisoners. The enemy had moved with great rapidity, and made his appearance at Resaca, and Hood had in person demanded its surrender. I had from Kingston re-enforced Resaca by two regiments of the Army of the Tennessee. I at first intended to move the army into the Chattooga Valley, to interpose between the enemy and his line of retreat down the Coosa, but feared that General Hood would, in that event, turn eastward by Spring Place, and down the Federal Road, and therefore moved against him at Resaca. Colonel Weaver at Resaca, afterward re-enforced by General Raum's brigade, had repulsed the enemy from Resaca, but he had succeeded in breaking the railroad from Tilton to Dalton, and as far north as the Tunnel.

Arriving at Resaca on the evening of the 14th, I determined to strike Hood in flank, or force him to battle, and directed the Army of the Tennessee, General Howard, to move to Snake Creek Gap, which was held by the enemy, while General Stanley, with the 4th and 14th Corps, moved by Tilton across the mountains to the rear of Snake Creek Gap, in the neighborhood of Villanow.

The Army of the Tennessee found the enemy occupying our old lines in the Snake Creek Gap, and on the 15th skirmished for the purpose of holding him there until Stanley could get to his rear. But the enemy gave way about noon, and was followed through the Gap, escaping before General Stanley had reached the farther end of the Pass. The next day, the 16th, the armies moved directly toward La Fayette, with a view to cut off Hood's retreat. We found him intrenched in Ship's Gap, but the leading division (Wood's) of the 15th Corps rapidly carried the advanced posts held by two companies of a South Carolina regiment, making them prisoners. The remaining eight companies escaped to the main body near La Fayette. The next morning we passed over into the valley of the Chattooga, the Army of the Tennessee moving in pursuit by La Fayette and Alpine toward Blue Pond; the Army of the Cumberland by Summerville and Melville Post-office to Gaylesville; and the Army of the Ohio and Garrard's cavalry from Villanow, Dirttown Valley, and Goover's Gap to Gaylesville. Hood, however, was little encumbered with trains, and marched with great rapidity, and had succeeded in getting into the narrow gorge formed by the Lookout Range abutting against the Coosa River in the neighborhood of Gadsden. He evidently wanted to avoid a fight.

On the 19th all the armies were grouped about Gaylesville, in the rich valley of the Chattooga, abounding in corn and meat, and I determined to pause in my pursuit of the enemy, to watch his movements, and live on the country. I hoped that Hood would turn toward Guntersville and Bridgeport. The Army of the Tennessee was posted near Little River, with instructions to feel forward in support of the cavalry, which was ordered to watch Hood in the neighborhood of Will's Valley, and to give me the earliest notice possible of his turning northward. The Army of the Ohio was posted at Cedar Bluff, with orders to lay a pontoon across the Coosa, and to feel forward to centre, and down in the direction of Blue Mountain. The Army of the Cumberland was held in reserve at Gaylesville, and all the troops were instructed to draw heavily for supplies from the surrounding country. In the mean time communications were opened to Rome, and a heavy force set to work in repairing the damages done to our railroads. Atlanta was abundantly supplied with provisions, but forage was scarce; and General Slocum was instructed to send strong foraging parties out in the direction of South River and collect all the corn and fodder possible, and to put his own trains in good condition for farther service.

Hood's movements and strategy had demonstrated that he had an army capable of endangering at all times my communications, but unable to meet me in open fight. To follow him would simply amount to being decoyed away from Georgia, with little prospect of overtaking and overwhelming him. To remain on the defensive, would have been bad policy for an army of so great value as the one I then commanded; and I was forced to adopt a course more fruitful in results than the naked one of following him to the southwest. I had previously submitted to the Commander-in-Chief a general plan, which amounted substantially to the destruction of Atlanta and the railroad back to Chattanooga, and sallying forth from Atlanta through the heart of Georgia, to capture one or more of the great Atlantic sea-ports. This I renewed from Gaylesville, modified somewhat by the change of events.

On the 26th of October, satisfied that Hood had moved westward from Gadsden across Sand Mountain, I detached the 4th Corps, Major General Stanley, and ordered him to proceed to Chattanooga and report to Major General Thomas at Nashville.

Subsequently, on the 30th of October, I also detached the 23d Corps, Major General Schofield, with the same destination, and delegated to Major General Thomas full power over all the troops subject to my command, except the four corps with which I designed to move into Georgia. This gave him the two divisions under A. J. Smith, then in Missouri, but *en route* for Tennessee, the two corps named, and all the garrisons in Tennessee, as also all the cavalry of my military division, except one division under Brigadier General Kilpatrick, which was ordered to rendezvous at Marietta.

Brevet Major General Wilson had arrived from the Army of the Potomac, to assume command of the cavalry of my army, and I dispatched him back to Nashville with all dismounted detachments, and orders as rapidly as possible to collect the cavalry serving in Kentucky and Tennessee, to mount, organize, and equip them, and report to Major General Thomas for duty. These forces I judged would enable General Thomas to defend the railroad from Chattanooga back, including Nashville and Decatur, and give him an army with which he could successfully cope with Hood, should the latter cross the Tennessee northward.

By the 1st of November Hood's army had moved from Gadsden, and made its appearance in the neighborhood of Decatur, where a feint was made; he then passed on to Tuscumbia, and laid a pontoon bridge opposite Florence. I then began my preparations for the march through Georgia, having received the sanction of the Commander-in-Chief for carrying into effect my plan, the details of which were explained to all my corps commanders and heads of staff departments, with strict injunctions of secrecy. I had also communicated full details to General Thomas, and had informed him I would not leave the neighborhood of Kingston until he felt perfectly confident that he was entirely prepared to cope with Hood, should he carry into effect his threatened invasion of Tennessee and Kentucky. I estimated Hood's force at thirty-five thousand infantry and ten thousand cavalry.

I moved the Army of the Tennessee by slow and easy marches on the south of the Coosa back to the neighborhood of the Smyrna campground, and the 14th Corps, General Jeff. C. Davis, to Kingston, whither I repaired in person on the 2d of November. From that point I directed all surplus artillery, all baggage not needed for my contemplated march, all the sick and wounded, refugees, etc., to be sent back to Chattanooga; and the 14th Corps above mentioned, with Kilpatrick's cavalry, were put in the most efficient condition possible for a long and difficult march. This operation consumed the time until the 11th of November, when, every thing being ready, I ordered General Corse, who still remained at Rome, to destroy the bridges there, all founderies, mills, shops, warehouses, or other property that could be useful to an enemy, and to move to Kingston.

At the same time the railroad in and about Atlanta, and between the Etowah and the Chattahoochee, was ordered to be utterly destroyed. The garrisons from Kingston northward were also ordered to draw back to Chattanooga, taking with them all public property and all railroad stock, and to take up the rails from Resaca back, saving them, ready to be replaced whenever future interests should demand.

The railroad between the Etowah and the Oostenaula was left untouched, because I thought it more than probable that we would find it necessary to re-occupy the country as far forward as the line of the Etowah.

Atlanta itself is only of strategic value as long as it is a railroad centre; and as all the railroads leading to it are destroyed, as well as all its founderies, machine shops, warehouses, depots, etc., etc., it is of no more value than any other point in Northern Georgia; whereas the line of the Etowah, by reason of its rivers and natural features, possesses an importance which will always continue. From it all parts of Georgia and Alabama can be reached by armies marching with trains down the Coosa or the Chattahoochee valleys.

On the 12th of November my army stood detached and cut off from all communication from the rear. It was composed of four corps: the 15th and 17th, constituting the right wing, under Major General O. O. Howard; the 14th and 20th Corps, constituting the left wing, under Major General H. W. Slocum, of an aggregate strength of sixty thousand infantry, one cavalry division, in aggregate strength five thousand five hundred, under Brigadier General Judson Kilpatrick, and the artillery reduced to the minimum, one gun per one thousand men.

The whole force was moved rapidly, and grouped about Atlanta on the 14th November.

In the mean time, Captain O. M. Poe had thoroughly destroyed Atlanta, save its mere dwelling-houses and churches, and the right wing, with General Kilpatrick's cavalry, was put in motion in the direction of Jonesboro' and McDonough, with orders to make a strong feint on Macon, to cross the Ocmulgee about Planters' Mills, and rendezvous in the neighborhood of Gordon in seven days, exclusive of the day of march. On the same day General Slocum moved with the 20th Corps by Decatur and Stone Mountain, with orders to tear up the railroad from Social Circle to Madison, to burn the large and important railroad bridge across the Oconee, east of Madison, and turn south and reach Milledgeville on the seventh day, exclusive of the day of march. In person I left Atlanta on the 16th, in company with the 14th Corps, Brevet Major General Jeff. C. Davis, by Lithonia, Covington, and Shady Dale, directly on Milledgeville. All the troops were provided with good wagon trains, loaded with ammunition and supplies, approximating twenty days' bread, forty days' sugar and coffee, a double allowance of salt for forty days, and beef cattle equal to forty days' supplies. The wagons were also supplied with about three days' forage in grain. All were instructed, by a judicious system of foraging, to maintain this order of things as long as possible, living chiefly if not solely upon the country, which I knew to abound in corn, sweet potatoes, and meats.

My first object was of course to place my army in the very heart of Georgia, interposing between Macon and Augusta, and obliging the enemy to divide his forces to defend not only those points, but Millen, Savannah, and Charleston. All my calculations were fully realized. During the 22d, General Kilpatrick made a good feint on Macon, driving the enemy within his intrenchments, and then drew back to Griswoldville, where Walcott's brigade of infantry joined him to cover that flank, while Howard's trains were closing up, and his men scattered, breaking up railroads. The enemy came out of Macon and attacked Walcott in position, but was so roughly handled that he never repeated the experiment. On the eighth day after leaving Atlanta, namely, on the 23d, General Slocum occupied Milledgeville and the important bridge across the Oconee there, and Generals Howard and Kilpatrick were in and about Gordon.

General Howard was then ordered to move eastward, destroying the railroad thoroughly in his progress, as far as Tennille Station, opposite Sandersville, and General Slocum to move to Sandersville by two roads. General Kilpatrick was ordered to Milledgeville and thence move rapidly eastward, to break the railroad which leads from Millen to Augusta, then to turn upon Millen and rescue our prisoners of war supposed to be confined at that place.

I accompanied the 20th Corps from Milledgeville to Sandersville, approaching which place on the 25th, we found the bridges across Buffalo Creek burned, which delayed us three hours. The next day we entered Sandersville, skirmishing with Wheeler's cavalry, which offered little opposition to the advance of the 20th and 14th Corps, entering the place almost at the same moment.

General Slocum was then ordered to tear up and destroy the Georgia Central Railroad from Station 13 (Tennille) to Station 10, near the crossing of the Ogeechee, one of his corps substantially following the railroad, the other by way of Louisville, in support of Kilpatrick's cavalry. In person I shifted to the right wing, and accompanied the 17th Corps, General Blair, on the south of the railroad till abreast of Station $9\frac{1}{2}$ (Barton)—General Howard in person, with the 15th Corps, keeping farther to the right and about one day's march ahead, ready to turn against the flank of any enemy who should oppose our progress. At Barton I learned that Kilpatrick's cavalry had reached the Augusta Railroad about Waynesboro', where he ascertained that our prisoners had been removed from Millen, and therefore the purpose of rescuing them, upon which we had set our hearts, was an impossibility. But as Wheeler's cavalry had hung around him, and as he had retired to Louisville to meet our infantry, in pursuance of my instructions, not to risk battle unless at great advantage, I ordered him to leave his wagons and all encumbrances with the left wing, and moving in the direction of Augusta, if Wheeler gave him the opportunity, to indulge him with all the fighting he wanted. General Kilpatrick, supported by Baird's division of infantry of the 14th Corps, again moved in the direction of Waynesboro', and encountering Wheeler in the neighborhood of Thomas's Station, attacked him in position, driving him from three successive lines of barricades handsomely through Waynesboro' and across Briar Creek, the bridges over which he burned, and then, with Baird's division, rejoined the left wing, which in the mean time had been marching by easy stages of ten miles a day in the direction of Lumpkin's Station and Jacksonboro'.

The 17th Corps took up the destruction of the railroad at the Ogeechee near Station 10, and continued it to Millen, the enemy offering little or no opposition, although preparations had seemingly been made at Millen.

On the 3d of December, the 17th Corps, which I accompanied, was at Millen; the 15th Corps, General Howard, was south of the Ogeechee, opposite Station 7 (Scarboro'); the 20th Corps, General Slocum, on the Augusta Railroad, about four miles north of Millen, near Buckhead Church; and the 14th Corps, General Jeff. C. Davis, in the neighborhood of Lumpkin's Station, on the Augusta Railroad.

All were ordered to march in the direction of Savannah, the 15th Corps to continue south of the Ogeechee, the 17th to destroy the railroad as far as Ogeechee Church, and four days were allowed to reach the line from Ogeechee Church to the neighborhood of Halley's Ferry on the Savannah River. All the columns reached their destination on time, and continued to march on their several roads—General Davis following the Savannah River road, General Slocum the middle road by way of Springfield, General Blair the railroad, and General Howard still south and west of the Ogeechee, with orders to cross to the east bank opposite "Eden Station," or Station No. 2.

As we approached Savannah, the country became more marshy and difficult, and more obstructions were met in the way of felled trees where the roads crossed the creek-swamps on narrow causeways. But our pioneer companies were well organized, and removed these obstructions in an incredibly short time. No opposition from the enemy worth speaking of was encountered until the heads of the columns were within fifteen miles of Savannah, where all the roads leading to the city were obstructed more or less by felled timber, with earth-works and artillery. But these were easily turned and the enemy driven away, so that by the 10th of December the enemy was driven within his lines at Savannah. These followed substantially a swampy creek which empties into the Savannah River about three miles above the city, across to the head of a corresponding stream which empties into the Little Ogeechee. These streams were singularly favorable to the enemy as a cover, being very marshy, and bordered by rice-fields, which were flooded either by the tide-water or by inland ponds, the gates to which were controlled and covered by his heavy artillery. The only approaches to the city were by five narrow causeways, namely, the two railroads, and the Augusta, the Louisville, and the Ogeechee dirt roads, all of which were commanded by heavy ordnance, too strong for us to fight with our light field-guns. To assault an enemy of unknown strength at such a disadvantage appeared to me unwise, especially as I had so successfully brought my army, almost unscathed, so great a distance, and could surely attain the same result by the operation of time.

I therefore instructed my army commanders to closely invest the city from the north and west, and to reconnoitre well the ground in their fronts respectively, while I gave my personal attention to opening communication with our fleet, which I knew was waiting for us in Tybee, Wassaw, and Ossabaw Sounds.

In approaching Savannah, General Slocum struck the Charleston Railroad near the bridge, and occupied the river bank as his left flank, where he had captured two of the enemy's river boats, and had prevented two others (gun-boats) from coming down the river to communicate with the city; while General Howard, by his right flank, had broken the Gulf Railroad at Fleming's and Way Station, and occupied the railroad itself down to the Little Ogeechee near Station 1, so that no supplies could reach Savannah by any of its accustomed channels.

We, on the contrary, possessed large herds of cattle, which we had brought along or gathered in the country, and our wagons still contained a reasonable amount of breadstuffs and other necessaries, and the fine rice-crops of the Savannah and Ogeechee Rivers furnished to our men and animals a large amount of rice and rice-straw.

We also held the country to the south and west of the Ogeechee as foraging ground.

Still, communication with the fleet was of vital importance, and I directed General Kilpatrick to cross the Ogeechee by a pontoon bridge, to reconnoitre Fort McAllister, and to proceed to St. Catharine's Sound in the direction of Sunbury or Kilkenny Bluff, and open communication with the fleet. General Howard had previously, by my direction, sent one of his best scouts down the Ogeechee in a canoe for a like purpose. But more than this was necessary. We wanted the vessels and their contents, and the Ogeechee River, a navigable stream close to the rear of our camps, was the proper avenue of supply.

The enemy had burned the road-bridge across the Ogeechee, just below the mouth of the Camochee, known as "King's Bridge." This was reconstructed in an incredibly short time in the most substantial manner by the 58th Indiana, Colonel Buel, under the direction of Captain Reese, of the Engineer Corps, and on the morning of the 13th December, the second division of the 15th Corps, under command of Brigadier General Hazen, crossed the bridge to the west bank of the Ogeechee, and marched down with orders to carry by assault Fort McAllister, a strong inclosed redoubt, manned by two companies of artillery and three of infantry; in all, about two hundred men, and mounting twenty-three guns *en barbette*, and one mortar.

General Hazen reached the vicinity of Fort McAllister about one P.M., deployed his division about the place, with both flanks resting upon the river, posted his skirmishers judiciously behind the trunks of trees whose branches had been used for abattis, and about five P.M. assaulted the place with nine regiments at three points, all of them successfully. I witnessed the assault from a rice-mill on the opposite bank of the river, and can bear testimony to the handsome manner in which it was accomplished.

Up to this time we had not communicated with our fleet. From the signal-station at the rice-mill our officers had looked for two days over the rice-fields and salt marsh in the direction of Ossabaw Sound, but could see nothing of it. But while watching the preparations for the assault on Fort McAllister, we discovered in the distance what seemed to be the smoke-stack of a steamer, which became more and more distinct, until about the very moment of the assault she was plainly visible below the fort, and our signal was answered. As soon as I saw our colors fairly planted upon the walls of McAllister, in company with General Howard, I went in a small boat down to the fort, and met General Hazen, who had not yet communicated with the gun-boat below, as it was shut out to him by a point of timber. Determined to communicate that night, I got another small boat and a crew, and pulled down the river till I found the tug Dandelion, Captain Williamson, U.S.N., who informed me that Captain Duncan, who had been sent by General Howard, had succeeded in reaching Admiral Dahlgren and General Foster, and that he was expecting them hourly in Ossabaw Sound. After making communications to those officers, and a short communication to the

War Department, I returned to Fort McAllister that night, and before daylight was overtaken by Major Strong, of General Foster's staff, advising me that General Foster had arrived in the Ogeechee, near Fort McAllister, and was very anxious to meet me on board his boat. I accordingly returned with him, and met General Foster on board the steamer Nemaha, and, after consultation, determined to proceed with him down the sound, in hopes to meet Admiral Dahlgren. But we did not meet him until we reached Wassaw Sound, about noon. I there went on board the admiral's flag-ship, the Harvest Moon, after having arranged with General Foster to send us from Hilton Head some siege ordnance, and some boats suitable for navigating the Ogeechee River. Admiral Dahlgren very kindly furnished me with all the data concerning his fleet and the numerous forts that guarded the inland channels between the sea and Savannah. I explained to him how completely Savannah was invested at all points save only the plank-road on the South Carolina shore, known as the "Union Causeway," which I thought I could reach from my left flank across the Savannah River. I explained to him that if he would simply engage the attention of the forts along Wilmington Channel at Beaulieu and Rosedew, I thought I could carry the defenses of Savannah by assault as soon as the heavy ordnance arrived from Hilton Head.

On the 15th the admiral carried me back to Fort McAllister, whence I returned to our lines in the rear of Savannah.

Having received and carefully considered all the reports of division commanders, I determined to assault the lines of the enemy as soon as my heavy ordnance came from Port Royal, first making a formal demand for surrender. On the 17th, a number of thirty-pounder Parrott guns having reached King's Bridge, I proceeded in person to the headquarters of Major General Slocum on the Augusta Road, and dispatched thence into Savannah, by flag of truce, a formal demand for the surrender of the place, and on the following day received an answer from General Hardee, refusing to surrender.

In the mean time, farther reconnoissances from our left flank had demonstrated that it was impracticable or unwise to push any considerable force across the Savannah River, for the enemy held the river opposite the city with iron-clad gun-boats, and could destroy any pontoons laid down by us between Hutchinson's Island and the South Carolina shore, which would isolate any force sent over from that flank. I therefore ordered General Slocum to get into position the siege-guns and make all the preparations necessary to assault, and to report to me the earliest moment when he could be ready, while I should proceed rapidly round by the right and make arrangements to occupy the Union Causeway from the direction of Port Royal. General Foster had already established a division of troops on the peninsula or neck between the Coosahatchie and Tullifinney Rivers, at the head of Broad River, from which position he could reach the railroad with his artillery.

I went to Port Royal in person, and made arrangements to re-enforce that command by one or more divisions under a proper officer, to assault and carry the railroad, and thence turn toward Savannah until it occupied the causeway in question. I went on board the admiral's flagship, the Harvest Moon, which put to sea the night of the 20th. But the wind was high, and increased during the night, so that the pilot judged Ossabaw Bar impassable, and ran into Tybee, whence we proceeded through the inland channels into Wassaw Sound, and thence through Romney Marsh. But the ebb tide caught the Harvest Moon, and she was unable to make the passage. Admiral Dahlgren took me in his barge, and pulling in the direction of Vernon River, we met the army tug Red Legs, bearing a message from my adjutant, Captain Dayton, of that morning, the 21st, to the effect that our troops were in possession of the enemy's lines, and were advancing without opposition into Savannah, the enemy having evacuated the place during the previous night.

Admiral Dahlgren proceeded up the Vernon River in his barge, while I transferred to the tug, in which I proceeded to Fort McAllister, and thence to the rice-mill; and on the morning of the 22d rode into the city of Savannah, already occupied by our troops.

I was very much disappointed that Hardee had escaped with his garrison, and had to content myself with the material fruits of victory without the cost of life which would have attended a general assault. The substantial results will be more clearly set forth in the tabular statements of heavy ordnance and other public property acquired, and it will suffice here to state, that the important city of Savannah, with its valuable harbor and river, was the chief object of the campaign.

With it we acquired all the forts and heavy ordnance in its vicinity, with large stores of ammunition, shot and shells, cotton, rice, and other valuable products of the country. We also gain locomotives and cars, which, though of little use to us in the present condition of the railroads, are a serious loss to the enemy, as well as four steamboats gained, and the loss to the enemy of the iron-clad Savannah, one ram, and three transports blown up or burned by them the night before.

Formal demand having been made for the surrender, and having been refused, I contend that every thing within the line of intrenchments belongs to the United States, and I shall not hesitate to use it, if necessary, for public purposes. But, inasmuch as the inhabitants generally have manifested a friendly disposition, I shall disturb them as little as possible consistently with the military rights of present and future military commanders, without remitting in the least our just rights as captors.

After having made the necessary orders for the disposition of the troops in and about Savannah, I ordered Captain O. M. Poe, chief engineer, to make a thorough examination of the enemy's works in and about Savannah, with a view to making it conform to our future uses. New lines of defenses will be built, embracing the city proper, Forts Jackson, Thunderbolt, and Pulaski retained, with slight modifications in their armament and rear defenses. All the rest of the enemy's forts will be dismantled and destroyed, and their heavy ordnance transferred to Hilton Head, where it can be more easily guarded.

Our base of supplies will be established in Savannah as soon as the very difficult obstructions placed in the river can be partially removed. These obstructions at present offer a very serious impediment to the commerce of Savannah, consisting of crib-work of logs and timber heavily bolted together, and filled with the cobble-stones which formerly paved the streets of Savannah. All the channels below the city were found more or less filled with torpedoes, which have been removed by order of Admiral Dahlgren, so that Savannah already fulfills the important part it was designed in our plans for the future.

In thus sketching the course of events connected with this campaign, I have purposely passed lightly over the march from Atlanta to the seashore, because it was made in four or more columns, sometimes at a distance of fifteen or twenty miles from each other, and it was impossible for me to attend but one. Therefore I have left it to the army and corps commanders to describe in their own language the events which attended the march of their respective columns. These reports are herewith submitted, and I beg to refer to them for farther details. I would merely sum up the advantages which I conceive have accrued to us by this march.

Our former labors in North Georgia had demonstrated the truth that no large army, carrying with it the necessary stores and baggage, can overtake and capture an inferior force of the enemy in his own country; therefore no alternative was left me but the one I adopted, namely, to divide my forces, and with the one part act offensively against the enemy's resources, while with the other I should act defensively, and invite the enemy to attack, risking the chances of battle.

In this conclusion I have been singularly sustained by the results. General Hood, who, as I have heretofore described, had moved to the westward, near Tuscumbia, with a view to decoy me away from Georgia, finding himself mistaken, was forced to choose either to pursue me, or to act offensively against the other part, left in Tennessee. He adopted the latter course, and General Thomas has wisely and well fulfilled his part of the grand scheme, in drawing Hood well up into Tennessee until he could concentrate all his own troops, and then turn upon Hood, as he has done, and destroy or fatally cripple his army. That part of my army is so far removed from me, that I leave, with perfect confidence, its management and history to General Thomas.

I was thereby left with a well-appointed army to sever the enemy's only remaining railroad communications eastward and westward, for over one hundred miles, namely, the Georgia State Railroad, which is broken up from Fairburn Station to Madison and the Oconee, and the Central Railroad from Gordon clear to Savannah, with numerous breaks on the latter road from Gordon to Eatonton, and from Millen to Augusta, and the Savannah and Gulf Railroad. We have also consumed the corn and fodder in the region of country thirty miles on either side of a line from

Atlanta to Savannah, as also the sweet potatoes, cattle, hogs, sheep, and poultry, and have carried away more than ten thousand horses and mules, as well as a countless number of their slaves. I estimate the damage done to the State of Georgia and its military resources at one hundred millions of dollars; at least twenty millions of which has inured to our advantage, and the remainder is simple waste and destruction. This may seem a hard species of warfare, but it brings the sad realities of war home to those who have been directly or indirectly instrumental in involving us in its attendant calamities.

The campaign has also placed this branch of my army in a position from which other great military results may be attempted, besides leaving in Tennessee and North Alabama a force which is amply sufficient to meet all the chances of war in that region of our country.

Since the capture of Atlanta my staff is unchanged, save that General Barry, chief of artillery, has been absent, sick, since our leaving Kingston. Surgeon Moore, United States Army, is chief medical director, in place of Surgeon Kittoe, relieved to resume his proper duties as a medical inspector.

Major Hitchcock, A.A.G., has also been added to my staff, and has been of great assistance in the field and office.

Captain Dayton still remains as my adjutant general. All have, as formerly, fulfilled their parts to my entire satisfaction.

In the body of my army I feel a just pride. Generals Howard and Slocum are gentlemen of singular capacity and intelligence, thorough soldiers and patriots, working day and night, not for themselves, but for their country and their men.

General Kilpatrick, who commanded the cavalry of this army, has handled it with spirit and dash to my entire satisfaction, and kept a superior force of the enemy's cavalry from even approaching our infantry columns or wagon trains. His report is full and graphic. All the division and brigade commanders merit my personal and official thanks, and I shall spare no efforts to secure them commissions equal to the rank they have exercised so well. As to the rank and file, they seem so full of confidence in themselves, that I doubt if they want a compliment from me; but I must do them the justice to say that, whether called on to fight, to march, to wade streams, to make roads, clear out obstructions, build bridges, make "corduroy," or tear up railroads, they have done it with alacrity and a degree of cheerfulness unsurpassed. A little loose in foraging, they "did some things they ought not to have done," yet, on the whole, they have supplied the wants of the army with as little violence as could be expected, and as little loss as I calculated. Some of these foraging parties had encounters with the enemy which would in ordinary times rank as respectable battles.

The behavior of our troops in Savannah has been so manly, so quiet, so perfect, that I take it as the best evidence of discipline and true courage. Never was a hostile city, filled with women and children, occupied by a large army with less disorder, or more system, order, and good government. The same general and generous spirit of confidence and good feeling pervades the army which it has ever afforded me especial pleasure to report on former occasions.

I avail myself of this occasion to express my heartfelt thanks to Admiral Dahlgren and the officers and men of his fleet, as also to General Foster and his command, for the hearty welcome given us on our arrival at the coast, and for their ready and prompt co-operation in all measures tending to the result accomplished.

I send herewith a map of the country through which we have passed; reports from General Howard, General Slocum, and General Kilpatrick, and their subordinates respectively, with the usual lists of captured property, killed, wounded, and missing, prisoners of war taken and rescued, as also copies of all papers illustrating the campaign, all of which are respectfully submitted by Your obedient servant,

W. T. SHERMAN, Major General.

II.

Report of the Campaign of the Carolinas.

Headquarters of the Military Division of the Mississippi,
Goldsboro', N. C., April 4th, 1865.

GENERAL,—I must now endeavor to group the events of the past three months connected with the armies under my command, in order that you may have as clear an understanding of the late campaign as the case admits of. The reports of the subordinate commanders will enable you to fill up the picture.

I have heretofore explained how, in the progress of our arms, I was enabled to leave in the West an army under Major General George H. Thomas of sufficient strength to meet emergencies in that quarter, while in person I conducted another army, composed of the 14th, 15th, 17th, and 20th Corps, and Kilpatrick's division of cavalry, to the Atlantic slope, aiming to approach the grand theatre of war in Virginia by the time the season would admit of military operations in that latitude. The first lodgment on the coast was made at Savannah, strongly fortified and armed, and valuable to us as a good sea-port, with its navigable stream inland. Near a month was consumed there in refitting the army, and in making the proper disposition of captured property, and other local matters; but by the 15th of January I was all ready to resume the march. Preliminary to this, General Howard, commanding the right wing, was ordered to embark his command at Thunderbolt, transport it to Beaufort, South Carolina, and thence by the 15th of January make a lodgment on the Charleston Railroad at or near Pocotaligo. This was accomplished punctually, at little cost, by the 17th Corps, Major General Blair, and a dépôt for supplies was established near the mouth of Pocotaligo Creek, with easy water communication back to Hilton Head.

The left wing, Major General Slocum, and the cavalry, Major General Kilpatrick, were ordered to rendezvous about the same time near Robertsville and Coosahatchie, South Carolina, with a dépôt of supplies at Pureysburg or State's Ferry, on the Savannah River. General Slocum had a good pontoon bridge constructed opposite the city, and the "Union Causeway," leading through the low rice-fields opposite Savannah, was repaired and "corduroyed;" but before the time appointed to start, the heavy rains of January had swelled the river, broken the pontoon bridge, overflowed the whole "bottom," so that the causeway was four feet under water, and General Slocum was compelled to look higher up for a passage over the Savannah River. He moved up to Sister's Ferry, but even there the river, with its overflowed bottoms, was near three miles wide, and he did not succeed in getting his whole wing across until during the first week of February.

In the mean time General Grant had sent me Grover's division of the 19th Corps to garrison Savannah, and had drawn the 23d Corps, Major General Schofield, from Tennessee, and sent it to re-enforce the commands of Major Generals Terry and Palmer, operating on the coast of North Carolina, to prepare the way for my coming.

On the 18th of January I transferred the forts and city of Savannah to Major General Foster, commanding the Department of the South, imparted to him my plans of operation, and instructed him how to follow my movements inland by occupying in succession the city of Charleston and such other points along the sea-coast as would be of any military value to us. The combined naval and land forces under Admiral Porter and General Terry had, on the 15th of January, captured Fort Fisher and the Rebel forts at the mouth of Cape Fear River, giving me an additional point of security on the sea-coast. But I had already resolved in my own mind, and had so advised General Grant, that I would undertake at one stride to make Goldsboro', and open communication with the sea by the Newbern Railroad, and had ordered Colonel W. W. Wright, superintendent of military railroads, to proceed in advance to Newbern, and to be prepared to extend the railroad out from Newbern to Goldsboro' by the 15th of March.

On the 19th of January all preparations were complete, and the orders of march were given. My chief quartermaster and Commissary Generals Easton and Beckwith were ordered to complete the supplies at Sister's Ferry and Pocotaligo, and then to follow our movement coastwise, looking for my arrival at Goldsboro'. North Carolina, about March 15th, and opening communication with me from Morehead City.

On the 22d of January I embarked from Savannah for Hilton Head, where I held a conference with Admiral Dahlgren, United States Navy, and Major General Foster, commanding the Department of the South, and next proceeded to Beaufort, riding out thence on the 24th to Pocotaligo, where the 17th Corps, Major General Blair, was encamped. The 15th Corps was somewhat scattered—Wood's and Hazen's divisions at Beaufort, John E. Smith marching from Savannah by the coast road, and Corse still at Savannah, cut off by the storms and freshet in the river. On the 25th a demonstration was made against the Combahee Ferry and Railroad Bridge across the Salkahatchie, merely to amuse the enemy, who had evidently adopted that river as his defensive line against our supposed *objective*, the city of Charleston. I reconnoitred the line in person, and saw that the heavy rains had swollen the river, so that water stood in the swamps for a breadth of more than a mile at a depth of from one to twenty feet. Not having the remotest intention of approaching Charleston, a comparatively small force was able, by seeming preparations to cross over, to keep in their front a considerable force of the enemy disposed to contest our advance on Charleston. On the 27th I rode to the camp of General Hatch's division of Foster's command, on the Tullafinney and Coosahatchie Rivers, and directed those places to be evacuated, as no longer of any use to us. That division was then moved to Pocotaligo to keep up the feints already begun, until we should, with the right wing, move higher up and cross the Salkahatchie about River's or Broxton's Bridge.

On the 29th I learned that the roads back of Savannah had at last become sufficiently free of the flood to admit of General Slocum putting his wing in motion, and that he was already approaching Sister's Ferry, whither a gun-boat, the Pontiac, Captain Luce, kindly furnished by Admiral Dahlgren, had preceded him to cover the crossing. In the mean time three divisions of the 15th Corps had closed up at Pocotaligo, and the right wing had loaded its wagons and was ready to start. I therefore directed General Howard to move one corps, the 17th, along the Salkahatchie, as high up as River's Bridge, and the other, the 15th, by Hickory Hill, Loper's Cross-roads, Anglesey Post-office, and Beaufort's Bridge. Hatch's division was ordered to remain at Pocotaligo, feigning at the Salkahatchie Railroad Bridge and Ferry, until our movement turned the enemy's position and forced him to fall behind the Edisto.

The 17th and 15th Corps drew out of camp on the 31st of January, but the real march began on the 1st of February. All the roads northward had for weeks been held by Wheeler's cavalry, who had, by details of negro laborers, felled trees, burned bridges, and made obstructions to impede our march. But so well organized were our pioneer battalions, and so strong and intelligent our men, that obstructions seemed only to quicken their progress. Felled trees were removed and bridges rebuilt by the heads of columns before the rear could close up. On the 2d of February the 15th Corps reached Loper's Cross-roads, and the 17th was at River's Bridge. From Loper's Cross-roads I communicated with General Slocum, still struggling with the floods of the Savannah River at Sister's Ferry. He had two divisions of the 20th Corps, General Williams's, on the east bank, and was enabled to cross over on his pontoons the cavalry of Kilpatrick. General Williams was ordered to Beaufort's Bridge by way of Lawtonville and Allandale, Kilpatrick to Blackville *via* Barnwell, and General Slocum to hurry the crossing at Sister's Ferry as much as possible, and overtake the right wing on the South Carolina

Railroad. General Howard, with the right wing, was directed to cross the Salkahatchie and push rapidly for the South Carolina Railroad at or near Midway. The enemy held the line of the Salkahatchie in force, having infantry and artillery intrenched at River's and Beaufort's Bridges. The 17th Corps was ordered to carry River's Bridge, and the 15th Corps Beaufort's Bridge. The former position was carried promptly and skilfully by Mower's and Giles A. Smith's divisions of the 17th Corps, on the 3d of February, by crossing the swamp, nearly three miles wide, with water varying from knee to shoulder deep. The weather was bitter cold, and Generals Mower and Smith led their divisions in person on foot, waded the swamp, made a lodgment below the bridge, and turned on the Rebel brigade which guarded it, driving it in confusion and disorder toward Branchville. Our casualties were 1 officer and 17 men killed, and 70 men wounded, who were sent to Pocotaligo. The line of the Salkahatchie being thus broken, the enemy retreated at once behind the Edisto at Branchville, and the whole army was pushed rapidly to the South Carolina Railroad at Midway, Bamberg (or Lowry's Station), and Graham's Station. The 17th Corps, by threatening Branchville, forced the enemy to burn the railroad bridge, and Walker's Bridge below, across the Edisto. All hands were at once set to work to destroy railroad track. From the 7th to the 10th of February this work was thoroughly prosecuted by the 17th Corps from the Edisto up to Bamberg, and by the 15th Corps from Bamberg up to Blackville. In the mean time General Kilpatrick had brought his cavalry rapidly by Barnwell to Blackville, and had turned towards Aiken, with orders to threaten Augusta, but not to be drawn needlessly into a serious battle. This he skilfully accomplished, skirmishing heavily with Wheeler's cavalry, first at Blackville and afterward at Williston and Aiken. General Williams, with two divisions of the 20th Corps, marched to the South Carolina Railroad at Graham's Station on the 8th, and General Slocum reached Blackville on the 10th. The destruction of the railroad was continued by the left wing from Blackville up to Windsor. By the 11th of February all the army was on the railroad all the way from Midway to Johnson's Station, thereby dividing the enemy's forces, which still remained at Branchville and Charleston on the one hand, Aiken and Augusta on the other.

We then began the movement on Orangeburg. The 17th Corps crossed the south fork of Edisto River at Binnaker's Bridge and moved straight for Orangeburg, while the 15th Corps crossed at Holman's Bridge and moved to Poplar Springs in support. The left wing and cavalry were still at work on the railroad, with orders to cross the South Edisto at New and Guignard's Bridges, move to the Orangeburg and Edgefield Road, and there await the result of the attack on Orangeburg. On the 12th the 17th Corps found the enemy intrenched in front of the Orangeburg Bridge, but swept him away by a dash, and followed him, forcing him across the bridge, which was partially burned. Behind the bridge was a battery in position, covered by a cotton and earth rampart, with wings as far as could be seen. General Blair held one division (Giles

A. Smith's) close up to the Edisto, and moved the other two to a point about two miles below, where he crossed Force's division by a pontoon bridge, holding Mower's in support. As soon as Force emerged from the swamp the enemy gave ground, and Giles Smith's division gained the bridge, crossed over, and occupied the enemy's parapet. He soon repaired the bridge, and by four P.M. the whole corps was in Orangeburg, and had begun the work of destruction on the railroad. Blair was ordered to destroy this railroad effectually up to Lewisville, and to push the enemy across the Congaree and force him to burn the bridges, which he did on the 14th; and without wasting time or labor on Branchville or Charleston, which I knew the enemy could no longer hold, I turned all the columns straight on Columbia.

The 17th Corps followed the State Road, and the 15th crossed the North Edisto from Poplar Springs at Schilling's Bridge, above the mouth of "Cawcaw Swamp" Creek, and took a country road which came into the State Road at Zeigler's. On the 15th, the 15th Corps found the enemy in a strong position at Little Congaree Bridge (across Congaree Creek), with a *tête-de-pont* on the south side, and a well constructed fort on the north side, commanding the bridge with artillery. The ground in front was very bad, level, and clear, with a fresh deposit of mud from a recent overflow. General Charles R. Wood, who commanded the leading division, succeeded, however, in turning the flank of the *tête-de-pont* by sending Stone's brigade through a cypress swamp to the left; and following up the retreating enemy promptly, he got possession of the bridge and the fort beyond. The bridge had been partially damaged by fire, and had to be repaired for the passage of artillery, so that night closed in before the head of the column could reach the bridge across Congaree River in front of Columbia. That night the enemy shelled our camps from a battery on the east side of the Congaree above Granby. Early next morning (February 16th) the head of column reached the bank of the Congaree opposite Columbia, but too late to save the fine bridge which spanned the river at that point. It was burned by the enemy. While waiting for the pontoons to come to the front, we could see people running about the streets of Columbia, and occasionally small bodies of cavalry, but no masses. A single gun of Captain De Grass's battery was firing at their cavalry squads, but I checked his firing, limiting him to a few shots at the unfinished State-house walls, and a few shells at the railroad dépôt, to scatter the people who were seen carrying away sacks of corn and meal that we needed. There was no white flag or manifestation of surrender. I directed General Howard not to cross directly in front of Columbia, but to cross the Saluda at the factory, three miles above, and afterward Broad River, so as to approach Columbia from the north. Within an hour of the arrival of General Howard's head of column at the river opposite Columbia, the head of column of the left wing also appeared, and I directed General Slocum to cross the Saluda at Zion Church, and thence to take roads direct for Winnsboro', breaking up *en route* the railroads and bridges about Alston.

General Howard effected a crossing of the Saluda near the factory on the 16th, skirmishing with cavalry, and the same night made a flying bridge across Broad River, about three miles above Columbia, by which he crossed over Stone's brigade of Wood's division, 15th Corps. Under cover of this brigade a pontoon bridge was laid on the morning of the 17th. I was in person at this bridge, and at 11 A.M. learned that the Mayor of Columbia had come out in a carriage and made formal surrender of the city to Colonel Stone, 25th Iowa Infantry, commanding third brigade, first division, 15th Corps. About the same time, a small party of the 17th Corps had crossed the Congaree in a skiff, and entered Columbia from a point immediately west. In anticipation of the occupation of the city, I had made written orders to General Howard touching the conduct of the troops. These were to destroy absolutely all arsenals and public property not needed for our own use, as well as all railroads, dépôts, and machinery useful in war to an enemy, but to spare all dwellings, colleges, schools, asylums, and harmless private property. I was the first to cross the pontoon bridge, and in company with General Howard rode into the city. The day was clear, but a perfect tempest of wind was raging. The brigade of Colonel Stone was already in the city, and was properly posted. Citizens and soldiers were on the streets, and general good order prevailed. General Wade Hampton, who commanded the Confederate rear-guard of cavalry, had, in anticipation of our capture of Columbia, ordered that all cotton, public and private, should be moved into the streets and fired, to prevent our making use of it. Bales were piled every where, the rope and bagging cut, and tufts of cotton were blown about in the wind, lodged in the trees and against houses, so as to resemble a snow-storm. Some of these piles of cotton were burning, especially one in the very heart of the city near the court-house, but the fire was partially subdued by the labor of our soldiers. During the day, the 15th Corps passed through Columbia and out on the Camden Road. The 17th did not enter the town at all; and, as I have before stated, the left wing and cavalry did not come within two miles of the town.

Before one single public building had been fired by order, the smouldering fires set by Hampton's order were rekindled by the wind, and communicated to the buildings around. About dark they began to spread, and got beyond the control of the brigade on duty within the city. The whole of Wood's division was brought in, but it was found impossible to check the flames, which by midnight had become unmanageable, and raged until about four A.M., when, the wind subsiding, they were got under control. I was up nearly all night, and saw Generals Howard, Logan, Wood, and others laboring to save houses, and to protect families thus suddenly deprived of shelter and of bedding and wearing apparel. I disclaim on the part of my army any agency in this fire, but, on the contrary, claim that we saved what of Columbia remains unconsumed. And, without hesitation, I charge General Wade Hampton with having burned his own city of Columbia, not with a malicious intent, or as the manifestation of a silly "Roman stoicism," but from folly and want of sense, in filling it with lint, cotton, and tinder. Our officers and men on duty worked well to extinguish the flames; but others not on duty, including the officers who had long been imprisoned there, rescued by us, may have assisted in spreading the fire after it had once begun, and may have indulged in unconcealed joy to see the ruin of the capital of South Carolina. During the 18th and 19th, the arsenal, railroad depôts, machine-shops, founderies, and other buildings were properly destroyed by detailed working parties, and the railroad track torn up and destroyed to Kingsville and the Wateree Bridge, and up in the direction of Winnsboro'.

At the same time, the left wing and cavalry had crossed the Saluda and Broad Rivers, breaking up railroad about Alston, and as high up as the bridge across Broad River on the Spartanburg Road, the main body moving straight for Winnsboro', which General Slocum reached on the 21st of February. He caused the railroad to be destroyed up to Blackstakes Depôt, and then turned to Rocky Mount, on the Catawba River. The 20th Corps reached Rocky Mount on the 22d, laid a pontoon bridge, and crossed over during the 23d. Kilpatrick's cavalry followed, and crossed over in a heavy rain during the night of the 23d, and moved up to Lancaster, with orders to keep up the delusion of a general movement on Charlotte, North Carolina, to which General Beauregard and all the cavalry of the enemy had retreated from Columbia. I was also aware that Cheatham's corps of Hood's old army was aiming to make a junction with Beauregard at Charlotte, having been cut off by our rapid movement on Columbia and Winnsboro'. From the 23d to the 26th we had heavy rains, swelling the rivers and making the roads almost impassable. The 20th Corps reached Hanging Rock on the 26th, and waited there for the 14th Corps to get across the Catawba. The heavy rains had so swollen the river that the pontoon bridge broke, and General Davis had very hard work to restore it and get his command across. At last he succeeded, and the left wing was all put in motion for Cheraw.

In the mean time, the right wing had broken up the railroad to Winnsboro', and thence turned for Pea's Ferry, where it was crossed over the Catawba before the heavy rains set in, the 17th Corps moving straight on Cheraw via Young's Bridge, and the 15th Corps by Tiller's and Kelly's Bridges. From this latter corps detachments were sent into Camden to burn the bridge over the Wateree, with the railroad depôt, stores, etc. A small force of mounted men under Captain Duncan was also dispatched to make a dash and interrupt the railroad from Charleston to Florence, but it met Butler's division of cavalry, and, after a sharp night skirmish on Mount Elon, was compelled to return unsuccessful. Much bad road was encountered at Lynch's Creek, which delayed the right wing about the same length of time as the left wing had been at the Catawba.

On the 2d of March, the leading division of the 20th Corps entered Chesterfield, skirmishing with Butler's division of cavalry, and the next day about noon the 17th Corps entered Cheraw, the enemy retreating across the Pedee and burning the bridge at that point. At Cheraw we found much ammunition and many guns, which had been brought from Charleston on the evacuation of that city. These were destroyed, as also the railroad trestles and bridges down as far as Darlington. An expedition of mounted infantry was also sent down to Florence, but it encountered both cavalry and infantry, and returned, having only broken up in part the branch road from Florence to Cheraw.

Without unnecessary delay the columns were again put in motion, directed on Fayetteville, North Carolina, the right wing crossing the Pedee at Cheraw and the left wing and cavalry at Sneedsboro'. General Kilpatrick was ordered to keep well on the left flank, and the 14th Corps, moving by Love's Bridge, was given the right to enter and occupy Fayetteville first. The weather continued unfavorable and the roads bad, but the 14th and 17th Corps reached Fayetteville on the 11th of March, skirmishing with Wade Hampton's cavalry, that covered the rear of Hardee's retreating army, which, as usual, had crossed Cape Fear River, burning the bridge. During the march from the Pedee, General Kilpatrick had kept his cavalry well on the left and exposed flank. During the night of the 9th March his three brigades were divided to picket the roads. General Hampton, detecting this, dashed in at daylight and gained possession of the camp of Colonel Spencer's brigade, and the house in which General Kilpatrick and Colonel Spencer had their quarters. The surprise was complete, but General Kilpatrick quickly succeeded in rallying his men on foot in a swamp near by, and, by a prompt attack, well followed up, regained his artillery, horses, camp, and every thing, save some prisoners whom the enemy carried off, leaving their dead on the ground.

The 12th, 13th, and 14th were passed at Fayetteville, destroying absolutely the United States Arsenal and the vast amount of machinery which had formerly belonged to the old Harper's Ferry United States Arsenal. Every building was knocked down and burned, and every piece of machinery utterly broken up and ruined, by the 1st regiment Michigan engineers, under the immediate supervision of Colonel O. M. Poe, chief engineer. Much valuable property of great use to an enemy was here destroyed or cast into the river.

Up to this period, I had perfectly succeeded in interposing my superior army between the scattered parts of my enemy. But I was then aware that the fragments that had left Columbia under Beauregard had been re-enforced by Cheatham's corps from the West and the garrison of Augusta, and that ample time had been given to move them to my front and flank about Raleigh. Hardee had also succeeded in getting across Cape Fear River ahead of me, and could therefore complete the junction with the other armies of Johnston and Hoke in North Carolina. And the whole, under the command of the skillful and experienced Joe Johnston, made up an army superior to me in cavalry, and formidable enough in artillery and infantry to justify me in extreme caution in making the last step necessary to complete the march I had undertaken. Previous to reaching Fayetteville, I had dispatched to Wilmington from Laurel Hill Church two of our best scouts with intelligence of our position and my general plans. Both of these messengers reached Wilmington, and on the morning of the 12th of March the army tug Davidson, Captain Ainsworth, reached Fayetteville from Wilmington, bringing me full intelligence of events from the outer world. On the same day, this tug carried back to General Terry, at Wilmington, and General Schofield, at Newbern, my dispatches to the effect that on Wednesday, the 15th, we would move for Goldsboro', feigning on Raleigh, and ordering them to march straight for Goldsboro', which I expected to reach about the 20th. The same day, the gun-boat Eolus, Captain Young, United States Navy, also reached Fayetteville, and through her I continued to have communication with Wilmington until the day of our actual departure. While the work of destruction was going on at Fayetteville, two pontoon bridges were laid across Cape Fear River, one opposite the town, the other three miles below.

General Kilpatrick was ordered to move up the plank road to and beyond Averysboro'. He was to be followed by four divisions of the left wing, with as few wagons as possible; the rest of the train, under escort of the two remaining divisions of that wing, to take a shorter and more direct road to Goldsboro'. In like manner, General Howard was ordered to send his trains, under good escort, well to the right, toward Faison's Dépôt and Goldsboro', and to hold four divisions light, ready to go to the aid of the left wing if attacked while in motion. The weather continued very bad, and the roads had become mere quagmire. Almost every foot of it had to be corduroyed to admit the passage of wheels. Still, time was so important that punctually, according to order, the columns moved out from Cape Fear River on Wednesday, the 15th of March. I accompanied General Slocum, who, preceded by Kilpatrick's cavalry, moved up the river or plank road that day to Kyle's Landing, Kilpatrick skirmishing heavily with the enemy's rear-guard about three miles beyond, near Taylor's Hole Creek. At General Kilpatrick's request, General Slocum sent forward a brigade of infantry to hold a line of barricades. Next morning, the column advanced in the same order, and developed the enemy, with artillery, infantry, and cavalry, in an intrenched position in front of the point where the road branches off toward Goldsboro' through Bentonville. On an inspection of the map, it was manifest that Hardee, in retreating from Fayetteville, had halted in the narrow, swampy neck between Cape Fear and South Rivers, in hopes to hold me to save time for the concentration of Johnston's armies at some point to his rear, namely, Raleigh, Smithfield, or Goldsboro'. Hardee's force was estimated at 20,000 men. It was necessary to dislodge him, that we might have the use of the Goldsboro' Road, as also to keep up the feint on Raleigh as long as possible. General Slocum was therefore ordered to press and carry the position, only difficult by reason of the nature of the ground, which was so soft that horses would sink every where, and even men could hardly make their way over the common pine barren.

The 20th Corps, General Williams, had the lead, and Ward's division the advance. This was deployed, and the skirmish line developed the position of a brigade of Charleston heavy artillery armed as infantry (Rhett's) posted across the road behind a light parapet, with a battery of guns enfilading the approach across a cleared field. General Williams sent a brigade (Casey's) by a circuit to his left that turned this line, and by a quick charge broke the brigade, which rapidly retreated back to a second line, better built and more strongly held. A battery of artillery (Winnager's) well posted, under the immediate direction of Major Reynolds, chief of artillery of 20th Corps, did good execution on the retreating brigade, and, on advancing Ward's division over this ground, General Williams captured three guns and 217 prisoners, of which 68 were wounded, and left in a house near by with a Rebel officer, four men, and five days' rations. One hundred and eight Rebel dead were buried by us. As Ward's division advanced, he developed a second and stronger line, when Jackson's division was deployed forward on the right of Ward, and the two divisions of Jeff. C. Davis's (14th) Corps on the left well toward the Cape Fear. At the same time, Kilpatrick, who was acting in concert with General Williams, was ordered to draw back his cavalry and mass it on the extreme right, and, in concert with Jackson's right, to feel forward for the Goldsboro' Road. He got a brigade on the road, but it was attacked by McLaw's Rebel division furiously, and, though it fought well and hard, the brigade drew back to the flank of the infantry. The whole line advanced late in the afternoon, drove the enemy well within his intrenched line, and pressed him so hard that next morning he was gone, having retreated in a miserable stormy night over the worst of roads. Ward's division of infantry followed to and through Averysboro', developing the fact that Hardee had retreated, not on Raleigh, but on Smithfield. I had the night before directed Kilpatrick to cross South River at a mill-dam to our right rear and move up on the east side toward Elevation. General Slocum reports his aggregate loss in this affair, known as that of Averysboro', at 12 officers and 65 men killed, and 477 wounded. We lost no prisoners. The enemy's loss can be inferred from his dead (108) left for us to bury. Leaving Ward's division to keep up a show of pursuit, Slocum's column was turned to the right, built a bridge across the swollen South River, and took the Goldsboro' Road, Kilpatrick crossing to the north in the direction of Elevation, with orders to move eastward, watching that flank. In the mean time, the wagon trains and guards, as also Howard's column, were wallowing along the miry roads toward Bentonville and Goldsboro'. The enemy's infantry, as before stated, had retreated on Smithfield, and his cavalry retreated across our front in the same direction, burning the bridges across Mill Creek. I continued with the head of Slocum's column, and camped the night of the 18th with him on the Goldsboro' Road, twenty-seven miles from Goldsboro', about five miles from Bentonville, and where the road from Clinton to Smithfield crosses the Goldsboro' Road. Howard was at Lee's Store, only two miles south, and both columns had pickets three miles forward, to where the two roads came together and became common to Goldsboro'.

P 2

All the signs induced me to believe that the enemy would make no farther opposition to our progress, and would not attempt to strike us in flank while in motion. I therefore directed Howard to move his right wing by the new Goldsboro' Road, which goes by way of Falling Creek Church. I also left Slocum and joined Howard's column, with a view to open communications with General Schofield, coming up from Newbern, and Terry from Wilmington. I found General Howard's column well strung out, owing to the very bad roads, and did not overtake him in person until he had reached Falling Creek Church, with one regiment forward to the cross-roads near Cox's Bridge across the Neuse. I had gone from General Slocum about six miles, when I heard artillery in his direction, but was soon made easy by one of his staff officers overtaking me, explaining that his leading division (Carlin's) had encountered a division of Rebel cavalry (Dibbrell's), which he was driving easily. But soon other staff officers came up, reporting that he had developed near Bentonville the whole of the Rebel army, under General Johnston himself. I sent him orders to call up the two divisions guarding his wagon trains, and Hazen's division of the 15th Corps, still back near Lee's Store, to fight defensively until I could draw up Blair's corps, then near Mount Olive Station, and, with the three remaining divisions of the 15th Corps, come up on Johnston's left rear from the direction of Cox's Bridge. In the mean time, while on the road, I received couriers from both Generals Schofield and Terry. The former reported himself in possession of Kinston, delayed somewhat by want of provisions, but able to march so as to make Goldsboro' on the 21st; and Terry was at or near Faison's Dépôt. Orders were at once dispatched to Schofield to push for Goldsboro', and to make dispositions to cross Little River in the direction of Smithfield as far as Millard; to General Terry to move to Cox's Bridge, lay a pontoon bridge, and establish a crossing; and to General Blair to make a night march to Falling Creek Church; and at daylight, the right wing, General Howard, less the necessary wagon guards, was put in rapid motion on Bentonville. By subsequent reports, I learned that General Slocum's head of column had advanced from its camp of March 18th, and first encountered Dibbrell's cavalry, but soon found his progress impeded by infantry and artillery. The enemy attacked his head of column, gaining a temporary advantage, and took three guns and caissons of General Carlin's division, driving the two leading brigades back on the main body. As soon as General Slocum realized that he had in his front the whole Confederate army, he promptly deployed the two divisions of the 14th Corps, General Davis, and rapidly brought up on their left the two divisions of the 20th Corps, General Williams. These he arranged on the defensive, and hastily prepared a line of barricades. General Kilpatrick also came up at the sound of artillery, and massed on the left. In this position, the left wing received six distinct assaults by the combined forces of Hoke, Hardee, and Cheatham, under the immediate command of General Johnston himself, without giving an inch of ground, and doing good execution on the enemy's ranks, especially with our artillery, the enemy having little or none.

Johnston had moved by night from Smithfield with great rapidity and without unnecessary wheels, intending to overwhelm my left flank before it could be relieved by its co-operating columns. But he "reckoned without his host." I had expected just such a movement all the way from Fayetteville, and was prepared for it. During the night of the 19th, General Slocum got up his wagon train with its guard of two divisions, and Hazen's division of the 15th Corps, which re-enforcement enabled him to make his position impregnable. The right wing found Rebel cavalry watching its approach, but unable to offer any serious opposition, until our head of column encountered a considerable body behind a barricade at the forks of the road near Bentonville, about three miles east of the battle-field of the day before. This body of cavalry was, however, quickly dislodged, and the intersection of the roads secured. On moving forward the 15th Corps, General Logan found that the enemy had thrown back his left flank, and had constructed a line of parapet connecting with that toward General Slocum, in the form of a bastion, its salient on the main Goldsboro' Road, interposing between General Slocum on the west and General Howard on the east, while the flanks rested on Mill Creek, covering the road back to Smithfield. General Howard was instructed to proceed with due caution until he had made strong connection on his left with General Slocum. This he soon accomplished, and by four P.M. of the 20th a complete and strong line of battle confronted the enemy in his intrenched position, and General Johnston, instead of catching us in detail, was on the defensive, with Mill Creek and a single bridge to his rear. Nevertheless, we had no object to accomplish by a battle, unless at an advantage, and therefore my general instructions were to press steadily with skirmishers alone, to use artillery pretty freely on the wooded space held by the enemy, and to feel pretty strongly the flanks of his position, which were, as usual, covered by the endless swamps of this region of country. I also ordered all empty wagons to be sent at once to Kinston for supplies, and all other impediments to be grouped near the Neuse, south of Goldsboro', holding the real army in close contact with the enemy, ready to fight him if he ventured outside his parapets and swampy obstructions.

Thus matters stood about Bentonville on the 21st of March. On the same day General Schofield entered Goldsboro' with little or no opposition, and General Terry had got possession of the Neuse River at Cox's Bridge, ten miles above, with a pontoon bridge laid and a brigade across; so that the three armies were in actual connection, and the great object of the campaign was accomplished.

On the 21st a steady rain prevailed, during which General Mower's division of the 17th Corps, on the extreme right, had worked well to the right around the enemy's flank, and had nearly reached the bridge across Mill Creek, the only line of retreat open to the enemy. Of course, there was extreme danger that the enemy would turn on him all his reserves, and, it might be, let go his parapets to overwhelm Mower. Accordingly, I ordered at once a general attack by our skirmish line from left to right. Quite a noisy battle ensued, during which General Mower was enabled to regain his connection with his own corps by moving to his left rear. Still, he had developed a weakness in the enemy's position of which advantage might have been taken; but that night the enemy retreated on Smithfield, leaving his pickets to fall into our hands, with many dead unburied, and wounded in his field hospitals. At daybreak of the 22d, pursuit was made two miles beyond Mill Creek, but checked by my order. General Johnston had utterly failed in his attempt, and we remained in full possession of the field of battle.

General Slocum reports the losses of the left wing about Bentonville at 9 officers and 145 men killed, 51 officers and 816 men wounded, and 3 officers and 223 men missing, taken prisoners by the enemy; total, 1247. He buried on the field 167 rebel dead, and took 338 prisoners.

General Howard reports the losses of the right wing at 2 officers and 35 men killed, 12 officers and 289 men wounded, and 1 officer and 60 men missing; total, 399. He also buried 100 rebel dead and took 1287 prisoners.

The cavalry of Kilpatrick was held in reserve, and lost but few, if any, of which I have no report as yet. Our aggregate loss at Bentonville was 1646.

I am well satisfied that the enemy lost heavily, especially during his assaults on the left wing during the afternoon of the 19th; but as I have no data save his dead and wounded left in our hands, I prefer to make no comparisons.

Thus, as I have endeavored to explain, we had completed our march on the 21st, and had full possession of Goldsboro', the real "objective," with its two railroads back to the sea-ports of Wilmington and Beaufort, North Carolina. These were being rapidly repaired by strong working parties, directed by Colonel W. W. Wright, of the Railroad Department. A large number of supplies had already been brought forward to Kinston, to which place our wagons had been sent to receive them. I therefore directed General Howard and the cavalry to remain at Bentonville during the 22d, to bury the dead and remove the wounded, and on the following day, all the armies to the camps assigned them about Goldsboro', there to rest and receive the clothing and supplies of which they stood in need. In person I went, on the 22d, to Cox's Bridge, to meet General Terry, whom I met for the first time, and on the following day rode into Goldsboro', where I found General Schofield and his army. The left wing came in during the same day and next morning, and the right wing followed on the 24th, on which day the cavalry moved to Mount Olive Station and General Terry back to Faison's. On the 25th the Newbern Railroad was finished, and the first train of cars came in, thus giving us the means of bringing from the dépôt at Morehead City full supplies to the army.

It was all-important that I should have an interview with the General-in-Chief; and, presuming that he could not at this time leave City Point, I left General Schofield in chief command, and proceeded with all expedition by rail to Morehead City, and thence by steamer to City Point, reaching General Grant's headquarters on the evening of the 27th of March. I had the good fortune to meet General Grant, the President, Generals Meade, Ord, and others of the Army of the Potomac, and soon learned the general state of the military world, from which I had been in a great measure cut off since January. Having completed all necessary business, I re-embarked on the navy steamer Bat, Captain Barnes, which Admiral Porter placed at my command, and returned *via* Hatteras Inlet and Newbern, reaching my own headquarters in Goldsboro' during the night of the 30th. During my absence, full supplies of clothing and food had been brought to camp, and all things were working well.

I have thus rapidly sketched the progress of our columns from Savannah to Goldsboro', but for more minute details must refer to the reports of subordinate commanders and of staff officers, which are not yet ready, but will in due season be forwarded and filed with this report. I can not even with any degree of precision recapitulate the vast amount of injury done the enemy, or the quantity of guns and materials of war captured and destroyed. In general terms, we have traversed the country from Savannah to Goldsboro', with an average breadth of forty miles, consuming all the forage, cattle, hogs, sheep, poultry, cured meats, corn meal, etc. The public enemy, instead of drawing supplies from that region to feed his armies, will be compelled to send provisions from other quarters to feed the inhabitants. A map herewith, prepared by my chief engineer, Colonel Poe, with the routes of the four corps and cavalry, will show at a glance the country traversed. Of course, the abandonment to us by the enemy of the whole sea-coast, from Savannah to Newbern, North Carolina, with its forts, dock-yards, gun-boats, etc., was a necessary incident to our occupation and destruction of the inland routes of travel and supply; but the real object of this march was to place this army in a position easy of supply, whence it could take an appropriate part in the spring and summer campaign of 1865. This was completely accomplished on the 21st of March, by the junction of the three armies and occupation of Goldsboro'.

In conclusion, I beg to express in the most emphatic manner my entire satisfaction with the tone and temper of the whole army. Nothing seems to dampen their energy, zeal, or cheerfulness. It is impossible to conceive a march involving more labor and exposure, yet I can not recall an instance of bad temper by the way, or hearing an expression of doubt as to our perfect success in the end. I believe that this cheerfulness and harmony of action reflects upon all concerned quite as much real honor and fame as "battles gained" or "cities won," and I therefore commend all—generals, staff, officers, and men, for these high qualities, in addition to the more soldierly ones of obedience to orders, and the alacrity they have always manifested when danger summoned them "to the front." I have the honor to be your obedient servant,

W. T. SHERMAN, Major General Commanding.

Major General H. W. HALLECK, Chief of Staff, Washington City, D. C.

III.

Gen. Sherman's Testimony before the Committee on the War.

Washington, May 22d, 1865.

Major General Sherman being sworn and examined:

By the Chairman—Q. What is your rank in the army? A. I am major general in the regular army.

Q. As your negotiation with the rebel General Johnston in relation to his surrender has been the subject of much public comment, the committee desire you to state all the facts and circumstances in regard to it, or which you wish the public to know. A. On the 15th day of April last I was at Raleigh, in command of three armies: the Army of the Ohio, the Army of the Cumberland, and the Army of the Tennessee; my enemy was General Joseph E. Johnston, of the Confederate Army, who commanded 50,000 men, retreating along the railroad from Raleigh by Hillsboro', Greensboro', Salisbury, and Charlotte; I commenced pursuit by crossing the curve of that road in the direction of Ashboro' and Charlotte; after the head of my column had crossed the Cape Fear River at Aven's Ferry, I received a communication from General Johnston, and answered it, copies of which I most promptly sent to the War Department, with a letter addressed to the Secretary of War, as follows:

"Headquarters Military Division of the Mississippi,
in the Field, Raleigh, N. C., April 15th, 1865.

"General U. S. GRANT and Secretary of War,—I send copies of a correspondence to you with General Johnston, which I think will be followed by terms of capitulation. I will grant the same terms General Grant gave General Lee, and be careful not to complicate any points of civil policy. If any cavalry has retreated toward me, caution them to be prepared to find our work done. It is now raining in torrents, and I shall await General Johnston's reply here, and will prepare to meet him in person at Chapel Hill.

"I have invited Governor Vance to return to Raleigh, with the civil officers of his state. I have met ex-Governor Graham, Messrs. Badger, Moore, Holden, and others, all of whom agree that the war is over, and that the states of the South must resume their allegiance, subject to the Constitution and laws of Congress, and must submit to the national arms. This great fact was admitted, and the details are of easy arrangement. W. T. SHERMAN, Major General."

I met General Johnston in person at a house five miles from Durham Station, under a flag of truce. After a few preliminary remarks he said to me, since Lee had surrendered his army at Appomattox Court-house, of which he had just been advised, he looked upon farther opposition by him as the greatest possible of crimes; that he wanted to know whether I could make him any general concessions; any thing by which he could maintain his hold and control of his army, and prevent its scattering;

any thing to satisfy the great yearning of their people; if so, he thought he could arrange terms satisfactory to both parties. He wanted to embrace the condition and fate of all the armies of the Southern Confederacy to the Rio Grande, to make one job of it, as he termed it.

I asked him what his powers were — whether he could command and control the fate of all the armies to the Rio Grande. He answered that he thought he could obtain the power, but he did not possess it at that moment; he did not know where Mr. Davis was, but he thought if I could give him the time he could find Mr. Breckinridge, whose orders would be obeyed every where, and he could pledge to me his personal faith that whatever he undertook to do would be done.

I had had frequent correspondence with the late President of the United States, with the Secretary of War, with General Halleck, and with General Grant, and the general impression left upon my mind, that if a settlement could be made, consistent with the Constitution of the United States, the laws of Congress, and the proclamation of the President, they would not only be willing, but pleased to terminate the war by one single stroke of the pen.

I needed time to finish the railroad from the Neuse Bridge up to Raleigh, and thought I could put in four or five days of good time in making repairs to my road, even if I had to send propositions to Washington; I therefore consented to delay twenty-four hours, to enable General Johnston to procure what would satisfy me as to his authority and ability as a military man, to do what he undertook to do; I therefore consented to meet him the next day, the 17th, at twelve noon, at the same place.

We did meet again; after a general interchange of courtesies, he remarked that he was then prepared to satisfy me that he could fulfill the terms of our conversation of the day before. He then asked me what I was willing to do; I told him, in the first place, I could not deal with any body except men recognized by us as "belligerents," because no military man could go beyond that fact. The Attorney General has since so decided, and any man of common sense so understood it before; there was no difference upon that point as to the men and officers accompanying the Confederate armies. I told him that the President of the United States, by a published proclamation, had enabled every man in the Southern Confederate Army, of the rank of colonel and under, to procure and obtain amnesty, by simply taking the oath of allegiance to the United States, and agreeing to go to his home and live in peace. The terms of General Grant to General Lee extended the same principles to the officers, of the rank of Brigadier General and upward, including the highest officer in the Confederate Army, viz., General Lee, the commander-in-chief. I was therefore willing to proceed with him upon the same principles.

Then a conversation arose as to what form of government they were to have in the South? Were the states there to be dissevered, and were the people to be denied representation in Congress? Were the people there to be, in the common language of the people of the South, slaves to the people of the North? Of course I said, "No; we desire that you shall regain your position as citizens of the United States, free and equal to us in all respects, and wish representation upon the condition of submission to the lawful authority of the United States as defined by the Constitution, the United States courts, and the authorities of the United States supported by those courts." He then remarked to me that General Breckinridge, a major general in the Confederate Army, was near by, and, if I had no objection, he would like to have him present. I called his attention to the fact, that I had on the day before explained to him that any negotiations between us must be confined to belligerents. He replied that he understood that perfectly. "But," said he, "Breckinridge, whom you do not know, save by public rumor, as Secretary of War, is, in fact, a major general; I give you my word for that. Have you any objection to his being present as a major general?" I replied, "I have no objection to any military officer you desire being present as a part of your personal staff." I myself had my own officers near me at call.

Breckinridge came a stranger to me, whom I had never spoken to in my life, and he joined in the conversation; while that conversation was going on a courier arrived and handed to General Johnston a package of papers; he and Breckinridge sat down and looked over them for some time and put them away in their pockets; what they were I know not, but one of them was a slip of paper, written, as General Johnston told me, by Mr. Reagan, Postmaster General of the Southern Confederacy; they seemed to talk about it *sotto voce*, and finally handed it to me; I glanced over it; it was preceded by a preamble, and closed with a few general terms; I rejected it at once.

We then discussed matters; talked about slavery, talked about every thing. There was a universal assent that slavery was as dead as any thing could be; that it was one of the issues of the war long since determined; and even General Johnston laughed at the folly of the Confederate government in raising negro soldiers, whereby they gave us all the points of the case. I told them that slavery had been treated by us as a dead institution, first by one class of men from the initiation of the war, and then from the date of the Emancipation Proclamation of President Lincoln, and finally by the assent of all parties. As to reconstruction, I told them I did not know what the views of the administration were. Mr. Lincoln, up to that time, in letters and by telegrams to me, encouraged me by all the words which could be used in general terms to believe, not only in his willingness, but in his desires that I should make terms with civil authorities, governors, and legislatures, even as far back as 1863. It then occurred to me that I might write off some general propositions, meaning little, or meaning much, according to the construction of parties—what I would term "glittering generalities"— and send them to Washington, which I could do in four days. That would enable the new President to give me a clew to his policy in the important juncture which was then upon us, for the war was over; the highest military authorities of the Southern Confederacy so confessed to me openly, unconcealedly, and repeatedly. I therefore drew up the memorandum (which has been published to the world) for the purpose of referring it to the proper executive authority of the United States, and enabling him to define to me what I might promise, simply to cover the pride of the Southern men, who thereby became subordinate to the laws of the United States, civil and military. I made no concessions to General Johnston's army or the troops under his direction and immediate control; and if any concessions were made in those general terms, they were made because I then believed, and now believe, they would have delivered into the hands of the United States the absolute control of every Confederate officer and soldier, all their muster-rolls, and all their arms. It would save us all the incidental expense resulting from the military occupation of that country by provost-marshals, provost-guards, military governors, and all the machinery by which alone military power can reach the people of a civilized country. It would have surrendered to us the armies of Dick Taylor and Kirby Smith, both of them capable of doing infinite mischief to us by exhausting the resources of the whole country upon which we were to depend for the future extinguishment of our debt, forced upon us by their wrongful and rebellious conduct. I never designed to shelter a human being from any liability incurred in consequence of past acts to the civil tribunals of our country, and I do not believe a fair and manly interpretation of my terms can so construe them, for the words "United States courts," "United States authorities," "limitations of executive power," occur in every paragraph. And if they seemingly yield terms better than the public would desire to be given to the Southern people, if studied closely and well it will be found that there is an absolute submission on their part to the government of the United States, either through its executive, legislative, or judicial authorities. Every step in the programme of these negotiations was reported punctually, clearly, and fully, by the most rapid means of communication that I had. And yet I neglected not one single precaution necessary to reap the full benefits of my position in case the government amended, altered, or absolutely annulled those terms. As those matters were necessarily mingled with the military history of the period, I would like at this point to submit to the committee my official report, which has been in the hands of the proper officer, Brigadier General Rawlings, Chief of Staff of the Army of the United States, since about the 12th instant. It was made by me at Manchester, Va., after I had returned from Savannah, whither I went to open up the Savannah River and reap the fruits of my negotiations with General Johnston, and to give General Wilson's force in the interior a safe and sure base from which he could draw the necessary supply of clothing and food for his command. It was only after I had fulfilled all this that I learned, for the first time, through the public press, that my conduct had been animadverted upon, not only by the Secretary of War, but by General Halleck, and the press of the country at large. I did feel hurt and annoyed that Mr. Stanton coupled with the terms of my memorandum, confided to him, a copy of a telegram to General Grant which he had never sent to me. He knew, on the contrary, that when he was at Savannah, that I had negotiations with civil parties there, for he was present in my room when those parties were conferring with me, and I wrote him a letter setting forth many points of it, in which I said I aimed to make a split in Jeff. Davis's dominions, by segregating Georgia from their course. Those were civil negotiations, and, far from being discouraged from making them, I was encouraged by Secretary Stanton himself to make them.

By coupling the note to General Grant with my memorandum, he gave the world fairly and clearly to infer that I was in possession of it. Now, I was not in possession of it, and I have reason to know that Mr. Stanton knew I was not in possession of it. Next met me General Halleck's telegram, indorsed by Mr. Stanton, in which they publicly avowed an act of perfidy—namely, the violation of my terms, which I had a right to make, and which, by the laws of war and by the laws of Congress, is punishable by death and no other punishment. Next, they ordered an army to pursue my enemy, who was known to be surrendering to me, in the presence of General Grant himself, their superior officer; and, finally, they sent orders to General Wilson and to General Thomas—my subordinates, acting under me on a plan of the most magnificent scale, admirably executed—to defeat my orders, and to thwart the interests of the government of the United States. I did feel indignant; I do feel indignant. As to my honor, I can protect it. In my letter of the 15th of April I used this language: "I have invited Governor Vance to return to Raleigh, with the civil officers of his state." I did so because President Lincoln had himself encouraged me to a similar course with the Governor of Georgia when I was in Atlanta. And here was the opportunity which the Secretary of War should have taken to put me on my guard against making terms with civil authorities, if such were the settled policy of our government. Had President Lincoln lived, I know he would have sustained me.

The following is my report, which I desire to have incorporated into and made part of my testimony.

IV.

General Sherman's Report of Operations in North Carolina, and Surrender of Johnston's Army.

Headquarters of the Military Division of the Mississippi, } in the Field, City Point, Virginia, May 9th, 1865.

GENERAL,—My last official report brought the history of events, as connected with the armies in the field subject to my immediate command, down to the 1st of April, when the Army of the Ohio, Major General J. M. Schofield commanding, lay at Goldsboro', with detachments distributed so as to secure and cover our routes of communication and supply back to the sea at Wilmington and Morehead City; Major General A. H. Terry, with the 10th Corps, being at Faison's Dépôt; the Army of the Tennessee, Major General O. O. Howard commanding, was encamped to the right and front of Goldsboro', and the Army of Georgia, Major General H. W. Slocum commanding, to its left and front; the cavalry, Brevet Major General J. Kilpatrick commanding, at Mount Olive. All were busy in repairing the wear and tear of our then recent and hard march from Savannah, and in replenishing clothing and stores necessary for a farther progress

I had previously, by letter and in person, notified the Lieutenant General commanding the armies of the United States, that the 10th of April would be the earliest possible moment at which I could hope to have all things in readiness, and we were compelled to use our railroads to the very highest possible limit in order to fulfill that promise. Owing to a mistake in the railroad department in sending locomotives and cars of the five-foot guage, we were limited to the use of the few locomotives and cars of the four foot eight and a half inch guage already in North Carolina, with such of the old stock as was captured by Major General Terry at Wilmington and on his way up to Goldsboro'. Yet such judicious use was made of these, and such industry displayed in the railroad management, by Generals Easton and Beckwith, and Colonel Wright and Mr. Van Dyne, that by the 10th of April our men were all reclad, the wagons reloaded, and a fair amount of forage accumulated ahead.

In the mean time, Major General George Stoneman, in command of a division of cavalry operating from East Tennessee in connection with Major General George H. Thomas, in pursuance of my orders of January 21st, 1865, had reached the railroad about Greensboro', North Carolina, and had made sad havoc with it, and had pushed along it to Salisbury, destroying *en route* bridges, culverts, dépôts, and all kinds of rebel supplies, and had extended the break in the railroad down to the Catawba Bridge. This was fatal to the hostile armies of Lee and Johnston, who depended on that road for supplies, and as their ultimate line of retreat. Major General J. H. Wilson, also in command of the cavalry corps organized by himself under special field orders No. —, of October 24th, 1864, at Gaylesville, Alabama, had started from the neighborhood of Decatur and Florence, Alabama, and moved straight into the heart of Alabama, on a route prescribed for General Thomas after he had defeated General Hood at Nashville, Tennessee; but the roads being too heavy for infantry, General Thomas had devolved that duty on that most energetic young cavalry officer, General Wilson, who, imbued with the proper spirit, has struck one of the best blows of the war at the waning strength of the Confederacy. His route was one never before touched by our troops, and afforded him abundance of supplies as long as he was in motion, namely, by Tuscaloosa, Selma, Montgomery, Columbus, and Macon. Though in communication with him, I have not been able to receive, as yet, his full and detailed reports, which will in due time be published and appreciated. Lieutenant General Grant, also in immediate command of the armies about Richmond, had taken the initiative in that magnificent campaign which, in less than ten days, compelled the evacuation of Richmond, and resulted in the destruction and surrender of the entire Rebel army of Virginia under command of General Lee.

The news of the battles about Petersburg reached me at Goldsboro' on the 6th of April. Up to that time my purpose was to move rapidly northward, feigning on Raleigh and striking straight for Burkesville, thereby interposing between Johnston and Lee. But the auspicious events in Virginia had changed the whole military problem, and, in the expressive language of Lieutenant General Grant, "the Confederate Armies of Lee and Johnston" became the "strategic points." General Grant was fully able to take care of the former, and my task was to capture or destroy the latter. Johnston at that time, April 6th, had his army well in hand about Smithfield, interposing between me and Raleigh. I estimated his infantry and artillery at 35,000, and his cavalry from 6000 to 10,000. He was superior to me in cavalry, so that I held General Kilpatrick in reserve at Mount Olive, with orders to recruit his horses and be ready to make a sudden and rapid march on the 10th of April.

At daybreak of the day appointed, all the heads of columns were in motion straight against the enemy—Major General H. W. Slocum taking the two direct roads for Smithfield; Major General O. O. Howard making a circuit by the right, and feigning up the Weldon Road to disconcert the enemy's cavalry; Generals Terry and Kilpatrick moving on the west side of the Neuse River, and aiming to reach the rear of the enemy between Smithfield and Raleigh. General Schofield followed General Slocum in support.

All the columns met, within six miles of Goldsboro', more or less cavalry, with the usual rail barricades, which were swept before us as chaff, and by 10 A.M. of the 11th the 14th Corps entered Smithfield, the 20th Corps close at hand. Johnston had rapidly retreated across the Neuse River, and, having his railroad to lighten up his trains, could retreat faster than we could pursue. The rains had also set in, making the resort to corduroy absolutely necessary to pass even ambulances. The enemy had burned the bridge at Smithfield, and as soon as possible Major General Slocum got up his pontoons and crossed over a division of the 14th Corps. We there heard of the surrender of Lee's army at Appomattox Court-house, Virginia, which was announced to the armies in orders, and created universal joy. Not an officer or soldier of my armies but expressed a pride and satisfaction that it fell to the lot of the armies of the Potomac and James so gloriously to overwhelm and capture the entire army that had held them so long in check, and their success gave new impulse to finish up our task. Without a moment's hesitation we dropped our trains and marched rapidly in pursuit to and through Raleigh, reaching that place at 7.30 A.M. of the 13th, in a heavy rain. The next day the cavalry pushed on through the rain to Durham's Station, the 15th Corps following as far as Morrisville Station, and the 17th Corps to Jones's Station. On the supposition that Johnston was tied to his railroad as a line of retreat by Hillsboro', Greensboro', Salisbury, Charlotte, etc., I had turned the other columns across the bend of that road toward Ashboro'. (See Special Field Orders, No. 55.) The cavalry, Brevet Major General J. Kilpatrick commanding, was ordered to keep up a show of pursuit toward the "Company's Shops," in Alamance County; Major General O. O. Howard to turn to the left by Hackney's Cross-roads, Pittsboro', St. Lawrence, and Ashboro'; Major General H. W. Slocum to cross Cape Fear River at Aven's Ferry, and move rapidly by Carthage, Caledonia, and Cox's Mills; Major General J. M. Schofield was to hold Raleigh and the road back, and with his spare force to follow an intermediate route.

By the 15th, though the rains were incessant and the roads almost impracticable, Major General Slocum had the 14th Corps, Brevet Major General Davis commanding, near Martha's Vineyard, with a pontoon bridge laid across Cape Fear River at Aven's Ferry, with the 20th Corps, Major General Mower commanding, in support, and Major General Howard had the 15th and 17th Corps stretched out on the roads toward Pittsboro', while General Kilpatrick held Durham's Station and Chapel Hill University.

Johnston's army was retreating rapidly on the roads from Hillsboro' to Greensboro', he himself at Greensboro'. Although out of place as to time, I here invite all military critics who study the problems of war to take their maps and compare the position of my army on the 15th and 16th of April with that of General Halleck about Burkesville and Petersburg, Virginia, on the 26th of April, when, according to his telegram to Secretary Stanton, he offered to relieve me of the task of "cutting off Johnston's retreat." Major General Stoneman at the time was at Statesville, and Johnston's only line of retreat was by Salisbury and Charlotte. It may be that General Halleck's troops can outmarch mine, but there is nothing in their past history to show it; or it may be that General Halleck can inspire his troops with more energy of action. I doubt that also, save and except in this single instance, when he knew the enemy was ready to surrender or disperse, as advised by my letter of April 18th, addressed to him when chief of staff at Washington City, and delivered at Washington on the 21st instant by Major Hitchcock of my staff.

Thus matters stood at the time I received General Johnston's first letter and made my answer of April 14th, copies of which were sent with all expedition to Lieutenant General Grant and the Secretary of War, with my letter of April 15th. I agreed to meet General Johnston in person at a point intermediate between our pickets on the 17th at noon, provided the position of the troops remained *statu quo*. I was both willing and anxious thus to consume a few days, as it would enable Colonel Wright to finish our railroad to Raleigh.

Two bridges had to be built and twelve miles of new road made. We had no iron except by taking up that on the branch from Goldsboro' to

Weldon. Instead of losing by time, I gained in every way; for every hour of delay possible was required to reconstruct the railroad to our rear and improve the condition of our wagon roads to the front, so desirable in case the negotiations failed and we be forced to make the race of near two hundred miles to head off or catch Johnston's army, then retreating toward Charlotte.

At noon of the day appointed, I met General Johnston for the first time in my life, although we had been interchanging shots constantly since May, 1863.

Our interview was frank and soldier-like, and he gave me to understand that farther war on the part of the Confederate troops was folly, that *the cause* was lost, and that every life sacrificed after the surrender of Lee's army was the "highest possible crime." He admitted that the terms conceded to General Lee were magnanimous, and all he could ask; but he did want some general concessions that would enable him to allay the natural fears and anxieties of his followers, and enable him to maintain his control over them until they could be got back to the neighborhood of their homes, thereby saving the State of North Carolina the devastations inevitably to result from turning his men loose and unprovided on the spot, and our pursuit across the state.

He also wanted to embrace in the same general proposition the fate of all the Confederate armies that remained in existence. I never made any concession as to his own army, or assumed to deal finally and authoritatively in regard to any other, but it did seem to me that there was presented a chance for peace that might be deemed valuable to the government of the United States, and was at least worth the few days that would be consumed in reference.

To push an army whose commmander had so frankly and honestly confessed his inability to cope with me were cowardly, and unworthy the brave men I led.

Inasmuch as General Johnston did not feel authorized to pledge his power over the armies in Texas, we adjourned to meet the next day at noon. I returned to Raleigh, and conferred freely with all my general officers, *every one* of whom urged me to conclude terms that might accomplish so complete and desirable an end. All dreaded the weary and laborious march after a fugitive and dissolving army back toward Georgia, almost over the very country where we had toiled so long. There was but one opinion expressed; and, if contrary ones were entertained, they were withheld, or indulged in only by that class who shun the fight and the march, but are loudest, bravest, and fiercest when danger is past. I again met General Johnston on the 18th, and we renewed the conversation. He satisfied me then of his *power* to disband the Rebel armies in Alabama, Mississippi, Louisiana, and Texas, as well as those in his immediate command, namely, North Carolina, South Carolina, Florida, and Georgia.

The points on which he expressed especial solicitude were, lest their states were to be dismembered and denied representation in Congress, or any separate political existence whatever, and that the absolute disarming his men would leave the South powerless, and exposed to depredations by wicked bands of assassins and robbers.

President Lincoln's Message of 1864; his Amnesty Proclamation; General Grant's terms to General Lee, substantially extending the benefits of that proclamation to all officers above the rank of colonel; the invitation to the Virginia Legislature to reassemble in Richmond by General Weitzel, with the approval of Mr. Lincoln and General Grant, then on the spot; a firm belief that I had been fighting to re-establish the Constitution of the United States; and last, and not least, the general and universal desire to close a war any longer without organized resistance, were the leading facts that induced me to pen the "memorandum" of April 18th, signed by myself and General Johnston.

It was designed to be, and so expressed on its face, as a mere "basis" for reference to the President of the United States and constitutional Commander-in-Chief, to enable him, if he chose, at one blow to dissipate the military power of the Confederacy which had threatened the national safety for years. It admitted of modification, alteration, and change. It had no appearance of an ultimatum, and by no false reasoning can it be construed into a usurpation of power on my part. I have my opinions on the questions involved, and will stand by the memorandum; but this forms no part of a military report. Immediately on my return to Raleigh I dispatched one of my staff, Major Hitchcock, to Washington, enjoining him to be most prudent and careful to avoid the spies and informers that would be sure to infest him by the way, and to say nothing to any body until the President could make known to me his wishes and policy in the matter.

The news of President Lincoln's assassination on the 14th of April (wrongly reported to me by telegraph as having occurred on the 11th) reached me on the 17th, and was announced to my command on the same day in Special Field Orders, No. 56. I was duly impressed with its horrible atrocity and probable effect upon the country; but when the property and interests of millions still living were involved, I saw no good reason to change my course, but thought rather to manifest real respect for his memory by following after his death that policy which, if living, I feel certain he would have approved, or, at least, not rejected with disdain. Up to that hour I had never received one word of instruction, advice, or counsel as to the "plan or policy" of government, looking to a restoration of peace on the part of the Rebel states of the South. Whenever asked for an opinion on the points involved, I had always evaded the subject. My letter to the Mayor of Atlanta has been published to the world, and I was not rebuked by the War Department for it.

My letter to Mr. N—— W——, at Savannah, was shown by me to Mr. Stanton before its publication, and all that my memory retains of his answer is that he said, like my letters generally, it was sufficiently "emphatic, and could not be misunderstood."

But these letters asserted my belief that, according to Mr. Lincoln's proclamations and messages, when the people of the South had laid down their arms and submitted to the lawful power of the United States, *ipso facto* the war was over as to them; and, farthermore, that if any state in rebellion would conform to the Constitution of the United States, "cease war," elect Senators and Representatives to Congress, if admitted (of which each House of Congress alone is the judge), that state became *instanter* as much in the Union as New York or Ohio. Nor was I rebuked for this expression, though it was universally known and commented on at the time. And again, Mr. Stanton in person, at Savannah, speaking of the terrific expenses of the war and difficulty of realizing the money necessary for the daily wants of government, impressed me most forcibly with the necessity of bringing the war to a close as soon as possible for *financial reasons.*

On the evening of April 23d, Major Hitchcock reported his return to Morehead City with dispatches, of which fact General Johnston, at Hillsboro', was notified, so as to be ready in the morning for an answer. At 6 o'clock A.M. on the 24th, Major Hitchcock arrived, accompanied by General Grant and members of his staff, who had not telegraphed the fact of his coming over our exposed road for prudential reasons.

I soon learned that the memorandum was disapproved, without reasons assigned, and I was ordered to give the forty-eight hours' notice, and resume hostilities at the close of that time, governing myself by the substance of a dispatch then inclosed, dated March 3d, 12 noon, at Washington, District of Columbia, from Secretary Stanton to General Grant, at City Point, but not accompanied by any part of the voluminous matter so liberally lavished on the public in the New York journals of the 24th of April. That was the *first* and only *time* I ever saw that telegram, or had one word of instruction on the important matter involved in it; and it does seem strange to me that every bar-room loafer in New York can read in the morning journals "official" matter that is withheld from a General whose command extends from Kentucky to North Carolina.

Within an hour a courier was riding from Durham's Station toward Hillsboro' with notice to General Johnston of the suspension of the truce, and renewing my demand for the surrender of the armies under his immediate command (see two letters, April 24th, 6 A.M.), and at 12 noon I had the receipt of his picket officer. I therefore published my Orders, No. 62, to the troops, terminating the truce at 12 M. on the 26th, and ordered all to be in readiness to march at that hour on the routes prescribed in Special Field Order, No. 55, April 14th, from the positions held April 18th.

General Grant had orders from the President, through the Secretary of War, to direct military movements, and I explained to him the exact position of the troops, and he approved of it most emphatically; but he did not relieve me, or express a wish to assume command. All things were in readiness, when, on the evening of the 25th, I received another letter from General Johnston, asking another interview to renew negotiations.

General Grant not only approved, but urged me to accept, and I appointed a meeting at our former place at noon of the 26th, the very hour fixed for the renewal of hostilities. General Johnston was delayed by an accident to his train, but at 2 P.M. arrived. We then consulted, concluded, and signed the final terms of capitulation.

These were taken by me back to Raleigh, submitted to General Grant, and met his immediate approval and signature. General Johnston was not even aware of the presence of General Grant at Raleigh at the time.

Thus was surrendered to us the second great army of the so-called Confederacy; and though undue importance has been given to the so-called negotiations which preceded it, and a rebuke and public disfavor cast on me wholly unwarranted by the facts, I rejoice in saying it was accomplished without farther ruin and devastation to the country, without the loss of a single life to those gallant men who had followed me from the Mississippi to the Atlantic, and without subjecting brave men to the ungracious task of pursuing a fleeing foe that did not want to fight. As for myself, I know my motives, and challenge the instance during the past four years where an armed and defiant foe stood before me that I did not go in for a fight, and I would blush for shame if I had ever insulted or struck a fallen foe. The instant the terms of surrender were approved by General Grant, I made my Orders, No. 65, assigning to each of my subordinate commanders his share of the work, and, with General Grant's approval, made Special Field Orders, No. 66, putting in motion my old army (no longer required in Carolina) northward for Richmond. General Grant left Raleigh at 9 A.M. of the 27th, and I glory in the fact that during his three-days' stay with me, I did not detect in his language or manner one particle of abatement in the confidence, respect, and affection that have existed between us throughout all the varied events of the past war; and, though we have honestly differed in opinion in other cases as well as this, still we respected each other's honest convictions.

I still adhere to my then opinions, that by a few general concessions, "glittering generalities," all of which in the end must and will be conceded to the organized states of the South, that this day there would not be an armed battalion opposed to us within the broad area of the dominions of the United States. Robbers and assassins must, in any event, result from the disbandment of large armies, but even these should be and could be taken care of by the local civil authorities without being made a charge on the national treasury.

On the evening of the 28th, having concluded all business requiring my personal attention at Raleigh, and having conferred with every army commander and delegated to him the authority necessary for his future action, I dispatched my headquarter wagons by land along with the 17th Corps, the office in charge of General Webster from Newbern, to Alexandria, Virginia, by sea, and in person, accompanied only by my personal staff, hastened to Savannah to direct matters in the interior of South Carolina and Georgia. I had received across the Rebel telegraph wires cipher dispatches from General Wilson at Macon to the effect that he was in receipt of my Orders, No. 65, and would send General Upton's division to Augusta, and General McCook's division to Tallahassee, to receive the surrender of those garrisons, take charge of the public property, and execute the paroles required by the terms of surrender. He reported a sufficiency of forage for his horses in Southwest Georgia, but asked me to send him a supply of clothing, sugar, coffee, etc., by way of Augusta, Georgia, whence he could get it by rail. I therefore went rapidly to Goldsboro' and Wilmington, reaching the latter city at 10 A.M. of the 29th, and the same day embarked for Hilton Head in the blockade runner "Russia," Captain A. M. Smith. I found General Q. A. Gillmore, commanding Department of the South, at Hilton Head, on the evening of April 30th, and ordered him to send to Augusta at once what clothing and small stores he could spare for General Wilson, and to open up a line of certain communication and supply with him at Macon. Within an hour the captured steam-boats "Jeff. Davis" and "Amazon," both adapted to the shallow and crooked navigation of the Savannah River, were being loaded, the one at Savannah and the other at Hilton Head. The former started up the river on the 1st of May, in charge of a very intelligent officer (whose name I can not recall) and forty-eight men, all the boat could carry, with orders to occupy temporarily the United States Arsenal at Augusta and open up communication with General Wilson at Macon, in the event that General McCook's division of cavalry was not already there. The "Amazon" followed next day, and General Gillmore had made the necessary orders for a brigade of infantry, to be commanded by General Molyneaux, to follow by a land march to Augusta as its permanent garrison. Another brigade of infantry was ordered to occupy Orangeburg, South Carolina, the point farthest in the interior that can at present be reached by rail from the seacoast (Charleston).

On the 1st of May I went on to Savannah, where General Gillmore also joined me, and the arrangements ordered for the occupation of Augusta were consummated.

At Savannah I found the city in the most admirable police, under direction of Brevet Major General Grover, and the citizens manifested the most unqualified joy to hear that, so far as they were concerned, the war was over. All classes, Union men as well as former Rebels, did not conceal, however, the apprehensions naturally arising from a total ignorance of the political conditions to be attached to their future state. Any thing at all would be preferable to this dread uncertainty.

On the evening of the 2d of May I returned to Hilton Head, and there, for the first time, received the New York papers of April 28th, containing Secretary Stanton's dispatch of 9 A.M. of the 27th of April to General Dix, including General Halleck's, from Richmond, of 9 P.M. of the night before, which seems to have been rushed with extreme haste before an excited public, namely, morning of the 28th. You will observe from the dates that these dispatches were running back and forth from Richmond and Washington to New York, and there published, while General Grant and I were together in Raleigh, North Carolina, adjusting, to the best of our ability, the terms of surrender of the only remaining formidable Rebel army in existence at the time east of the Mississippi River. Not one word of intimation had been sent to me of the displeasure of the government with my official conduct, but only the naked disapproval of a skeleton memorandum sent properly for the action of the President of the United States.

The most objectionable features of my memorandum had already (April 24th) been published to the world in violation of official usage, and the contents of my accompanying letters to General Halleck, General Grant, and Mr. Stanton, of even date, though at hand, were suppressed.

In all these letters I had stated clearly and distinctly that Johnston's army would *not* fight, but, if pushed, would "disband" and "scatter" into small and dangerous guerrilla parties, as injurious to the interests of the United States as to the Rebels themselves; that all parties admitted that the Rebel cause of the South was abandoned, that the negro was free, and that the temper of all was most favorable to a lasting peace. I say all these opinions of mine were withheld from the public with a seeming purpose; and I do contend that my official experience and former services, as well as my past life and familiarity with the people and geography of the South, entitled my opinions to at least a decent respect.

Although this dispatch (Mr. Stanton's of April 27th) was printed "official," it had come to me only in the questionable newspaper paragraph headed, "Sherman's Truce Disregarded."

I had already done what General Wilson wanted me to do, namely, had sent him supplies of clothing and food, with clear and distinct orders and instructions how to carry out in Western Georgia the terms for the surrender of arms and paroling of prisoners made by General Johnston's capitulation of April 26th, and had properly and most opportunely ordered General Gillmore to occupy Orangeburg and Augusta, strategic points of great value at all times, in peace or war; but, as the Secretary had taken upon himself to order my subordinate Generals to disobey my "orders," I explained to General Gillmore that I would no longer confuse him or General Wilson with "orders" that might conflict with those of the Secretary, which, as reported, were sent, not through me, but in open disregard of me and of my lawful authority.

It now becomes my duty to paint in justly severe character the still more offensive and dangerous matter of General Halleck's dispatch of April 26th to the Secretary of War, embodied in his to General Dix of April 27th.

General Halleck had been chief of staff of the army at Washington, in which capacity he must have received my official letter of April 18th, wherein I wrote clearly that if Johnston's army about Greensboro' were "pushed" it would "disperse," an event I wished to prevent. About that time he seems to have been sent from Washington to Richmond to command the new Military Division of the James, in assuming charge of which, on the 22d, he defines the limits of his authority to be the "Department of Virginia, the Army of the Potomac, and such part of North Carolina *as may not be occupied by the command of Major General Sherman.*" (See his General Orders, No. 1.) Four days later, April 26th, he reports to the Secretary that he has ordered Generals Meade, Sheridan, and Wright to invade that part of North Carolina which *was* occupied by my command, and pay "no regard to any truce or orders of" mine. They were ordered to "*push* forward, regardless of any orders save those of Lieutenant General Grant, and cut off Johnston's retreat." He knew at the time he penned that dispatch and made those orders, that Johnston was not retreating, but was halted under a forty-eight hours' truce with me, and was laboring to surrender his command and prevent its dispersion into guerrilla bands, and that I had on the spot a magnificent army at my command, amply sufficient for all purposes required by the occasion.

The plan for cutting off a retreat from the direction of Burkesville and Danville is hardly worthy one of his military education and genius. When he contemplated an act so questionable as the violation of a "truce" made by competent authority within his sphere of command, he should have gone himself and not have sent subordinates, for he knew I was bound in honor to *defend* and *maintain* my *own* truce and pledge of faith, even at the cost of many lives.

When an officer pledges the faith of his government, he is bound to defend it, and he is no soldier who would violate it knowingly.

As to Davis and his stolen treasure, did General Halleck, as chief of staff or commanding officer of the neighboring military division, notify me of the facts contained in his dispatch to the Secretary? No, he did not. If the Secretary of War wanted Davis caught, why not order it, instead of, by publishing in the newspapers, putting him on his guard to hide away and escape? No orders or instructions to catch Davis or his stolen treasure ever came to me; but, on the contrary, I was led to believe that the Secretary of War rather preferred he should effect an escape from the country, if made "unknown" to him. But even on this point I inclose a copy of my letter to Admiral Dahlgren, at Charleston, sent him by a fleet steamer from Wilmington on the 25th of April, two days before the bankers of Richmond had imparted to General Halleck the important secret as to Davis's movement, designed doubtless to stimulate his troops to march their legs off to catch *their* treasure for *their* own use.

I know now that Admiral Dahlgren did receive my letter on the 26th, and had acted on it *before* General Halleck had even thought of the matter; but I do not believe a word of the treasure story—it is absurd on its face—and General Halleck or any body has my full permission to chase Jeff. Davis and cabinet with their stolen treasure through any part of the country occupied by my command.

The last and most obnoxious feature of General Halleck's dispatch is wherein he goes out of his way and advises that my subordinates, Generals Thomas, Stoneman, and Wilson, should be instructed not to obey "Sherman's" commands.

This is too much; and I turn from the subject with feelings too strong for words, and merely record my belief that so much mischief was never before embraced in so small a space as in the newspaper paragraph headed "Sherman's Truce Disregarded," authenticated as "official" by Mr. Secretary Stanton, and published in the New York papers of April 28th.

During the night of May 2d, at Hilton Head, having concluded my business in the Department of the South, I began my return to meet my troops then marching toward Richmond from Raleigh. On the morning of the 3d we ran into Charleston Harbor, where I had the pleasure to meet Admiral Dahlgren, who had, in all my previous operations from Savannah northward, aided me with a courtesy and manliness that commanded my entire respect and deep affection; also General Hatch, who, from our first interview at his Tullifinney camp, had caught the spirit of the move from Pocotaligo northward, and had largely contributed to our joint success in taking Charleston and the Carolina coast. Any one who is not *satisfied* with war should go and see Charleston, and he will pray louder and deeper than ever that the country may in the long future be spared any more war. Charleston and secession being synonymous terms, the city should be left as a sample, so that centuries may pass away before that false doctrine is again preached in our Union.

We left Charleston on the evening of the 3d of May, and hastened with all possible speed back to Morehead City, which we reached at night of the 4th. I immediately communicated by telegraph with General Schofield at Raleigh, and learned from him the pleasing fact that the Lieutenant General commanding the armies of the United States had reached the Chesapeake in time to countermand General Halleck's orders, and prevent his violating my truce, invading the area of my command, and driving Johnston's surrendering army into fragments. General Johnston had fulfilled his agreement to the very best of his ability; and the officers charged with issuing the paroles at Greensboro' reported about thirty thousand (30,000) already made, and that the greater part of the North Carolina troops had gone home without waiting for their papers, but that all of them would doubtless come into some one of the military posts, the commanders of which are authorized to grant them. About eight hundred (800) of the Rebel cavalry had gone South, refusing to abide the terms of the surrender, and it was supposed they would make for Mexico. I would sincerely advise that they be encouraged to go and stay; they would be a nuisance to any civilized government, whether loose or in prison.

With the exception of some plundering on the part of Lee's and Johnston's disbanded men, all else in North Carolina was "quiet." When to the number of men surrendered at Greensboro' are added those at Tallahassee, Augusta, and Macon, with the scattered squads who will come in at other military posts, I have no doubt fifty thousand (50,000) armed men will be disarmed and restored to civil pursuits by the capitulation made near Durham's Station, North Carolina, on the 26th of April, and that, too, without the loss of a single life to us.

On the 5th of May I received and here subjoin a farther dispatch from General Schofield, which contains inquiries I have been unable to satisfy, similar to those made by nearly every officer in my command whose duty brings him in contact with citizens. I leave you to do what you think expedient to provide the military remedy.

"By telegraph from Raleigh, N. C., May 5th, 1865.
"To Major General W. T. Sherman, Morehead City:

"When General Grant was here, as you doubtless recollect, he said the lines had been extended to embrace this and other states south. The order, it seems, has been modified so as to include only Virginia and Tennessee. I think it would be an act of wisdom to open this state to trade at once. I hope the government will make known its policy as the organ of state governments without delay. Affairs must necessarily be in a very unsettled state until that is done; the people are now in a mood to accept almost any thing which promises a definite settlement.

"What is to be done with the freedmen, is the question of all, and is the all-important question. It requires prompt and wise action to prevent the negro from becoming a huge elephant on our hands. If I am to govern this state, it is important for me to know it at once. If another is to be sent here, it can not be done too soon; for he will probably undo the most that I shall have done. I shall be glad to hear from you freely when you have time to write.

"I will send your message to Wilson at once.

"J. M. SCHOFIELD, Major General."

I give this dispatch entire, to demonstrate how intermingled have become civil matters with the military, and how almost impossible it has become for an officer in authority to act a pure military part.

There are no longer armed enemies in North Carolina, and a soldier can deal with no other sort. The marshals and sheriffs with their *posses* (of which the military may become a part) are the only proper officers to deal with civil criminals and marauders. But I will not be drawn out in a discussion of this subject, but instance the case to show how difficult is the task become to military officers, when men of the rank, education, experience, nerve, and good sense of General Schofield feel embarrassed by them.

General Schofield, at Raleigh, has a well-appointed and well-disciplined command, is in telegraphic communication with the controlling parts of his department, and remote ones in the direction of Georgia, as well as with Washington, and has military possession of all strategic points.

In like manner, General Gillmore is well situated in all respects, except as to rapid communication with the seat of the general government. I leave him also with every man he ever asked for, and in full and quiet possession of every strategic point in his department; and General Wilson has in the very heart of Georgia the strongest, best appointed, and best equipped cavalry corps that ever fell under my command; and he has now, by my recent action, opened to him a source and route of supply by way of Savannah River that simplifies his military problem, so that I think I may with a clear conscience leave them and turn my attention once more to my special command, the army with which I have been associated through some of the most eventful scenes of this or any war.

I hope and believe none of these commanders will ever have reason to reproach me for any "orders" they may have received from me; and the President of the United States may be assured that all of them are in position, ready and willing to execute to the letter and in spirit any orders he may give. I shall henceforth cease to give them any orders at all, for the occasion that made them subordinate to me is past; and I shall confine my attention to the army composed of the 15th and 17th, the 14th and 20th Corps, unless the commanding General of the armies of the United States orders otherwise.

At four P. M. of May 9th I reached Manchester, on the James River, opposite Richmond, and found that all the four corps had arrived from Raleigh, and were engaged in replenishing their wagons for the resumption of the march toward Alexandria.

I have the honor to be your obedient servant,
     W. T. SHERMAN, Major General Commanding.
General JOHN A. RAWLINS, Chief of Staff, Washington, D. C.

V.

Testimony before the Committee on the War — Continued.

Q. Did you have, near Fortress Monroe, a conference with President Lincoln, and if so, about what time? A. I met General Grant and Mr. Lincoln on board a steam-boat lying at the wharf at City Point, and during the evening of the 27th of March; I resumed my visit to the President on board the same steamer anchored in the stream on the following day, General Grant being present on both occasions.

Q. In those conferences was any arrangement made with you and General Grant, or either of you, in regard to the manner of arranging business with the Confederacy in regard to the terms of peace? A. Nothing definite; it was simply a matter of general conversation, nothing specific and definite.

Q. At what time did you learn that President Lincoln had assented to the assembling of the Virginia Rebel Legislature? A. I knew of it on the 18th of April, I think, but I procured a paper with the specific order of General Weitzel, also a copy of the Amnesty Proclamation on the 20th of April.

Q. You did not know at that time that that arrangement had been rescinded by the President? A. No, sir; I did not know that until afterward; the moment I heard of that I notified General Johnston of it.

Q. Then at the time you entered into this arrangement with General Johnston, you knew that General Weitzel had approved of the calling together of the Rebel Legislature of Virginia by the assent of the President? A. I knew of it by some source unofficially; I succeeded in getting a copy of the paper containing General Weitzel's order on the 20th or 21st of April.

Q. But at the time of your arrangement you did not know that that order had been rescinded? A. No, sir; I learned that several days afterward, and at once sent word to General Johnston.

Q. At the time of your arrangement you also knew of the surrender of Lee's army and the terms of that surrender? A. I had that officially from General Grant; I got that at Smithfield on the 12th of April; I have what purports to be a letter from you to Johnston, which seems to imply that you intended to make the arrangement on the terms of Lee's surrender. The letter is as follows:

"Headquarters, Division of the Mississippi, in the Field, Raleigh, N. C., April 14th, 1865.

"General J. E. Johnston, Commanding Confederate Army:

"GENERAL,—I have this moment received your communication of this date. I am fully empowered to arrange with you any time for the suspension of farther hostilities as between the armies commanded by myself, and will be willing to confer with you to that end. I will limit the advance of my main column to-morrow to Morristown, and the cavalry to the University, and I expect you will maintain the present position of your forces until each has notice of a failure to agree.

"Thus a basis of action may be had. I undertake to abide by the same terms and conditions as were made by Generals Grant and Lee at Appomattox Court-house, of the 9th instant, relative to the two armies, and furthermore, to obtain from General Grant an order to suspend the movements of any troops from the direction of Virginia. General Stoneman is under my command, and my orders will suspend any devastation or destruction contemplated by him. I will add, that I really desire to save the people of North Carolina the damage they would sustain by the march of this army through the central or western parts of the state.

"I am, with respect, your obedient servant,

"W. T. SHERMAN, Major General."

Those were the terms as to his own army, but the concessions I made him were for the purpose of embracing other armies.

Q. And the writings you signed were to include other armies? A. The armies of Kirby Smith and Dick Taylor, so that afterward no man within the limits of the Southern Confederacy could claim to belong to any Confederate army in existence.

Q. The President addressed a note to General Grant, perhaps not to you, to the effect of forbidding officers of the army from entering into any thing but strictly military arrangements, leaving civil matters entirely to him? A. I never saw such a note signed by President Lincoln;

Mr. Stanton made such a note or telegram, and says it was by President Lincoln's dictation; he made it to General Grant, but never to me; on the contrary, while I was in Georgia, Mr. Lincoln telegraphed to me encouraging me to discuss matters with Governor Brown and Mr. Stephens.

Q. Then you had no notice of that order to General Grant? A. I had no knowledge of it, official or otherwise.

Q. In the published report of your agreement there is nothing about slavery, I believe? A. There was nothing said about slavery, because it did not fall within the category of military questions, and we could not make it so. It was a legal question which the President had disposed of, overriding all our actions. We had to treat the slave as *free*, because the President, our commander-in-chief, said he was free. For me to have renewed the question when that decision was made, would have involved the absurdity of an inferior undertaking to qualify the work of his superior.

Q. That was the reason why it was not mentioned? A. Yes, sir; subsequently I wrote a note to Johnston, stating that I thought it would be well to mention it for political effect when we came to draw up the final terms with precision; that note was written pending the time my memorandum was going to Washington, and before an answer had been returned.

Q. At the time you entered into those negotiations was Johnston in a condition to offer any effectual resistance to your army? A. He could not have resisted my army an hour if I could have got hold of him; but he could have escaped from me by breaking up into small parties, or by taking the country roads, traveling faster than any army with trains could have pursued.

Q. Then your object in negotiating was to keep his army from scattering into guerilla bands? A. That was my chief object; I so officially notified the War Department.

Q. And not because there was any doubt about the result of a battle? A. There was no question as to the result of a battle, and I knew it; every soldier knew it; Johnston said in the first five minutes of our conversation that any farther resistance on his part would be an act of folly, and all he wanted was to keep his army from dispersing.

By Mr. Loan—Q. In your examination by the chairman you stated that you were acting in pursuance of instructions from Mr. Lincoln, derived from his letters and telegrams at various times? A. Yes, sir.

Q. Have you any of these letters and telegrams which you can furnish to the committee? A. I can furnish you a copy of a dispatch to General Halleck from Atlanta, in which I stated that I had invited Governor Brown and Vice-president Stephens to meet us, and I can give you a copy of Mr. Lincoln's answer, for my dispatch was referred to him, in which he said he felt much interested in my dispatch, and encouraged me to allow their visit; but the letter to which I referred specifically was a longer letter, which I wrote to General Halleck from my camp on

Big Black, Mississippi, at General Halleck's instigation, in September, 1863, which was received in Washington, and submitted to Mr. Lincoln, who desired to have it published, to which I would not consent; in that letter I gave my opinions fully and frankly, not only upon the military situation, but also the civil policy necessary; Mr. Lincoln expressed himself highly pleased with my views, and desired to make them public, but I preferred not to do so.

Q. And by subsequent acts he induced you to believe he approved of these views? A. I *know* he approved of them, and always encouraged me to carry out those views.

By the Chairman—Q. The following is a letter published in the newspapers, purporting to have been addressed by you to Johnston, dated April 21st, 1865:

> "Headquarters of the Military Division of the Mississippi,
> in the Field, Raleigh, N. C., April 21st, 1865.
>
> "General J. E. Johnston, Commanding Confederate Army:
>
> "GENERAL,—I send you a letter for General Wilson, which, if sent by telegraph and courier, will check his career. He may mistrust the telegraph; therefore better send the original, for he can not mistake my handwriting, with which he is familar. He seems to have his blood up, and will be hard to hold. If he can buy corn, fodder, and rations down about Fort Valley, it will obviate the necessity of his going up to Rome or Dalton.
>
> "It is reported to me from Cairo that Mobile is in our possession, but it is not minute or official.
>
> "General Baker sent in to me, wanting to surrender his command, on the theory that the whole Confederate army was surrendered. I explained to him, or his staff officer, the exact truth, and left him to act as he thought proper. He seems to have disbanded his men, deposited a few arms about twenty miles from here, and himself awaits your action. I will not hold him, his men, or arms, subject to any condition other than the final one we may agree upon.
>
> "I shall look for Major Hitchcock back from Washington on Wednesday, and shall promptly notify you of the result. By the action of General Weitzel in relation to the Virginia Legislature, I feel certain we will have no trouble on the score of recognizing existing state governments. It may be the lawyers will want us to define more minutely what is meant by the guaranty of rights of persons and property. It may be construed into a compact for us to undo the past as to the rights of slaves and leases of plantations on the Mississippi of vacant and abandoned plantations. I wish you would talk to the best men you have on these points; and, if possible, let us in our final convention make these points so clear as to leave no room for angry controversy. I believe if the South would simply and publicly declare what we feel, that slavery is dead, that you would inaugurate an era of peace and prosperity that would soon efface the ravages of the past four years of war. Negroes would remain in the South, and afford you abundance of cheap labor,

which otherwise will be driven away; and it will save the country the senseless discussions which have kept us all in hot water for fifty years.

"Although, strictly, this is no subject for a military convention, yet I am honestly convinced that our simple declarations of a result will be accepted as good law every where. Of course, I have not a single word from Washington on this or any other point of our agreement, but I know the effect of such a step by us will be universally accepted.

"I am, with great respect, your obedient servant,

"W. T. SHERMAN, Major General U.S.A."

Q. This is the letter in which you say that it would be well to declare publicly that slavery is dead? A. Yes, sir, that is the letter.

By *Mr. Loan*—Q. Will you furnish the committee a copy of the letter written by you to Mr. Stanton in January last from Savannah? A. I will do so.

Mr. Chairman. And when the manuscript of your testimony is prepared it will be remitted to you for revision, and you can add to it any statement or papers that you may subsequently desire or consider necessary.

I have the above, and now subjoin copies of letters from my letter-book in the order of the bringing in the questions revised by this inquiry.

"Headquarters Middle Department of the Mississippi, in the Field, Raleigh, N. C., April 18th, 1865.

"Lieutenant General U. S. Grant, or Major General Halleck, Washington, D. C.:

"GENERAL,—I inclose herewith a copy of an agreement made this day between General Joseph E. Johnston and myself, which, if approved by the President of the United States, will produce peace from the Potomac to the Rio Grande. Mr. Breckinridge was present at the conference in the capacity of major general, and satisfied me of the ability of General Johnston to carry out to the full extent the terms of this agreement; and if you will get the President to simply indorse the copy and commission me to carry out the terms, I will follow them to the conclusion. You will observe that it is an absolute submission of the enemy to the lawful authorities of the United States, and disposes his army absolutely; and the point to which I attach most importance is, that the disposition and dispersement of the armies is done in such a manner as to prevent them breaking up into a guerrilla crew. On the other hand, we can retain just as much of an army as we please. I agree to the mode and manner of the surrender of armies set forth, as they give the state the means of suppressing guerrillas, which we could not expect to do if we strip them of all armies.

"Both Generals Johnston and Breckinridge admitted that slavery was dead, and I could not insist in embracing it in such a paper, because it can be made with the states in detail. I know that all the men of substance in the South sincerely want peace, and I do not believe they will resort to war again during this century. I have no doubt but that they will in the future be perfectly subordinate to the laws of the United States. The moment my action in this matter is approved, I can spare five corps, and will ask for and have General Schofield here with the 10th Corps, and go myself, with the 14th, 15th, 17th, 20th, and 23d Corps, *via* Burkesville and Gordonsville, to Frederick or Hagerstown, there to be paid and mustered out.

"The question of finance is now the chief one, and every soldier and officer not needed, to go home at work. I would like to be able to begin the march north by May 1st.

"I urge on the part of the President speedy action, as it is important to get the Confederate armies to their homes as well as our own.

"I am, with great respect, your obedient servant,

"W. T. SHERMAN, Major General Commanding."

"Headquarters Middle Department of the Mississippi, in the Field, Raleigh, N. C., April 18th, 1865.

"General H. W. Halleck, Chief of Staff, Washington, D. C. :

"GENERAL,—I received your dispatch describing the man Clark detailed to assassinate me. He had better be in a hurry, or he will be too late. The news of Mr. Lincoln's death produced a most intense effect on our troops. At first I feared it would lead to excesses, but now it has softened down, and can easily be quieted. None evince more feeling than General Johnston, who admitted that the act was calculated to stain his cause with a dark hue, and he contended that the loss was most severe to the South, who had begun to realize that Mr. Lincoln was the best friend the South had.

"I can not believe that even Mr. Davis was privy to the diabolical plot, but think it the emanation of a lot of young men of the South, who are very devils. I want to throw upon the South the care of this class of men, who will soon be as obnoxious to their industrious class as to us.

"Had I pushed Johnston's army to an extremity, it would have dispersed and done infinite mischief. Johnston informed me that General Stoneman had been at Salisbury, and was now about Statesville. I have sent him orders to come to me.

"General Johnston also informed me that General Wilson was at Columbus, Georgia, and he wanted me to arrest his progress. I leave that to you. Indeed, if the President sanctions my agreement with Johnston, our interest is to cease all destruction. Please give all orders necessary according to the views the Executive may take, and inform him, if possible, not to vary the terms at all, for I have considered every thing, and believe that the Confederate armies are dispersed. We can adjust all else fairly and well. I am yours, etc.,

"W. T. SHERMAN, Major General Commanding."

Lest confusion should result to the mind of the committee by the latter part of the above letter, I state it was addressed to General Halleck as chief of staff, when he was in the proper "line of order" to the Commander-in-Chief. The whole case changed when, on the 26th of April, he became the commander of the separate division of the James.

As stated in my testimony, General Grant reached Raleigh on the 24th, and on the 25th, on the supposition that I would start next day to chase Johnston's army, I wrote him the following letter, delivered in person:

"Headquarters Department of the Mississippi, in the Field,
Raleigh, N. C., April 25th, 1865.

"Lieutenant General U. S. Grant,—Present:

"GENERAL,—I received your letter of April 21st, with inclosures, yesterday, and was well pleased that you came along, as you must have observed that I held the military control, so as to adapt it to any phase the case might assume.

"It is but just that I should record the fact that I made my terms with General Johnston under the influence of the liberal terms you extended to the army of General Lee, at Appomattox Court-house, on the 9th, and the seeming policy of our government as evinced by the call of the Virginia Legislature and governor back to Richmond under your and President Lincoln's very eyes. It now appears this last act was done without any consultation with you or any knowledge of Mr. Lincoln, but, rather, in opposition to a previous policy well considered.

"I have not the least desire to interfere in the civil policy of our government, but would shun it as something not to my liking; but occasions arise when a prompt seizure of results is forced on military commanders not in immediate communication with the proper authority. It is possible that the terms signed by General Johnston and myself were not clear enough on the point well understood between us, that our negotiations did not apply to any parties outside the officers and men of the Confederate armies, which could easily have been remedied.

"No surrender of any army not actually at the mercy of the antagonist was ever made without 'terms,' and those always define the military status of the surrendered. Thus you stipulated that the officers and men of Lee's army should not be molested at their homes so long as they obeyed the laws at the place of their residence. I do not wish to discuss these points involved in our recognition of the state governments in actual existence, but will merely state my conclusion, to await the solution of the future.

"Such action on one point in no manner recognizes for a moment the so-called Confederate government, or makes us liable for its debts or acts. The laws and acts done by the several states during the period of rebellion are *void*, because done without the oath prescribed by our Constitution of the United States, which is a condition precedent. We have a right to use any sort of machinery to produce military results, and it is the commonest thing for military commanders to use the civil government *in actual existence* as a means to an end. I do believe he could and can use the present state governments lawfully, constitutionally, and as the very best possible means to produce the object desired, viz., entire and complete submission to the lawful authority of the United States.

"As to the punishment of past crimes, that is for the judiciary, and can in no manner of way be disturbed by our acts; and, so far as I can,

I will use my influence that Rebels shall suffer all the personal punishment provided by law, as also the civil liabilities accruing from this past act.

"What we now want is the new form of law, by which common men may regain their position of industry, so long disturbed by the war.

"I now apprehend that the Rebel army will disperse, and, instead of dealing with six or seven states, we will have to deal with numberless bands of desperadoes, headed by such men as Mosby, Forrest, Red Jackson, and others, who know not and care not for danger and its consequences. I am, with great respect, your obedient servant,

"W. T. SHERMAN, Major General."

On the same day I wrote and mailed to the Secretary of War the following:

"Headquarters Middle Division of the Mississippi, in the Field, Raleigh, N. C., April 25th, 1865.

"Hon. E. M. Stanton, Secretary of War, Washington:

"DEAR SIR,—I have been furnished a copy of your letter of April 21st to General Grant, signifying your disapprobation of the terms on which General Johnston proposed to disarm and disperse the insurgents on condition of amnesty, etc. I admit my folly in embracing in a military convention any civil matter; but unfortunately, such is the nature of our situation that they seem inextricably united, and I understand from you at Savannah that the financial state of the country demanded military success, and would warrant a little leaning to policy.

"When I had my conference with General Johnston, I had the public example before me of General Grant's terms to Lee's army, and General Weitzel's invitation to the Virginia Legislature to assemble. I still believe that General Grant, of the United States, has made a mistake, but that is none of my business. Mine is a different task, and I had flattered myself that, by four years of patient and unremitting and successful labor, I deserved no reminder such as is contained in the last paragraph of your letter to General Grant.

"You may assure the President that I heed his suggestion.

"I am truly, etc.,

"W. T. SHERMAN, Major General Commanding."

The last sentence refers to the fact that General Grant had been sent to Raleigh to direct military movements. That was the first time in my life I had ever had a word of reproof from the government of the United States, and I was naturally sensitive. But all I said to any one was to General Meigs, who came with General Grant: "It was not kind on the part of Mr. Secretary Stanton." The fact known did not gratify my military conduct. The first interview with General Johnston followed, and the terms of capitulation were agreed upon and signed, and General Grant started for Washington bearing the news.

When, on the 28th of April, I received in the New York *Times* the most extraordinary budget of Mr. Stanton, which for the first time startled me, and I wrote to General Grant this letter:

"Headquarters Military Division of the Mississippi,
in the Field, April 28th, 1865.
"Lieutenant General U. S. Grant, General-in-Chief, Washington, D. C.:

"GENERAL,—Since you left me yesterday, I have seen the New York *Times* of the 24th instant, containing a budget of military news, authenticated by the signature of the Secretary of War, which is grouped in such a way as to give very erroneous impressions. It embraces a copy of the basis of agreement between myself and General Johnston of April 18th, with commentaries which it will be time enough to discuss two or three years hence, after the government has experimented a little more in the machinery by which power reaches the scattered people of the vast country known as the South. But, in the mean time, I do think that my rank (if not past services) entitled me at least to the respect of keeping secret what was known to none but the cabinet until farther inquiry comes to be made, instead of giving publicity to documents I never saw, and drawing inferences wide of the truth.

"I never saw, or had furnished me, a copy of Mr. Stanton's dispatch to you of the 3d of March, nor did Mr. Stanton or any human being ever convey to me its substance, or any thing like it; but, on the contrary, I had seen General Weitzel in relation to the Virginia Legislature made in Mr. Lincoln's very person, and had failed to discover any other official hints of a plan of reconstruction, or any idea calculated to allay the fears of the people of the South after the destruction of their armies and civil authorities would leave them without any government at all.

"We should not drive a people in anarchy, and it is simply impossible for one military power to waste all the masses of this unhappy country.

"I confess I did not want to drive General Johnston's army into the hands of armed men going about without purpose, and capable only of indefinite mischief.

"But you saw on your arrival at Raleigh that I had my armies so disposed that his escape was only possible in a disorganized shape; and as you did not choose to direct military operations in this quarter, I infer that you were satisfied with the military situation.

"At all events, the moment I learned—what was proper enough—the disapproval of the President, I wished in such manner to compel the surrender of Johnston's whole army on the same terms you had prescribed to General Lee s army when you had it surrounded and in your absolute power.

"Mr. Stanton, in stating that my order to General Stoneman was likely to result in the escape of 'Mr. Davis to Mexico or Europe,' is in deep error.

"General Stoneman was not at Salisbury then, but had gone back to Statesville. Davis was supposed to be between us, and Stoneman was beyond him.

"By turning toward me, he was approaching Davis; and had he joined me as ordered, I then would have had a mounted force needed for that and other purposes. But even now I do not know that Mr. Stanton wants Davis caught. And as my official papers, deemed sacred, are hastily published to the world, it will be imprudent for me to state what has been done in this respect.

"As the editor of the *Times* has (it may be) logically and fairly drawn the inference from this singular document that I am insubordinate, I can only deny the intention. I have never in my life questioned or disobeyed an order, though many and many a time have I risked my life, my health, and reputation in obeying orders, or even hints, to execute plans and purposes not to my liking. It is not fair to withhold from me plans and policy (if any there be) and expect me to guess at them; for facts and events appear quite different from different stand-points. For four years I have been in camp dealing with soldiers; and I can assure you that the conclusion at which the cabinet arrived with such singular unanimity differs from mine. I conferred freely with the best officers in this army as to the points involved in this controversy, and, strange to say, they were singularly unanimous in the other conclusion; and they will learn with pain and sorrow that I am deemed insubordinate, and wanting in common sense; that I, who have labored day and night, winter and summer, for four years, and have brought an army of 70,000 men in magnificent condition across a country deemed impassable, and placed it just where it was wanted almost on the day appointed, have brought discredit on the government.

"I do not wish to boast of this; but I do say that it entitled me to the courtesy of being consulted before publishing to the world a proposition rightfully submitted to higher authority for adjudication, and then accompanied by statements which invited the press to be let loose on me.

"It is true that non-combatants—men who sleep in comfort and security while we watch on the distant lines—are better able to judge than we poor soldiers, who rarely see a newspaper, hardly can hear from our families, or stop long enough to get our pay. I envy not the task of reconstruction, and am delighted that the Secretary has relieved me of it.

"As you did not undertake to assume the management of the affairs of this army, I infer that on personal inspection your mind arrived at a different conclusion from that of Mr. Secretary Stanton. I will therefore go on and execute your orders to the conclusion, and when done will, with intense satisfaction, leave to the civil authorities the execution of the task of which they seem to me so jealous; but as an honest man and soldier, I invite them to follow my path; for they may see some things and hear some things that may disturb their philosophy.

"With sincere respect,
"W. T. SHERMAN, Major General Commanding.

"P.S.—As Mr. Stanton's singular paper has been published, I demand that this also be made public; though I am in no manner responsible to the press, but to the law and my proper superiors.

"W. T. SHERMAN, Major General Commanding."

Since my arrival at Washington I have learned from General Grant that this letter was received, but he preferred to withhold it until my arrival, as he knew I was making toward Washington with my army. Upon my arrival I did not insist on its publication till it was drawn out by this inquiry. I also append here the copy of a letter from Colonel T. S. Bowers, A.A.G., asking me to modify my report as to the point of violating my truce, with my answer.

"Headquarters Armies of the United States, }
Washington, May 25th, 1865. }
"Major General W. T. Sherman, Commanding Middle Division of the Mississippi:

"General Grant directed me to call your attention to the part of your report in which the necessity of maintaining your truce at the expense of many lives is spoken of. The General thinks that in making a truce the commander of an army can control only his own army, and that the hostile General must make his own arrangements with other armies acting against him.

"While independent generals acting against a common foe would naturally act in concert, the General claims that each must be the judge of his own duty and responsible for its execution.

"If you should wish, the report will be returned for any change you deem best.

"Very respectfully, your obedient servant,
"T. S. BOWERS, Assistant Adjutant General."

"Headquarters Military Division of the Mississippi, }
Washington, D. C., May 26th, 1865. }
"Colonel T. S. Bowers, Assistant Adjutant General, Washington, D. C.:

"COLONEL,—I had the honor to receive your letter of May 25th last evening, and I hasten to answer. I wish to precede it by renewing the assurance of my entire confidence and respect for the President and Lieutenant General Grant, and that in all matters I will be most willing to shape my official and private conduct to suit their wishes. The past is beyond my control, and the matters embraced in the official report to which you refer are finished. It is but just the reasons that actuated me, right or wrong, should stand on record; but in all future cases, should any arise, I will respect the decisions of General Grant, though I think them wrong.

"Suppose a guard has prisoners in charge and officers of another command should aim to rescue or kill them, is it not clear the guard must defend the prisoners as a safeguard? So jealous is the military law to protect and maintain *good faith* when pledged, that the law adjudges death, and no alternative punishment, to one who violates a safeguard in foreign ports. (See Articles of War, No. 55.) For murder, arson, treason, and the highest military crimes, the punishment prescribed by law is death or some minor punishment, but for the violation of a 'safeguard' death, and death alone, is the prescribed penalty I instance this to illustrate how, in military stipulations to an enemy, our government commands and enforces 'good faith.' In discussing this matter I would like to refer to many writers on military law, but am willing to take Halleck as the text. (See his chapter, No. xxvii.)

"In the very first article he states that *good faith* should always be observed between enemies in war, because when our faith has been pledged to him, so far as the promise extends, he ceases to be an enemy. He then defines the meaning of *compacts* and *conventions*, and says they are made sometimes for a general or a partial suspension of hostilities for the 'surrender of an army,' etc. They may be *special*, limited to particular places or to particular forces, but, of course, can only bind the armies subject to the General who makes the truce, and co-extensive only with the extent of his command. This is all I ever claimed, and it clearly covers the whole case: all of North Carolina was in my immediate command, with General Schofield, its department commander, and his army present with me. I never asked the truce to have effect beyond my own territorial command. General Halleck himself, in his Order No. 1, defines his own limits clearly enough, *viz.*, 'Such part of North Carolina as was not occupied by the command of Major General Sherman.' He could not pursue and cut off Johnston's retreat toward Salisbury and Charlotte without invading my command; and so patent was his purpose to defy and violate my truce, that Mr. Stanton's publication of the fact, not even yet recalled, modified, or explained, was headed, 'Sherman's Truce Disregarded,' that the whole world drew but one inference—it admits of no other. I never claimed that that truce bound Generals Halleck or Canby within the sphere of their respective commands as defined by themselves.

"It was a partial truce of very short duration, clearly within my limits and right, justified by events, and, as in the case of prisoners in my custody, or the violation of a safeguard given by me in my own territorial limits, I am bound to maintain good faith. I prefer not to change my report, but again repeat that in all future cases I am willing to be governed by the interpretation of General Grant, although I again invite his attention to the limits of my command, and those of General Halleck at the time, and the pointed phraseology of General Halleck's dispatch to Mr. Stanton, wherein he reports that he had ordered his Generals to pay no heed to *my orders* within the clearly defined area of my command. I am yours,   W. T. SHERMAN, Major General U.S.A. Commanding."

I now add the two letters written to Mr. Stanton at Savannah, and the dispatch from Atlanta mentioned in the body of my testimony, with Mr. Lincoln's answer:

'Headquarters Military Division of the Mississippi,
in the Field, Savannah, January 2d, 1865.

"Hon. Edwin M. Stanton, Secretary of War, Washington, D. C.:

"SIR,—I have just received from Lieutenant General Grant a copy of that part of your telegram to him of 26th December relating to cotton, a copy of which has been immediately furnished to General Eaton, my chief quartermaster, who will be strictly governed by it.

"I had already been approached by all the consuls and half the people of Savannah on this cotton question, and my invariable answer has been that all the cotton in Savannah was prize of war and belonged to the United States, and nobody should recover a bale of it with my consent; and that as cotton had been one of the chief causes of this war, it should help pay its expenses; that all cotton became tainted with treason from the hour the first act of hostility was committed against the United States, some time in December, 1860, and that no bill of sale subsequent to that date could convey title.

"My orders were that an officer of the Quartermaster's Department U.S.A. might furnish the holder, agent, or attorney a mere certificate of the fact of seizure, with description of the bales, marks, etc., the cotton then to be turned over to the agent of the Treasury Department, to be shipped to New York for sale; but since the receipt of your dispatch I have ordered General Eaton to make the shipment himself to the quartermaster at New York, where you can dispose of it at pleasure. I do not think the Treasury Department ought to bother itself with the prizes or captures of war.

"Mr. Barclay, former consul at New York—representing Mr. Molyneux, former consul, but absent since a long time—called on me in person with reference to cotton claims by English subjects. He seemed amazed when I told him I should pay no respect to consular certificates, and that in no event would I treat an English subject with more favor than one of our own deluded citizens; and that, for my part, I was unwilling to fight for cotton for the benefit of Englishmen openly engaged in smuggling arms and munitions of war to kill us; that, on the contrary, it would afford me great satisfaction to conduct my army to Nassau and wipe out that nest of pirates. I explained to him, however, that I was not a diplomatic agent of the general government of the United States, but that my opinion, so frankly expressed, was that of a soldier, which it would be well for him to heed. It appeared, also, that he owned a plantation on the line of investment of Savannah, which of course is destroyed, and for which he expected me to give him some certificate entitling him to indemnification, which I declined emphatically.

"I have adopted, in Savannah, rules concerning property, severe but just, founded upon the laws of nations and the practice of civilized governments; and of clearly of opinion that we should claim all the belligerent rights over conquered countries, that the people may realize the truth that war is no child's play.

"I embrace in this a copy of a letter dated December 31st, 1864, in answer to one from Solomon Cohen, a rich lawyer, to General Blair, his personal friend, as follows:

"'Major General F. P. Blair, Commanding 17th Army Corps:

"'GENERAL,—Your note, inclosing Mr. Cohen's of this date, I received, and I answer frankly through you his inquiries.

"'1st. No one can practice law as an attorney in the United States without acknowledging the supremacy of our government. If I am not in error, an attorney is as much an officer of the court as the clerk, and it would be a novel thing in a government to have a court to administer law that denied the supremacy of the government itself.

"'2d. No one will be allowed the privileges of a merchant; or, rather, to trade is a privilege which no one should seek of the government without in like manner acknowledging its supremacy.

"'3d. If Mr. Cohen remains in Savannah as a denizen, his property, real and personal, will not be disturbed, unless its temporary use be necessary for the military authorities of the city. The title to property will not be disturbed in any event, until adjudicated by the Courts of the United States.

"'4th. If Mr. Cohen leaves Savannah under my Special Order, No. 143, it is a public acknowledgment that he "adheres to the enemies of the United States," and all his property becomes forfeited to the United States. But, as a matter of favor, he will be allowed to carry with him clothing and furniture for the use of himself, family, and servants, and will be transported within the enemy's lines, but not by way of Port Royal.

"'These rules will apply to all parties, and from them no exception will be made.

"'I have the honor to be, General, your obedient servant,

"W. T. SHERMAN, Major General.'"

"This letter was in answer to specific inquiries. It is clear and specific, and covers all the points; and should I leave before my orders are executed, I will endeavor to impress upon my successor, General Foster, their wisdom and propriety.

"I hope the course I have taken in these matters will meet your approbation, and that the President will not refund to parties claiming cotton or other property without the strongest evidence of loyalty and friendship on the part of the claimant, or unless some other positive end is to be gained.

"I am, with great respect, your obedient servant,

"W. T. SHERMAN, Major General Commanding.

"Headquarters of the Military Division of the Mississippi,
in the Field, Savannah, January 19th, 1865.

"Hon. E. M. Stanton, Secretary of War, Washington, D. C.:

"SIR,—When you left Savannah, a few days ago, you forgot the map which General Geary had prepared for you, showing the route by which his division entered the city of Savannah, being the first troops to occupy that city. I now send it to you. I avail myself of the opportunity also to inclose you copies of all my official orders touching trade and intercourse with the people of Georgia, as well as for the establishment of the negro settlements. Delegations of the people of Georgia continue to come, and I am satisfied that a little judicious handling, and by a little respect being paid to their prejudices, we can create a schism in Jeff. Davis's dominions. All that I have conversed with realize the truth that slavery, as an institution, is defunct, and the only questions that remain are, what disposition shall be made of the negroes themselves. I confess myself unable to offer a complete solution for these questions, and prefer to leave it to the slower operations of time. We have given the initiative, and can afford to wait the working of the experiment.

"As to trade matters, I also think it is to our interest to keep the people somewhat dependent on the articles of commerce to which they have been hitherto accustomed. General Grover is now here, and will, I think, be able to manage this matter judiciously, and may gradually relax, and invite cotton to come in in large quantities.

"But at first we should manifest no undue anxiety on that score, for the Rebels would at once make use of it as a power against us. We should assume a tone of perfect contempt for cotton and every thing else in comparison with the great object of the war—the restoration of the Union, with all its rights and power. If the Rebels burn cotton as a war measure, they simply play into our hands, by taking away the only product of value they now have to exchange in foreign ports for war ships and munitions. By such a course, also, they alienate the feelings of the large class of small farmers that look to their little parcels of cotton to exchange for food and clothing for their families. I hope the government will not manifest too much anxiety to obtain cotton in large quantities, and, especially, that the President will not indorse the contracts for the purchase of large quantities of cotton. Several contracts, involving from six to ten thousand bales, indorsed by Mr. Lincoln, have been shown me, but were not in such a form as to amount to an order for me to facilitate their execution.

"As to treasury trade agents and agents to take charge of confiscated and abandoned property, whose salaries depend on their fees, I can only say that, as a general rule, they are mischievous and disturbing elements to a military government, and it is almost impossible for us to study the law and regulations so as to understand fully their powers and duties. I rather think the Quartermaster's Department of the army could better fulfill all their duties, and accomplish all that is aimed at by the law. Yet, on this subject, I will leave Generals Foster and Grover to do the best they can.

"I am, with great respect, your obedient servant,
"W. T. SHERMAN, Major General Commanding."

"Headquarters of the Middle Division of the Mississippi, in the Field, Atlanta, Georgia, September 15th, 1864.
"Major General Halleck, Washington, D. C.:

"My report is done, and will be forwarded as soon as I get a few more of the subordinate reports. I am awaiting a courier from General Grant. All well, and troops in fine healthy camps, and supplies coming forward finely. Governor Brown has disbanded his militia to gather the corn and sorghum of the state. I have reason to believe that he and Stephens want to visit me, and I have sent them a hearty invitation. I will exchange two thousand prisoners with Hood, but no more.

"W. T. SHERMAN, Major General Commanding."

"Washington, D. C., September 17th, 1864—10 A.M.

"MAJOR GENERAL SHERMAN,—I feel great interest in the subjects of your dispatch mentioning corn and sorghum, and contemplated a visit to you. A. LINCOLN, President U.S."

"I have not possession here of all my official records, most of which are out West, and I have selected the above from my more recent letter books, and I offer them to show how prompt and full have been my official reports, and how unnecessary was all the clamor made touching my action and opinions at the time the basis of agreement of April 18th was submitted to the President.

"All of which is most respectfully submitted,

"W. T. SHERMAN, Major General United States Army.

VI.

Major General Barry's Report of the Campaign of the Carolinas.

Artillery Headquarters, Military Division of the Mississippi,
Goldsboro', N. C., March 31st, 1865.

GENERAL,—I have the honor to report the operations of the artillery of the armies under your command during the Carolina campaign of February and March, 1865.

In consideration of the peculiarities of the campaign, involving long and rapid marches over bad roads, and at an inclement season of the year, the same precautions which were so advantageously taken for your Savannah campaign of last autumn were again observed. The number of guns was reduced to one per thousand effective bayonets, and each artillery carriage was provided with eight draught animals.

The whole number of field batteries was sixteen, comprising sixty-eight guns, which were distributed and of calibres as follows:

		20-pounder Parrotts.	12-pounders	3-inch Rifles.	Total.
Right Wing	15th Army Corps	4	10	4	18
	17th Army Corps		4	10	14
Left Wing	14th Army Corps		8	8	16
	20th Army Corps		8	8	16
Cavalry Division				4	4
Total		4	30	34	68

Including the reserve supply, each gun was furnished with three hundred and fifty rounds of ammunition.

A careful and critical personal inspection, made a few days preceding our departure from Savannah, satisfied me that in all essentials the artillery was in excellent condition for any kind of work. The result fully justified these expectations. During the whole march the artillery supplied itself, unaided by infantry or cavalry, with provisions for its officers and men, forage for its animals, and, to a great extent, with fresh horses and mules captured in the country. A tabular statement is appended to this report, showing the extent to which this unusual artillery service was performed.

No gun or artillery carriage of any description was abandoned, disabled, or at any time even a temporary impediment to the march of the infantry columns—a fact the more creditable to the artillery, since in many places the roads were of the worst possible description.

Although the nature of your operations did not, except at the battles of Averysboro' and Bentonville, call for any general use of artillery, yet in support of skirmish lines, brushing away cavalry, and covering the crossings of several difficult and important rivers, it was advantageously used at the following named times and places, namely:

January 20th, 1865, Pocotaligo, 17th Army Corps.
January 22d, 1865, Combahee, 15th Army Corps.
January 29th, 1865, Robertsville, 20th Army Corps.
February 1st, 1865, Hickory Hill, 15th Army Corps.
February 2d, 1865, Lawtonville, 20th Army Corps.
February 2d, 1865, Whippy Swamp, 17th Army Corps.
February 3d, 1865, "Store" at Duck Creek, 15th Army Corps.
February 6th, 1865, Little Salkahatchie, 15th Army Corps.
February 9th, 1865, Binnaker's Bridge, 17th Army Corps.
February 11th, 1865, North Edisto, 17th Army Corps.
February 15th, 1865, Congaree Creek, 15th Army Corps.
February 16th, 1865, Columbia, 15th and 17th Army Corps.
February 17th, 1865, Columbia, 15th and 17th Army Corps.
February 17th, 1865, Broad River, 15th Army Corps.
March 16th, 1865, Little Rockfish Creek, 15th Army Corps.

At the battle of Averysboro', March 16th, the batteries of the 20th Corps were promptly and judiciously posted by Major Reynolds, the chief of artillery of that corps, and by the precision and rapidity of their fire did most excellent service in dislodging the enemy from his intrenched line, and the consequent capture of three of his guns.

At the battle of Bentonville, March 19th, 20th, and 21st, it was the fortune of the artillery to play a more conspicuous part. The batteries of the 15th and 20th Corps were hotly engaged on the 19th, and after the first temporary advantage gained by the enemy, in which the 19th Indiana Battery, not by any fault of its own, lost three of its guns (one of which was recaptured next day), they poured in a fire so steady, rapid, and effective, that all of the enemy's frequently repeated assaults were successfully repulsed. On the 20th, and particularly on the 21st, the batteries of the 15th Corps lent most efficient aid in advancing our own lines, in repelling the enemy's assaults, and in inflicting heavy loss upon him. Both of these fields of battle give abundant proof of the precision of our artillery fire.

The following tabular statements will exhibit the amounts of provisions and forage, and the number of animals captured by the unaided labors of the artillery, the casualties among officers, enlisted men, and animals, the expenditure of ammunition, and the number of guns lost by us and captured by the enemy:

PROVISIONS, ANIMALS, FORAGE, ETC.

By what Batteries procured.	Flour.	Corn Meal.	Bacon	Beef, etc.	Potatoes.	Corn.	Hay and Fodder	Horses.	Mules
	lbs.	lbs.	lbs.	lbs.	lbs.	lbs.	lbs.		
20th Corps..	8,000	10,000	25,000	50,000	50,000	350,000	300,000	96	602
14th Corps..	3,000	5,200	4,360	8,065		217,920	91,800	53	85
15th Corps..	4,900	5,700	23,000	2,300	37,440	499,000	90,000	50	63
17th Corps..	2,000	3,200	18,000			218,000	106,000	50	33
Total.....	17,900	24,100	70,360	60,365	87,440	1,284,920	587,800	249	783

CASUALTIES.

	Officers.				Enlisted Men.				Horses.		Mules.	
	Killed.	Wounded.	Missing.	Died.	Killed.	Wounded.	Missing.	Died.	Killed.	Wounded.	Killed.	Wounded.
14th Corps....	1				4	6	1		25			
20th Corps....					1	14	1			3		
15th Corps....						5	3					
17th Corps....					1	1	1					
Cav. Div......					1	1	13		10			
	1				7	27	19		35	3		

EXPENDITURE OF AMMUNITION.

Command.	Number of Rounds.
14th Army Corps	1007
20th Army Corps	832
Army of Tennessee	1665
Total	3504

GUNS CAPTURED AND LOST.

Place.	Number of Guns captured from the Enemy.	Number of Guns lost by us.
Columbia	43	
Cheraw	25	
Fayetteville	26	
Averysboro	3	
Bentons		2
Total	97	2

Of these all were serviceable, and about four fifths were field guns of recent and approved pattern.

If to the operations of your armies, the legitimate fruits of which they really are, be credited the guns captured at Charleston and Wilmington (excluding from the number of the latter those captured at Fort Fisher and the other forts at the mouth of Cape Fear River), the total artillery captured during the past ten months by troops under your immediate command will exceed 700 guns.

Throughout the campaign the ammunition, fuses, and primers proved unusually good and reliable, the only fault observed being sand cracks and insufficient bursting charges in a few of the twenty-pounder Parrott projectiles, want of care in the screwing of the Bohrmann fuse in twelve-pounder projectiles, and insufficient bursting charges in many of the Hotchkiss three-inch shell and case-shot. Ammunition and fuses received from St. Louis Arsenal appear to be more complained of (especially the fuses) than that received from other places.

In conclusion, I am gratified to be able to commend the officers and men for attention to their duties in preparation for the field and for good conduct after entering it, for the details of which I respectfully invite attention to the sub-reports which will be laid before you.

The services of the following named officers give evidence of industry, intelligence, and gallant conduct, and entitle them to notice and reward, namely:

Major Osborn, 1st New York Artillery, Chief of Artillery Army of Tennessee; Major Reynolds, 1st New York Artillery, Chief of Artillery 20th Army Corps; Major Waterhouse, 1st Illinois Artillery, Chief of Artillery 17th Army Corps; Lieutenant Colonel Ross, 1st Michigan Artillery, Chief of Artillery 15th Army Corps; Major Houghtaling, 1st Illinois Artillery, Chief of Artillery 14th Army Corps.

I respectfully ask that each of these officers, who have also served faithfully and creditably through the Atlanta and Savannah campaigns, be recommended for promotion by brevet.

The officers of my staff, Major Dickson, Inspector of Artillery; Captain Marshall, Assistant Adjutant General; Captain Merritt and Lieutenant Verplanck, Aides-de-Camp, at all times performed cheerfully and well the duties with which they were charged.

I am, General, very respectfully your obedient servant,

WILLIAM F. BARRY, Brevet Major General, Chief of Artillery.

Major General W. T. SHERMAN, Commanding Military Division of the Mississippi.

VII.

Report of Engineer's Department.

The following reports are generously furnished me by Colonel Poe, chief engineer for the division, and are taken from reports made to his superior officers. They will indicate the nature and extent of the organization of the Engineer Corps, and the tools they had to work with. It will be understood by every one that this small body was utterly unequal to the amount of work required for so large an army; directed and guided by the engineers, the intelligence, patience, and energy of both officers and men of the body of the army, accomplished the rest.

Headquarters Military Division of the Mississippi,
Chief Engineer's Office, Savannah, Ga., January 2d, 1865.

GENERAL,—In accordance with your directions, I have the honor of submitting the following memoranda showing the engineer organization during the recent campaign from Atlanta, Ga., to Savannah, Ga.:

First, Engineer troops and troops of the line on engineer duty: 1st Michigan Engineers and Mechanics, ten companies, 1500 men; 1st Missouri Engineers, five companies, 500 men; 58th Indiana Volunteers, (infantry) pontoniers, ten companies, 775 men : total, 2775 men.

R

Second, Pioneers: left wing, six divisions, each having a pioneer corps of the average strength of 100 men, 600 men; right wing, seven divisions, each having a pioneer corps of the average strength of 100 whites and 70 blacks, 1200 men: aggregate for engineer duty, 4575 men. Each of these pioneer corps carried a sufficient number of tools to work their full strength, and in the right wing they were supplied with a duplicate set, which was carried in wagons. In the left wing each brigade was provided with a tool wagon, loaded with about 350 intrenching tools. In addition to these, a good many tools were in the hands of the troops, but always within reach in case of emergency.

Third, Tool trains: the Michigan Engineers had a train of fifty wagons, of which twenty were loaded with tools, as follows: 1500 axes and helves, 1500 shovels, 700 picks and helves, 200 hatchets, and an ample supply of carpenters' and bridge-building tools, and extra saws and augers; also 100 hooks for twisting railroad iron, made upon a plan of my own. The remainder of the wagons carried subsistence and quartermaster's stores. The Missouri Engineers had a much smaller train, which was somewhat mixed up with the pontoon train, of which they had charge. They carried the following intrenching tools: 500 shovels, 500 axes; also an assortment of carpenters' and blacksmiths' tools.

Fourth, Pontoon trains: left wing pontoniers, 58th Indiana Volunteers (infantry), Colonel G. P. Buell commanding, strength, 775 men; materials, 51 pontoon boats (canvas) complete, 15 covers (extra), 10 anchors, 2000 lbs. rope, 37 horses, 505 mules, 54 government wagons, 3 ambulances, 2 tool wagons, 3 forges, 24 chess wagons, 16 balk wagons, 196 balk, 850 chess, and the necessary harness, etc., for the foraging teams. Length of bridge, by using small timber for balk, 850 feet. Right wing pontoniers, 1st Missouri Engineers, Lieutenant Colonel W. Tweeddale commanding, strength, 530 men; materials, 28 pontoon boats (canvas) complete, 28 boat wagons, 600 chess, 15 chess wagons, 196 balk (claw), 1 forge, 1 battery wagon, 2 tool wagons (a general assortment), 7 forage wagons, and a sufficient quantity of harness, rope, etc. Length of bridge, 580 feet. Total length of bridge, 1430 feet. About 3000 feet of bridge were built during the march. Respectfully submitted.

(Signed)   O. M. POE, Capt. Eng'rs., Chief Eng'r. M.D.M.
Major General J. G. BARNARD, Chief Eng. Armies of the U.S. in the Field.

VIII.

Extracts from Colonel Poe's Report of Operations in the Campaign of the Carolinas.

During the campaign from Atlanta to Savannah, our line of march was parallel to the water-courses; on this, it led at right angles to them all, and, as we expected, the difficulties encountered by us were much greater. It was chosen near the line of junction between the clay of the uplands and the sand of the lower country. This line cuts the streams at the head of navigation on each. It was hoped and expected that along this line the best roads and the minimum amount of swamps and mud would be found. This supposition proved entirely correct, as we found whenever it was necessary to depart much from this line. Still, it involved an immense amount of bridging of every kind known in active campaigning, and some four hundred miles of corduroying. The latter was a very simple affair where there were plenty of fence-rails, but, in their absence, involved the severest labor. It was found that a fence on each side of the road furnished enough rails for corduroying it, so as to make it passable. I estimate the amount of corduroying at fully one hundred miles for each army corps. This is a moderate estimate, and would make, for the four corps, some four hundred miles of corduroying. The cavalry did very little of this kind of work, as their trains moved with the infantry columns.

The right wing built fifteen pontoon bridges, having an aggregate length of 3720 feet, the left wing built about 4000 feet; being a total of $1\frac{1}{4}$ miles. There were no measurements of the amount of trestle-bridge built, but it was not so great.

The corduroying and building trestle-bridges was all done by the Michigan Engineers, the pioneer corps of the several subdivisions of the army, and by the troops themselves. The pontoniering was all done by engineer troops—that for the right wing being done by the Missouri Engineers, and that of the left wing by the 58th Indiana. The engineer organization was as follows:

Captain C. B. Reese, United States Engineers, chief engineer right wing; Lieutenant Amos Stickney, United States Engineers, assistant engineer right wing; Captain Kloslerman, United States Volunteers, chief engineer 15th Army Corps; Captain Kassak, A.D.C., chief engineer 17th Army Corps; Lieutenant William Ludlow, United States Engineers, chief engineer left wing; unassigned, 1st Regiment Michigan Engineers and Mechanics; pontoniers of right wing, 1st Regiment Missouri Engineers; pontoniers of left wing, 58th Regiment Indiana Volunteers. The Michigan Engineers were commanded by Colonel J. B. Yates, the Missouri Engineers by Lieutenant Colonel Wm. Tweeddale, and the 58th Indiana by Lieutenant Colonel J. Moore (lately by Brigadier General G. P. Buell). To one and all these officers I am under great obligations for efficient performance of duty, but far more than to any one else am I indebted to Captain Reese.

Pioneers were not organized with any system, as frequently an entire army corps was simply a body of pioneers.

The right wing was provided with 600 feet of canvas pontoon bridge, and the left wing with 850 feet, but lost 250 feet at the crossing of the Catawba, when the bridge was carried away by high water.

Surveys have been made of the entire line of march of each army corps, as well as the route pursued by headquarters military division. The latter was a very careful survey, made by Captain H. A. Ullfers, A.A.G., on duty in my office. The bearings were taken with prismatic compass, and the distances measured with an odometer. These surveys will be embodied in a map as soon as possible.

We found the maps of South Carolina tolerably accurate, but those of North Carolina were almost worthless. I have seen two state maps of North Carolina, one dated 1833, and the other 1857. They vie with each other in inaccuracy.

Messrs. Dorr, Rockwell, Harding, and Platt, of the Coast Survey, accompanied me on the campaign. They had but little opportunity to do plane-table work, owing to our rapid marching. They made a survey of Pocotaligo, and are now engaged upon one of this place.

This seems to be the proper time and place to urge upon the bureau the necessity of making a great effort to have the Engineer Department put upon the same footing with regard to rank and pay as the Quartermaster's Department, the Commissary's Department, and the Medical Department. It is only an act of simple justice, and certainly a bill authorizing it can be passed through Congress.

All of which is respectfully submitted.

O. M. POE, Capt. Eng'rs., Bt. Col. U.S.A., Chief Eng'r. M.D.M.

IX.

Quartermaster Reports.

It has been impossible to obtain a complete list of the supplies furnished the army by the Quartermaster's Department. It should be considered that this department was not called upon to furnish horses, mules, and other needs of a large army, in the same proportion that other armies required. The thousands of animals used in artillery, cavalry, and for transportation and food for men and animals, were taken from plantations as we passed. It is not an overestimate to say that the army must have been entirely refitted three times in this way in the course of the two late campaigns.

The first memorandum below of supplies provided is gathered from official papers kindly furnished me by the quartermaster general of the army, Major General Meigs.

For the reason that the army supplied itself from the enemy, renewing and adding to its stock of horses, mules, cattle, forage, etc., it was a most difficult task for the quartermaster general to make just estimates for the needs of the army when it should arrive at its new base. Under date of November 18th, there was ordered from New York 30,000 rations of grain and 30,000 rations of hay, to be forwarded daily until farther orders. On the same date there was ordered clothing for 30,000 men, and a supply of harness, wagons, ambulances, forges, etc. November 28th 150 barrels of salt were sent for use of animals.

As it appeared at this time that General Sherman was making for the

QUARTERMASTER'S STORES.

Atlantic coast, the shipment of supplies to Pensacola, which was one of General Sherman's alternatives, was stopped. It was not known where he would come out, and provision had been made for several places.

To those who are not familiar with the large figures which it is necessary to use in stating the amount of supplies furnished in a given time to the army, the following memorandum will appear enormous.

The statement of supplies forwarded from New York is furnished me by General Van Vliet, who has been, and is, at the head of the Quartermaster's Department in that city. When it is known that two thirds, if not seven eighths, of the supplies forwarded to the armies all over the country have gone through the New York office, I am sure the public will wonder at the perfect system, order, and quiet, which has characterized the performance of General Van Vliet's duties. The truth is, that the soldiers and the public are altogether too contented in feeling assured that the work has been done, and well done, to stop to inquire about the *savior faire.* And it has been one object of the writer of this story, in introducing these figures, to show to the people that praise and honor is due to others in the service besides those who are actually in the melee of battle.

December 6th, 1864, General Van Vliet, at New York, was ordered to estimate for supplies for Sherman's force of 60,000 men, 10,000 cavalry, 60 pieces artillery, and 30,000 horses and mules. He was also ordered to ship 30,000 sack coats, 30,000 blouses, 60,000 shirts, 60,000 pairs of drawers, 60,000 pairs of socks, 100,000 pairs of boots and shoes, 20,000 forage caps, 10,000 great-coats, 20,000 blankets, 10,000 waterproof blankets, 10,000 shelter tents, 100 hospital tents, 10,000 knapsacks, 20,000 haversacks, 10,000 canteens, 20,000 camp kettles, 5000 mess pans, 5000 felling axes (two handles each), 1000 hatchets (two handles each), 2000 spades, 2000 picks, wheel harness for 400 mules, head harness for 800 mules, 10,000 lbs. bar iron (assorted), 500 lbs. steel, 1000 lbs. harness leather, 40 sets shoeing tools, 40 extra harness, thread, wax, needles, and awls, 500 lbs. wrought nails, 20 buttresses, 200 horse-rasps, 100 large files (assorted), 50 shoeing knives (extra), 4000 lbs. manilla rope, 200 extra wagon wheels (assorted), 50 ambulance wheels, 100,000 lbs. horse and mule shoes, 10,000 lbs. nails.

December 6th there were forwarded 50 extra key bits, 500 tent-pins, 200 wagon tongues, 400 extra whiffle-trees, 50 extra double trees, 100 coupling-poles, 200 front rounds for wagons, 100 hind rounds for wagons, 200 mule hames ironed for use, 200 mule collars, 500 wagon bows, 100 wagon whips, 1000 open links for repairing trace-chains, 500 open rings.

390　APPENDIX.

Statement of Subsistence Stores furnished from New York by Colonel H. F. Clarke, A.D.C. and A.C.G.S., U.S.A., under Requisitions of Colonel A. Beckwith, Chief Commissary of Subsistence General Sherman's Army.

Date of Departure.	Destination.	Pork.	Bacon.	Ham.	Beef.	Flour.	Rations of Bread.	Beans.	Rice.	Hominy.	Corn Meal.	Coffee.	Tea.
1864. Oct. 31	Pensacola Harbor..	143,200	36,896	3,220	36,000	87,000	249,950	147,900	119,400		8,000	218,900	14,000
1865. Feb'y 8	Savannah, Ga......	2,113,067	559,446	142,400	1,060,083	1,233,478	4,664,800	2,632,326	69,810	418,420		3,533,624	732,623
" 25	Beaufort, N.C......	954,136	181,754	52,400	354,500	181,149	987,200	1,059,888				1,298,613	
March 9	Beaufort, N.C......	1,734,937	391,925	86,800	714,220	534,568	2,358,750	1,479,075				2,762,139	
" 14	Beaufort, N.C......	1,941,871	495,231	86,800	846,380	671,158	3,014,500	1,595,775				3,639,202	
" 30	Beaufort, N.C......	2,415,206	593,415	86,800	1,045,420	854,089	4,517,050	1,713,975				4,305,602	
April 15	Wilmington, N.C...	1,047,736	770,390		178,560	490,506	1,967,900	498,635		501,190		4,324,100	
" 21	Beaufort, N.C......					499,602	1,397,560					2,045,605	
	Total Rations..	10,350,153	3,058,157	468,420	4,235,163	4,501,493	19,157,700	9,027,654	179,210	919,610	8,000	22,147,785	746,623
	Total in Bulk...	Barrels. 38,813	Pounds. 2,293,575	Pounds. 343,800	Barrels. 26,456	Barrels. 25,900	Boxes. 383,154	Pounds. 1,354,125	Pounds. 17,990	Pounds. 91,960	Pounds. 10,000	Pounds. 1,771,616	Pounds. 105,700

Date of Departure.	Destination.	Sugar.	Vinegar.	Candles.	Soap.	Rations of Salt.	Pepper.	Molasses.	Des. Potatoes.	Des. Mixed Vegetables.	Whisky.	Remarks.
1864. Oct. 31	Pensacola Harbor..	252,000	254,000	272,000	250,000	261,300	250,000	7307	3800	27,000		
1865. Feb'y 8	Savannah, Ga......	4,011,265	2,063,000	3,009,800	3,046,500	6,118,998	3,750,000		6000	1,661,700	176,390	
" 25	Beaufort, N.C......	1,331,000	829,400	1,007,900	910,000	999,000	900,000				143,466	
March 9	Beaufort, N.C......	3,656,469	1,928,900	2,255,000	2,610,000	3,183,000	2,100,000				277,984	
" 14	Beaufort, N.C......	4,300,963	2,273,500	3,280,700	3,450,000	3,761,700	3,200,000				325,224	
" 30	Beaufort, N.C......	4,540,963	2,607,500	4,794,400	4,100,000	4,206,100	4,100,000				344,552	
April 15	Wilmington, N.C...	2,073,554	721,600	1,981,300	2,000,000	3,139,300	2,000,000					
" 21	Beaufort, N.C......	2,089,600				1,835,400						
	Total Rations..	22,259,814	10,687,900	16,601,100	16,366,500	23,504,798	16,300,000	7307	9800	1,658,700	1,267,638	
	Total in Bulk...	Pounds. 3,338,970	Gallons. 1,006,879	Pounds. 207,513	Pounds. 664,044	Pounds. 881,426	Pounds. 40,750	Galls. 22	Pounds. 918	Pounds. 103,668	Gallons. 59,614	

SUPPLIES OF ARMY STORES.

Abstract of Stores moved by Water from New York City by Brevet Brigadier General Stewart Van Vliet, Quartermaster U.S.A., for the use of the Army of Major General William T. Sherman, from November 6th, 1864, to April 30th, 1865, inclusive.

Destination.	Cannon and Howitzers.	Barrels of Powder.	Gun-carriages and Caissons, Battery Wagons, Forges, and Limbers.	Garrison Gins and Sling Carts.	Shot and Shell in Boxes.	Shot and Shell loose.	Ammunition in Boxes.	Ordnance Stores.	Artillery and portable Forges.	Locomotive Engines and Tenders.	Pails and Buckets.	Hardware, etc.	Paints, Oils, etc.	Clothing in Boxes and Bales.	Camp and Garrison Equipage.	Anvils and Vices.	Coal in Bags.	Army Wagons and Carts.	Extra Wheels and Wagon Poles.	Hospital Stores.	Ambulance and Medical Wagons.
Pensacola, Fla.	22	250	21		1,158	1299	71	76	13			60	20,498	3,492 1,243	210 979	300	326	50	100	336	50
Savannah, Ga.			{4 gins 10 carts}		11,022	2903	2936	47			11	14 30	7,500 12,969		13,902 15,950	23 38		81	2375	7,109 1,686	123 57
Wassaw Sound.		1	57					7689			5	16		791	12			60	16		77
Port Royal, S.C.	5	1430				229	3000	77 683			6			5700				90		719	20
Wilmington, N.C.			4				3980	26 312						2,329 820	1499	26	281		2491		338 103
Beaufort, N.C.												22	50	3,081	671	101		4,742 3,102		5,046 7,046	
Morehead City, N.C.												86 31	28 32	8,422					16	18,940	245 46
Newbern, N.C.																					5
Total....	27	1690	83		12,409	4992	9987	8915	13	11	574	431	301	32,380	3271	61	326	69,468	23,907	81,576	1092

Destination.	Harness and Leather in Boxes and Rolls.	Pile-drivers, Engines, and Machinery.	Telegraph Material (Wire; etc.).	Iron and Steel in Bars, Bundles, and Sheets.	Horse and Mule Shoes in Kegs.	Nails, Spikes, Bolts, Nuts, and Washers (in Kegs).	Axes, Adzes, Hatchets, etc.	Zinc, Brass, etc., in Sheets.	Shovels, Spades, and Forks.	Railroad Cars.	Railroad Iron in Bars.	Railroad Chains, Frogs, and Braces.	Oats in Bags.	Corn in Bags.	Lumber in Pieces.	Sundry Q. M. Stores in various Packages.
Pensacola, Fla.	184															
Savannah, Ga.	675		50	134	504	23 1004		1	465				31,702 14,705	9,202 14,705	546	
Wassaw Sound.																
Port Royal, S.C.	17			2740	1474	2012 20	466		534							
Wilmington, N.C.	53	{2 P. drivers 3 engines}	100						639							
Beaufort, N.C.	98		22	815 391		3620 476	180 41 25		4 40							
Morehead City, N.C.	17						3 3									
Newbern, N.C.																
Total....	1044		172	4050	1978	7259	690	29	1108							

The above stores were transported in 70 steamers, 2 ships, 7 barks, 5 brigs, and 44 schooners.
The above report was prepared by T. M. Hempstead, Transportation Clerk.

X.

Commissary Stores furnished the Army.

The subjoined statement shows the amount of supplies actually distributed by the Commissary Department from the time of the arrival of the army before Savannah until it arrived at Richmond.

In the first days at Savannah supplies were brought up the Ogeechee River, a stream shallow and unreasonably crooked. After the occupation of Savannah, they were brought forward in the first instance *via* Thunderbolt, and subsequently, when the obstructions were in some measure removed, directly up the Savannah River.

When the army arrived at Goldsboro' supplies for present need and for the future campaign were forwarded over a single line of railroad from Morehead City and Newbern.

It must be remembered that, in all the lines of communication mentioned above—by water at Savannah, and the single line of railroad to Goldsboro'—that these were used by all the departments for forwarding material, the Quartermaster, Commissary, Ordnance, Medical, and others. The Commissary Department alone employed 950 citizens, which included clerks, mechanics, and negro laborers. Extensive details of soldiers were also employed. At Morehead City a regular detail for fatigue duty alone was made, of 400 for the day and 200 for night duty.

This brief sketch will show the great labor performed, and the credit due the subordinate officers of these departments of the army, who are too often unappreciated. The work mentioned above was performed under the immediate direction of Captain Roots, a competent, untiring, energetic officer, acting under the orders of Colonel Beckwith.

SUPPLIES OF ARMY STORES. 393

Statement of Subsistence Stores delivered to General Sherman's Army from the time of striking the Atlantic Coast (about the middle of December) until they reached Richmond.

Where issued.	Pork. Bbls.	Ham. Pounds.	Bacon. Pounds.	Salt Beef. Bbls.	Hard Bread. Pounds.	Flour. Bbls.	Beans. Pounds.	Corn Meal. Bbls.	Rice. Pounds.	Tea. Pounds.	Coffee. Pounds.	Can- dles. Pds.	Brown Sugar. Pounds.	White Sugar. Pounds.	Vine- gar. Gallons.
Savannah, Ga., and vicinity	10,313	94,983	149,197	4363	4,735,100		7,972	348,002	460	115,312	10,686½		525,036	49,640	945,245	118,120	28,824½
Kingston, Neuse River, and Goldsboro'	4,360	131,700	404,175	1320	3,704,825		4,586	171,688		6,484		589,075	30,675	659,186	11,554
Raleigh	2,705	24,900	85,200	1914	1,164,950		1,485					118,434	640	124,539	
Total	17,378	251,583	637,572	6897½	9,604,875		14,043	519,690	460	115,312	17,170½	1,232,544	80,955	1,729,020	118,120	40,378½

Where issued.	Soap. Pounds.	Salt. Pounds.	Pepper. Pounds.	Whiskey. Galls.	Molasses. Gallons.	Pickles. Pounds.	Onions. Pounds.	Hops. Pounds.	Smoked Herring. Boxes.	Mack- erel. Barrels.	Codfish. Pounds.	Beef Cattle. No.	Pig's Feet. Pounds.	Pig's Tongues. HlF bbls.	Hay. Pounds.	Corn. Pounds.	Peaches. Cans.	Tomatoes. Pounds.
Savannah, Ga., and vicinity	154,074	231,730	7,980	30,795	12,459½				94,359	27,768		1784			63,059	1197	767,868	18,623	10,580	32,035
Kingston, Neuse River, and Goldsboro'	118,419	130,295	7,190	11,323	49,760				11,095						74,400				3,795
Raleigh		13,836		240														
Total	272,493	425,861	15,170	42,358	12,459½	76,940	29,520	105,454	27,758	2028	16	4	137,459	1197	767,868	18,623	10,580	35,830

Where issued.	Rasp- berries Cans.	Assorted Jellies. Cans.	Char- ries Cans.	Black- berries Cans.	Vege- tables Pds.	Pota- toes. Pds.	Hominy. Pounds.	Dried Beef. Pds.	Dried Peaches. Pounds.	Dried Apples. Pounds.	Fresh Potatoes. Pounds.
Savannah, Ga., and vicinity	192	72	240	107	500	15,610	1426	392	149	53	2028	16	4	6981	216

LOGAN H. ROOTS,
Capt. C. S. U. S. Vols., and C. C. S. Dépôts,
Military Division of the Mississippi.

XI.
Staff of General Sherman.

General Sherman's personal staff in the field consisted of Major McCoy, A.D.C.; Captain Audenried, A.D.C.; Major Hitchcock, A.A.G.; Captain Dayton, A.D.C., but performing faithfully the arduous duties of adjutant general; and Captain Nichols, A.A.D.C.

In addition to those already mentioned, as a part of the staff, there were the following officers who transacted the important duties of the office at Nashville: Brigadier General Webster, Lieutenant Colonel R. M. Sawyer, A.A.G.; Captain Rochester, A.A.G.; Captain Warner, A.Q.M.; Captain Coverdale, A.Q.M.; and Captain Jenny, A.A.D.C., in charge of the Engineer Bureau at Nashville.

Valuable & Interesting Books

PUBLISHED BY HARPER & BROTHERS, NEW YORK.

☞ HARPER & BROTHERS *will send their Books by Mail, postage free, to any part of the United States, on receipt of the Price.*

☞ HARPER'S CATALOGUE *and new* TRADE-LIST *may be obtained gratuitously, on application to the Publishers personally, or by letter, enclosing Five Cents.*

Brackett's United States Cavalry. History of the United States Cavalry from the Formation of the Federal Government to the 1st of June, 1863. To which is added a List of all the Cavalry Regiments, with the Names of their Commanders, which have been in the United States Service since the breaking out of the Rebellion. By ALBERT G. BRACKETT, Major First United States Cavalry, Colonel Ninth Illinois Volunteer Cavalry, late Chief of Cavalry of the Department of Missouri, Special Inspector of Cavalry, Department of the Cumberland. With Illustrations. 12mo. (*Nearly Ready.*)

Draper's American Civil Policy. Thoughts on the Future Civil Policy of America. By JOHN WILLIAM DRAPER, M.D., LL.D., Author of a "Treatise on Human Physiology," and of a "History of the Intellectual Development of Europe." Crown 8vo, Cloth. (*Shortly.*)

Napoleon's Life of Cæsar. The History of Julius Cæsar. By His Imperial Majesty NAPOLEON III. Vol. I. A new Elegant Library Edition, with wide Margins, on Superfine Calendered Paper, with Portrait and Colored Maps. 480 pages, 8vo, Cloth, $2 50. (*This is the only Edition with Maps.*)

Harper's Pictorial History of the Great Rebellion in the United States. 4to, 30 cents a Number.

Abbott's Sketches of Prison Life. Sketches of Prison Life, Showing how we lived and were treated at the Libby, Macon, Savannah, Charleston, Columbia, Charlotte, Raleigh, Goldsboro, and Andersonville. By A. O. ABBOTT, late Lieutenant First New York Dragoons. Illustrated. 12mo. (*In Press.*)

The Story of the Great March: Diary of General Sherman's Campaign through Georgia and the Carolinas. By Brevet Major GEORGE WARD NICHOLS, Aid-de-Camp to General Sherman. With a Map and Illustrations. 12mo, Cloth, $1 75.

Kinglake's Crimean War. The Invasion of the Crimea: its Origin, and an Account of its Progress down to the Death of Lord Raglan. By ALEXANDER WILLIAM KINGLAKE. With Maps and Plans. 2 vols. Vol. I. Maps, 12mo, Cloth, $2 00.

Abbott's Napoleon Bonaparte. The History of Napoleon Bonaparte. By JOHN S. C. ABBOTT. With Maps, Woodcuts, and Portraits on Steel. 2 vols., 8vo, Cloth, $10 00.

General Scott's Infantry Tactics; or, Rules for the Exercise and Manœuvres of the United States Infantry. Published by Authority. 3 vols., 24mo, Cloth, $3 00.

Butterfield's Camp and Outpost Duty. Camp and Outpost Duty for Infantry. With Standing Orders, Extracts from the Revised Regulations for the Army, Rules for Health, Maxims for Soldiers, and Duties of Officers. By Major-General DANIEL BUTTERFIELD, U. S. Army. 18mo, Cloth, 60 cents. (Suited for the Pocket.)

Szabad's Modern War. Modern War: its Theory and Practice. Illustrated from celebrated Campaigns and Battles. With Maps and Diagrams. By EMERIC SZABAD, Captain, U.S.A. 12mo, Cloth, $1 50.

Noyes's the Bivouac and Battle-field. The Bivouac and Battle-field; or, Campaign Sketches in Virginia and Maryland. By Captain GEORGE F. NOYES. 12mo, Cloth, $1 50.

General Marcy's Hand-Book for Overland Expeditions. The Prairie Traveller. A Hand-Book for Overland Expeditions. With Maps, Illustrations, and Itineraries of the Principal Routes between the Mississippi and the Pacific. By General RANDOLPH B. MARCY, U. S. Army. Published by Authority of the War Department. Small 12mo, Cloth, $1 00.

Russell's American Diary My Diary North and South. By WILLIAM HOWARD RUSSELL, LL.D. 8vo, Cloth, $1 00.

Creasy's Fifteen Decisive Battles. The Fifteen Decisive Battles of the World; from Marathon to Waterloo. By E. S. CREASY, A.M. 12mo, Cloth, $1 50.

A True Story of the Battle of Waterloo. By Rev. G. R. GLEIG. 12mo, Cloth, $1 25.

Alison's Life of Marlborough. Military Life of John, Duke of Marlborough. With Maps. 12mo, Cloth, $1 75.

Story of the Peninsular War. By General CHARLES W. VANE, Marquis of Londonderry, &c. New Edition, revised, with considerable Additions. 12mo, Cloth, $1 50.

Carleton's Buena Vista. The Battle of Buena Vista, with the Operations of the "Army of Occupation" for One Month. By Captain CARLETON. 12mo, Cloth, $1 25.

Motley's Dutch Republic. The Rise of the Dutch Republic. A History. By JOHN LOTHROP MOTLEY, LL.D., D.C.L. With a Portrait of William of Orange. 3 vols., 8vo, Cloth, $9 00.

Motley's United Netherlands. History of the United Netherlands: from the Death of William the Silent to the Synod of Dort. With a full View of the English-Dutch Struggle against Spain, and of the Origin and Destruction of the Spanish Armada. By JOHN LOTHROP MOTLEY, LL.D., D.C.L., Author of "The Rise of the Dutch Republic." 2 vols., 8vo, Cloth, $6 00.

Carlyle's Frederick the Great. History of Friedrich II., called Frederick the Great. By THOMAS CARLYLE. With Portraits and Maps. 6 vols., 12mo. (Vols. V. and VI. *in Press.*) Price per Vol., $2 00.

Alison's History of Europe. First Series.—From the Commencement of the French Revolution, in 1789, to the Restoration of the Bourbons in 1815. [In addition to the Notes on Chapter LXXVI., which correct the errors of the original work concerning the United States, a copious Analytical Index has been appended to this American Edition.] SECOND SERIES.—From the Fall of Napoleon, in 1815, to the Accession of Louis Napoleon, in 1852. A New Series. 8 vols., 8vo, Cloth, $16 00.

Hildreth's History of the United States. First Series.—From the First Settlement of the Country to the Adoption of the Federal Constitution. SECOND SERIES.—From the Adoption of the Federal Constitution to the End of the Sixteenth Congress. 6 vols., 8vo, Cloth, $18 00.

www.ingramcontent.com/pod-product-compliance
Lightning Source LLC
Chambersburg PA
CBHW031414230426
43668CB00007B/303